35 YEARS OF MUSIC
(originally published as *Music Observed*)

BOOKS BY B. H. HAGGIN

A Book of the Symphony (1937)
Music on Records (1938)
Music on Records (1941)
Music for the Man Who Enjoys "Hamlet" (1944)
Music in the Nation (1949)
The Listener's Musical Companion (1956)
Conversations with Toscanini (1959)
The Toscanini Musicians Knew (1967)
Ballet Chronicle (1971)
A Decade of Music (1973)
The New Listener's Companion and Record Guide (1974)

B. H. HAGGIN

35 YEARS
OF MUSIC

HORIZON PRESS   NEW YORK

Library of Congress Cataloging in Publication Data
Haggin, Bernard H.
　35 years of music.

　1964 ed. published under title Music observed.
　1. Musicians as authors.　2. Musical criticism.
3. Music—Analysis, appreciation.　I. Title.
ML90.H33　　1974　　　780'.8　　　74-12138
ISBN 0-8180-1213-7

Copyright © 1964, 1974, by B. H. Haggin

Copyright © 1962, 1964 by B. H. Haggin

Copyright © 1929, 1938, 1940, 1942, 1943, 1944, 1945, 1946, 1947, 1948, 1949, 1950, 1951, 1952, 1953, 1954, 1955, 1956, 1957 by *The Nation*

Copyright 1933, 1934 by *Hound & Horn*

Copyright © 1946, 1947, 1948, 1949 by the *New York Herald Tribune*

Copyright © 1957 by *Kenyon Review*

Copyright © 1958, 1959, 1960, 1961, 1962, 1963 by Hudson Review Inc.

Copyright © 1957, 1958, 1962, 1963 by *The New Republic*

Copyright © 1958 by *Playbill*

Copyright © 1963, 1964 by Yale University Press

PRINTED IN THE UNITED STATES OF AMERICA

35 YEARS OF MUSIC

Introduction

As I RECALL my beginning as a critic, I read, then I heard, or I heard and then read; in either case I found that what I heard was not described correctly by what I read; and at some point I began to express my disagreement in writing. When, for example, I heard Berlioz's *Symphonie Fantastique* I discovered that it was not the arid and banal work Richard Aldrich of the *Times* had said it was; in the same way I discovered that Mahler's Symphony No. 2 was not the horror Olin Downes had made it out to be in the *Times*. And the earliest of such discoveries concerned the music of Brahms.

Now and then, in the years that I have been writing, readers have deplored my prejudice against Brahms, some calling me opinionated and dogmatic and contending that such personal aberrations were something for a critic to keep strictly to himself, not to mislead others with in his writing. Something could be said about my correspondents' confidence that rational judgment of experience must lead to an estimate of Brahms as high as their own, and that my lower estimate must represent irrational prejudice; but I will limit myself to pointing out that actually—going for the first time, in 1915, to hear a symphony of Brahms, the Second, and going with the idea of it as a formidable musical labyrinth that I had got from Pitts Sanborn's writing about Brahms—I was intoxicated by what I heard, as I continued to be by everything I heard of Brahms, regarding his music as the greatest of all. This love affair continued for a dozen years, until one day when I was playing through the Cello Sonata Op. 99 I sud-

Introduction

denly became aware, at some point in the slow movement, that what I was hearing was synthetic and sterile substance being manipulated by formula to fill out structural pattern. Once I had heard it in this work I began to hear in others this pose of artistic creation, with its pretense of great emotions communicated in mechanically contrived large structures. And I was left with a few works—the sets of variations on themes of Haydn and Paganini and the final passacaglia of the Fourth Symphony, with a few other movements in the symphonies and a few of the songs—which I continued to like for the same reason as W. J. Turner, who explained once that he rated the Haydn Variations and the passacaglia of the Fourth highest in Brahms's work because in them Brahms is not "being a poet (in the Aristotelian sense) or a great creator; he is merely being a musician"—i.e. a musical craftsman—and that he liked Brahms when he is "entirely natural and self-forgetful" and "is not obsessed by the tramp of Beethoven behind him."

Since I liked these few works of Brahms, it seemed to me that my dislike of his other music couldn't be said to represent prejudice against him. Nor could I accept what my correspondents' position seemed to reduce itself to: that where my years of listening to the music and thinking about it led me to judgments different from theirs, and I refused to give up mine and accept theirs, I was prejudiced, opinionated, dogmatic, and should be silent. A long-developed and reasoned judgment, even when unfavorable, is not a prejudice; and though it is likely to be a strongly held and strongly expressed conviction, a man whose strongly held convictions are long-developed and reasoned judgments cannot be called opinionated, and his strong expression of such judgments cannot be called dogmatic. Not only must he be granted the right to his reasoned judgments, but his function, his duty, his sole usefulness as a critic, if he is one, is to state them—to state, that is, the reasons with the judgments. For criticism

Introduction

is not the mere opinion that this piece of music or this performance is good and that one is bad; it is the reasons for the opinion, in which the critic applies to what he has heard the insights that constitute his value to his readers.

There have been letters also in which readers accused me of having fallen for the Toscanini ballyhoo; and here again I will say that my high estimate of Toscanini's work came rather late, and that what I thought of him, early and late, represented my own response to what I heard. This began with a performance of *Madama Butterfly* in January 1914; and I wish I could say it so impressed me that I heard every subsequent performance of Toscanini's I could get to; but actually what impressed me was Farrar's looks, and it was her performances of Puccini and worse that I went to. Now historic performances of *Un Ballo in Maschera, Il Trovatore, Aida, Orfeo ed Eurydice, Tristan und Isolde, Die Meistersinger,* conducted by Toscanini, with Hempel, Destinn, Matzenauer, Fremstad, Homer, Caruso—these were available to me; but all I heard him do that last year before he left the Metropolitan was a few performances of Giordano's *Madame Sans-Gêne* with Farrar. When he came to the New York Philharmonic in 1926 I argued against what I regarded as the excessive excitement over him—not that I didn't hear the marvelous contours, textures and sonorities, but that I thought Mengelberg's shaping of the sound-time continuum produced more effective statements of Beethoven and Brahms. As late as 1933, when I had learned to dislike Mengelberg's plastic distortions, I contended that Toscanini produced beautiful sounds but the same beautiful sounds for all music, whereas Koussevitzky gave the right character to the music of each composer—not only of Tchaikovsky but of Beethoven and Brahms; and it took a few more years to find Koussevitzky's italicizing distortion of Beethoven, Brahms and Tchaikovsky impossible to listen to, and Toscanini's statements of their works the most deeply satisfying.

Introduction

What happened was that I learned to appreciate and require plastic economy and subtlety in performance; and I learned by hearing them long enough—which is to say, by my own experience.

Something similar happened with solo instrumentalists. A reader once attributed my criticisms of Heifetz, which he characterized as "snide and ill-mannered impertinence," to personal animosity; accused me of attempting to tear Heifetz down in order to elevate Szigeti, for personal reasons again, and of doing the same thing with Koussevitzky for the benefit of Toscanini and Beecham; and assured me that only the musical public, which had put Heifetz and Koussevitzky where they were, could remove them. Actually, Heifetz, when he first appeared here in 1917, was added to the celebrated performers I had begun to hear in 1914—Ysaye, Godowsky, Elman, Kreisler, Hofmann, Paderewski, Casals—who were the deities of the period, and whom I continued for years to accept as such. The inadequacies of perception and taste that caused me to be impressed by Hofmann kept me from being impressed by Schnabel when he first played in New York in 1923; and when, in 1930, I went to Brooklyn to hear him in Beethoven's Concerto No. 4 with the Boston Symphony, it was with no expectations but only out of curiosity; so that I was totally unprepared for a performance which produced the effect of revelation—in which, that is, as in a Toscanini performance of a Beethoven symphony, the clarifying articulation seemed literally to reveal the structure and expressive significance of the work for the first time. This and subsequent Schnabel performances made me aware also of the distinction, in a performance, between the playing of the instrument and the playing of the music, and thus of the distinction between a Hofmann who used the music to show what he could do with the piano, and a Schnabel who used the piano to illuminate the music. Similarly, Szigeti's performances—with their use of the violin

Introduction

in a powerful sculpturing of each large-spanned phrase with continuity of tension and outline from note to note, their creating of further continuity of tension and shape from phrase to phrase in the large structure—made me aware of the distinction in Heifetz's performances between his playing of the violin, with its dazzling tone and technique, and his playing of the music, with its mincing, wailing little swells on every two or three notes that kept breaking the line of the phrase, and its alternation, in a passage that should flow evenly, of now holding back and now hurrying forward, in a mannered and exaggerated expressive style that was as sentimental and vulgar in Beethoven as it would be in Liszt's *Liebestraum*. And I might add here that Toscanini's plastically coherent shaping of music made me aware of the distinction between the miracles of orchestral sonority that Stokowski and Koussevitzky produced with their orchestras, and the distortions and vulgarities they inflicted on many of the works they performed.

But as my reader's letter indicated, these were distinctions most people didn't make and didn't understand when someone else made them: what else was performance than the producing of the notes the composer had written; and how could a performance be wrong in which those notes were produced with dazzling beauty? For these people all performances by celebrated performers had equal validity; so that one could say Szigeti played Beethoven differently from Heifetz, or Beecham played Mozart differently from Koussevitzky, but not that one played the music well and the other poorly. And for them, therefore, my statement that Heifetz was guilty of phraseological vulgarities was "snide and ill-mannered impertinence." In this they failed to understand that I wasn't paid to genuflect before eminences or before the limited perceptions of the general public, but was paid, instead, to give the non-professional listeners who read me the benefit of my professional listener's sharper perceptions, by pointing out

Introduction

what those readers might otherwise not notice; and that if any of them couldn't hear what I pointed out or preferred to ignore it, this didn't mean I was wrong in hearing and reporting it.

Nor was this the only thing most people didn't understand about the critic's operation. A reader sent me one of my columns with *Records* crossed out and *Likes and Dislikes* substituted at the top, and with each statement that I liked or disliked something underlined throughout the piece. As though criticism properly was something other or more than personal likes and dislikes, and as though such likes and dislikes were mere whims. Actually criticism is as personal as the art it deals with: it begins with the critic's experience of, and response to, the work of art with his particular resources for the purpose; it ends with a formulation of his judgment that is a reasoned statement of like or dislike. My reader had underlined my dislike of Brahms's Violin Concerto and of Szigeti's performance; but he had paid no attention to the subsequent statement that "music as pretentious as the first movement, as saccharine as the second, should not be played with fussy, tremulous inflection that exaggerates its faults," which made the dislike not mere whim but reasoned judgment of my experience of the work and the performance.

And when, finally, I have commented on a statement of another critic, I have usually received a letter questioning the propriety of my doing so and contending that the proper activity of a music critic was to write about music, not about another critic's writing. Even an earlier publisher and editor of the *Nation*, who took it as a matter of course that the *Nation* should editorially rebuke the *Times* for a news report or an editorial she disapproved of, deplored my practice of criticizing the writing of other critics (I should add, however, that she lived up to the *Nation*'s proclaimed tradition by publishing what I wrote). But having begun to write my disagreement with what I read, I have continued to do so; and I have considered this part of my proper

Introduction

activity as a music critic—as it was part of the proper activity of the *Nation* to comment on something in the *Times*, and as it was part of the proper activity of a historian or a literary critic to discuss the writing of other historians or literary critics. The tradition among music critics in this country—that one never mentions a colleague except to pay him a compliment—may be a good one for the critics, but it has no other merit I can see, and it is a bad one for the public.

Since I may have given the impression that all I have had from readers is objections and dissents, let me add that there has also been evidence that my writing had counted for something in its readers' minds. And this is of course the return for his work that means most to a writer. [*Commentary*]

35 Years of Music

9 October 1929 "We Germans," said the widow of a well-known music historian proudly, "do not need Debussy; we have Schubert and Beethoven"; or—to bring the argument up to date—Reger, Mahler and Pfitzner, who also make Debussy superfluous. And this because, in the words of a Viennese musician, "We do not merely listen to the sounds and effects; we ask how do the chords move, what are the rhythms, how goes the counterpoint." For the German, that is, music is sweaty: the technical complexities, however sterile, of Reger, or the technical virtuosity, however impotent, of the Strauss of today. The German does not observe as a critic what Reger does not observe as a composer—"the difference," as Tovey has put it, "between analytical theory and the practical conditions of creative work"; he is a pedant who has yet to learn that one does better merely to listen to the effects than merely to ask how goes the counterpoint. But this pedantry makes him, in his own eyes, the most understanding of listeners. He reasons also that music is a racial product, therefore that German music can be understood only by Germans as French music can be understood only by Frenchmen. Nor can the traditions of its performance be acquired by musicians of other races, so that only in Germany does it sound as it should.

Now the Viennese simply carries this nonsense a step further: the music, the traditions, are not German but Viennese; hence even Furtwängler fails with Bruckner, and the Adolf Busch Quartet with Schubert; good German singers develop into great German singers when they come to the Vienna Opera; Furt-

9 October 1929

wängler achieves his most successful performances with the Vienna, not with the Berlin Philharmonic; this orchestra has not the tone even of the Vienna Symphony and gets only a pat on the head for its discipline (a quality which the Viennese affects to despise as Prussian and as one which robs the *interpretation of plasticity*). Hence, also, when the Viennese madly applauds a third-rate singer at the Opera or the dry, scratchy, pedantic Rosé Quartet, it may be that sheer love of music makes him uncritical, or that he is demonstrating how very critical he is, and that music has mysteries which are revealed only to Viennese performers and listeners—to whom one must add Viennese critics, whose ability to make small things appear big and simple things complicated is at times stupefying.

The Viennese, then, will not understand that what he had to teach has been learned; he will have it that he is still holding the torch, that the war which impoverished and humiliated him could not take away supremacy in the things that matter most—culture, manners, beauty and charm of women. His attitude is that of the impoverished aristocrat toward the *nouveau riche* whom he formerly looked down upon, particularly toward the German, to whom he always felt superior, and who has come out of the war better off than he. Today the Viennese finds it easier to be just to the Milan Scala company than to the Berlin Philharmonic.

The prevailing notion of America is that it has the money to command talent, but is not able really to appreciate it. A few Viennese, very conscious of their breadth of mind, concede that high standards and genuine understanding exist in America; but they expect Americans to concede that Viennese standards and understanding are superior to all. This an American who has come to Vienna to study will naturally do; and this done, his discernment is praised and he is flattered out of his senses. As a result, a more critical attitude encounters first amazement and

9 October 1929

then anger. When an American—in what he is reminded is the best musical society in Vienna—criticizes Furtwängler's performances, he is asked literally what he knows about it. When he characterizes the Viennese attitude toward the music Vienna does not hear or the American orchestras it has not heard as arrogant, he is told that as a visitor he is arrogant in presuming to judge Vienna's music or its Philharmonic even after hearing them, and that he will learn better when he has lived in the city long enough. As voices grow louder, the quiet confident arrogance of the beginning becomes angry and personally offensive: what he considered the finest performances at the Opera, those of Mozart and *Tristan* under Strauss, are characterized as "the worst, of course"; he is told the place for his taste is Berlin; he is asked to say on his honor whether he came to Vienna prejudiced; his word to the contrary is doubted at first; meanwhile the actual arguments are an affront to his intelligence. Not that he is argued with; he is simply told: for one thing that on racial grounds French music must be foreign to the Viennese—which is bad anthropology; and that therefore only the Americans, with no music of their own, can be musical internationalists—which is bad logic. Also, that he may not judge Reger without having studied the scores a few years—which is silly enough; but when he points out that he had not found this necessary for Beethoven, he is told that in his own lifetime Beethoven almost starved because his music was not understood—which is bad history. He is told not only nonsense, but contradictory nonsense, what with the necessity of being annihilated at every point: when he says that the Viennese get an inadequate idea of Debussy or Bloch from the performances they hear he is told that performance cannot obscure the quality of music; when he points out that America, on the contrary, has got its idea of Bruckner from Furtwängler, among others, he is told one does not hear the authentic Bruckner from Furtwängler.

April 1933

Curiously enough, when the battle is over, it appears that Furtwängler, since his American visits, has *not* been quite the same; that the Vienna Philharmonic *is* overworked; and so on. These, apparently, are things which the Viennese may admit among themselves, but which an American should not notice and has no right to speak of. [*The Nation*]

April 1933 Sibelius is no longer being neglected; he is being worse than neglected: conductors are digging out the feeblest, the dullest, the most barren of his works to set before their audiences —the incidental music for Strindberg's *Swan White* and Shakespeare's *The Tempest,* the symphonic poem *Tapiola.* One reason for this is that the critics are claiming too much for him—too much even for his best work, and certainly for his poorest. I have in mind not Cecil Gray's ad hoc—and sometimes mutually contradictory—generalizations, principles and definitions to support his absurdly exaggerated statements about the character and magnitude of these works of modest stature, and about the revolutionary innovations in the form of the first movement of the Second Symphony that actually is similar to the form of Brahms's Second; but rather the similarly absurd statements of so acute a critic as Constant Lambert in his brilliant book *Music Ho!* And Ernest Newman writes:

The surest and quickest way to win adherents for Sibelius is to familiarize the public first of all with his maturest works. Conductors and orchestras will also find this the best line of approach to him, for . . . it is in the later works that they will find the explanation of many a passage in the earliest works that by itself is far from clear; because while it *looks* like music of the usual kind it is in reality something quite different in meaning. . . . The conductor and orchestra who have got to the secret of the last four symphonies and of the splendid 'Tapiola' will then understand what Sibelius is driving at in certain parts of the first two symphonies.

But one important fact about Sibelius is that his thought is simple; which means that there is never any difficulty in knowing what he is saying, or whether he is saying anything at all (since there are times when he is saying nothing). There is, then, nothing obscure in the first two symphonies: their content is abundant and clear; and clear too is the difference between Sibelius's own ideas and his occasional derivations from others, which are to be expected in a first or second symphony. If in later symphonies Sibelius eliminates what is not his own, this does not permit or oblige us to deny its presence in the early ones and to assume that a passage in them which sounds like someone else is really an obscure form of Sibelius that becomes clear in the later ones. It is the *Sibelius* in the First or Second Symphony, not the someone else, that becomes the Sibelius of the Fifth or Seventh. As soon deny the conventional form of those early symphonies and contend that it conceals the form of the Fifth or Seventh. Nor is there any secret to get to in *Tapiola*: Newman simply cannot accept its clearly evident barrenness. The difficulty in grasping a content that is not there he ascribes to its being especially profound—a secret to which one must penetrate not only in *Tapiola* but in the first symphonies; which amounts to saying that one must read the barrenness of *Tapiola* into even the works that are not barren.

Much the same nonsense is written about the Fourth Symphony, and particularly its first movement. This, for Gray, is "the most compact and concise movement in symphonic literature. One can think of no other which says so much in such a small space." And Newman writes:

When his earlier symphonies are feeble . . . it is because he is padding in the Brahmsian manner, merely repeating a phrase at another height or in another key, instead of . . . leaping boldly from

April 1933

the point he wants to quit to the point he wants to reach. The amazing fourth symphony is a convulsive effort on Sibelius's part to build without the least fragment of mortar, bogus or real. This is a kind of Cyclopean architecture, block being laid on block without any other join than the surfaces of the material themselves.

This sort of thing comes from an unwillingness to believe what is indeed almost incredible: how little Sibelius says in this movement. There is no great content compressed into a small space: small as the space is, the content is even smaller; short as the movement is, it contains padding—padding in the Sibelius as well as the Brahms manner. An impressive introduction, built up by repetition of one idea at different levels, prepares one for something momentous, like the introduction of Brahms's First; and the similarity continues: with all his straining and sweating Brahms doesn't achieve anything momentous or significant in the rest of the movement; nor does Sibelius. The introduction leads to a heavy snort of the brass, which is of course intended to be something much more (Mr. Downes would say Sibelius shakes his fist at the sky), and which is repeated twice at higher levels without meaning any more the third time than the first. The third time it is accompanied by a vehement utterance of the high strings, which provides a conclusion; after which the entire passage is repeated at a different level. Then a few fragments of ideas, simple and uncompressed; and Sibelius has finished stating his material. Now the development: business of wild waving of arms in the strings, cries in the woodwinds, thunder in the kettledrums—all of it meaning exactly nothing, all of it padding in the Sibelius manner. The snorts of the brass are heard again, with the vehement utterance of the high strings; the fragments of ideas follow; and the movement is over. [*Hound & Horn*]

July 1934

July 1933 Elisabeth Rethberg's singing, in a program of *Lieder,* was the most exquisite, most perfect one could imagine. Its defect was that of Toscanini's performances: she brought to every song the same easy flow of beautiful sounds and perfect phrasing; and while many of the songs needed no more than this for the realization of their content, there were others for which it was not enough. A song like Schumann's *Widmung* demanded more intensity; and others the subtleties of color, accent, inflection that bring out in the music what is related to the poem. It is these subtleties that constitute the art of *Lieder*-singing; and a remarkable demonstration of this art is available on the records Elena Gerhardt has made for the Hugo Wolf Society. On these the voice is still lovely; but that is not the important thing: what was fascinating, always, was not the voice but the use of it by one of the most sensitive and subtle of musical intelligences; and today this is more fascinating than ever. [*Hound & Horn*]

July 1934 These stand out for me in the past season:
Toscanini's performance with the New York Philharmonic of the *Kyrie* of Bach's *B-Minor Mass.* I had known the music only as urged along by Albert Stoessel with the thought of four hours to go at the back of his mind; and so the effect of Toscanini's slow tempo was first shock, then revelation: I was hearing the sounds for the first time in their proper relations of time. And for the first time, also, in proper relations of volume: in place of unrelieved mass there was sensitive molding of beautiful tone. But there was also this revelation: by the time Bach was saying what he had to say for the seventh or whatever time it was, I knew it was several times too many. And I had the same feeling about the closing chorus of the *St. Matthew Passion,* on the same program.

1934-35

Mozart's Piano Concertos K.466 and 467 performed by Toscanini with Iturbi. Particularly the slow movement of K.467, one of Mozart's supreme utterances, in which Iturbi played the long line of melody with a largeness and nobility of style that I had never heard from him before. And the first movement of K.466, which I had never heard with the intensity and passion Toscanini imparted to it.

The production of *Four Saints in Three Acts* in all it aspects. Virgil Thomson's music was good for its purposes of providing a framework for what was done on the stage and pointing up what was said. [*Hound & Horn*]

Postscript, 1964 How good Thomson's music was I discovered at a concert performance in 1941. With no brilliant stage production to claim attention, I appreciated how the music—by separating and differentiating the flat repetitions of a Gertrude Stein verbal sequence—articulated them, gave them point, and imparted to them its own structure and climax. I appreciated also how, on the one hand, Thomson achieved humorous effect now by having the music highlight a Stein verbal incongruity, and now by presenting an incongruity of his own contriving between words with little import or weight and music with a great deal; and on the other hand how moving a result he produced when he put such music to words like the "led, said, wed, dead" sequence. The same treatment of the Stein text achieved similar delightful and moving results in *The Mother of Us All* a few years later.

1934-35 In a recent article Ernest Newman contended that the audiences which were praised for crowding into Queen's Hall on the Bach nights of the Promenade Concerts should be criticized instead for applauding with equal enthusiasm the poetry Bach produced when the exercise of his craftsmanship on the formulas of his style was stimulated and vivified by inspiration, and the mere workmanlike verse he turned out when the exercise was routine and mechanical. Newman's examples of this verse were the slow movement of the Clavier Concerto in F minor and the Brandenburg Concerto No. 1; but the example I would cite is the set of six Sonatas or Partitas for unaccompanied violin. Both as writing for the instrument and as music they are generally regarded as being among the great monuments of the violin literature; and as such they are not only among the test pieces with which a violinist demonstrates his technical and musical powers, but among those with which he can do this on the level of high art, as against the level of Wieniawski and Vieuxtemps. And it is true that to keep the melody flowing with continuity that is not broken by the occasional chords is as difficult as trying to walk with ease and dignity with a ball and chain attached to one leg; and that a performance like Szigeti's which achieves this is a demonstration of impressive technical and musical powers. But in most of the works—except for the great Chaconne of the Sonata No. 4 (Partita No. 2) and the superb Prelude of the Sonata No. 6 (Partita No. 3)—I hear only the expressive eloquence of Szigeti's playing, implying an expressiveness in the music that is not really there; which is to say that to my ears Bach's craftsmanship merely goes through the motions of creation and produces only the external appearance of expressiveness. But other listeners are impelled by the name Bach to accept the appearance as reality—to hear an expressive content that isn't there and that they contend is difficult to hear because it lies deep below the music's surface and is especially profound—"the passionate, yet untroubled, meditation of a great mind" beyond

1934-35 (1964)

"the composition's formidable technical frontiers," as one critic put it recently. [*Brooklyn Eagle*]

1934-35   Interest in last night's repetition of *Tristan und Isolde* at the Metropolitan centered in the Isolde of Kirsten Flagstad, who had made a triumphant debut as Sieglinde in last Saturday's performance of *Die Walküre*. Mme. Flagstad had a triumph last night, and fully deserved the cheers: I have never heard the part sung as well. The voice, of beautiful quality, was used with complete absence of effort and strain, and therefore retained its quality even in notes of the utmost fullness, and its carrying power even in notes of the utmost delicacy. Sounding young after twenty years' use, it was as fresh at the end of the opera as at the beginning. Moreover it was used with musical sensitiveness and dramatic expressiveness. And add to all this the fact that Mme. Flagstad looked the part perfectly and acted it intelligently, if not arrestingly. In the long stretches of singing without action there can be only the projective force of a compelling personality, which Barbara Kemp and Frida Leider, for example, had, and which Mme. Flagstad has not.

[*Brooklyn Eagle*]

Postscript 1964   Flagstad had made her debut the preceding Saturday without any advance statement from the Metropolitan alerting press and public about her extraordinary voice—for the simple reason that Gatti-Casazza and Bodanzky, at her audition in Europe, had not been impressed and had engaged her without enthusiasm. And since I disliked the *Ring* music dramas I had sent someone else to review this *Walküre*. But switching on my radio that afternoon for Geraldine Farrar's intermission comment, I heard the concluding duet of Act 1, and was overwhelmed by the sheer splendor of Flagstad's voice, its seemingly effortless deployment in the long-breathed phrases, and the musical intelligence and taste which governed this use of it. I went to the *Tristan*, therefore, prepared for the exciting marvels I heard, which included the sensational two high C's that, in the frenzied first moments of the second-act duet, Flagstad attacked squarely, produced fully, and held securely, entirely in her stride, as though they were an octave lower. And I am at a loss to account for the pallid, unexcited description of the singing I wrote after the performance that night.

1934-35   Ballet is not my field; but I think I may speak, without presuming, of aspects of George Balanchine's work that have delighted me in *Pastorale, The Prodigal Son* and *The Ball*, which I saw performed by the Diaghilev company; in *Concurrence* and *Cotillon*, which were done last year by the Monte Carlo company; and now in the various productions of the American Ballet.

My delight is in the unfailing inventiveness, the wit, the impress of a distinctive mind not only on movement of Balanchine's own devising (and his use of the body as a plastic medium is very much his own) but on traditional material. Not only is a piece of revue hokum like *Errante* distinguished at certain points by strokes of what someone has felicitously named *fantaisie Balanchine*—for example, Tamara Geva slipping off William Dollar's body as they are being carried off the stage; Geva flinging Charles Laskey's body about the stage; Geva's hands moving up the extended arms of Dollar and Laskey (all this, I am aware, will make sense only to those who have seen it). On the traditional steps of classical ballet also—in *Serenade, Mozartiana, Reminiscence*—are superimposed groupings, patterns of movement, and

1935-36

strokes of imagination and wit that are fascinating. Each time that Balanchine creates a *pas de deux* for ballerina and supporting male dancer, for example, it is something new and amazing. In *The Prodigal Son* it was the seduction, which ended in an interlocking of the two bodies. In *Cotillon* it was the strange and ominous *Hand of Fate* episode (to the extraordinary music of Chabrier). And the *pas de deux* in *Mozartiana* has features of its own. [*Brooklyn Eagle*]

Postscript 1964 I had also seen *Apollo* when it was first performed by the Diaghilev company; but this ballet, which has come to be, for me, the most beautiful and wonderful of all, baffled me completely that first time with its originality of movement and metaphor.

1935-36 Ordinarily the occasions which impress themselves on a reviewer in the course of a season and remain in his memory as great artistic events are extremely few (though enough to make him aware of the inadequacy of most of the things he is called on to appraise). And though the past season proved in the end to be extraordinary in this respect, its first months were normal. In this early period the few outstanding events were the debut of the pianist Webster Aitken, the recital of Joseph Szigeti and the first appearances in song recital of Kirsten Flagstad. Szigeti demonstrated again his extraordinary qualities as musician and violinist —the vitality, the fire, the unfailing purity and distinction of style, the equal purity of tone. At Flagstad's Carnegie Hall recital one was impressed by the richness, the subtlety of the flawless musicianship and taste that governed the succession of marvelous sounds and gave them shape and significance; at the closer range of Town Hall one was moved by the quality of the person, and perceived what had not been apparent before—how deeply the person was involved in what the singer did, how intimately feeling was related to each phrase that was sung; and having perceived this in Town Hall, one was able to perceive it later in the Metropolitan. But it is possible to consider Aitken's debut more important, for it introduced a pianist still in his twenties, with the matured and disciplined equipment of an artist twice his age, who chose to concern himself with matters like Beethoven's *Diabelli Variations* and met with ease and security their every requirement of technique and understanding.

In January Sir Thomas Beecham took over the Philharmonic-Symphony and, in the time he could spare from exhibiting the worst of English music, amazed one with the style of his performance of Mozart—the dynamic quality not only of the brilliant flourishes but of the bold accents and nuances in the phrasing of melody. Also memorable was a performance of Berlioz's *Symphonie Fantastique*, this time with the Philadelphia Orchestra, that resulted from the meeting of two highly individual minds whose similarity manifests itself most obviously in the dynamic quality of their phrasing—Berlioz's in his music, Sir Thomas's in his performance of music. And one must consider noteworthy an occasion at which the Philadelphia Orchestra is led by a conductor who not only can reveal its technical excellence but can use this excellence in the service of fine musical purpose.

In January too there began one of the outstanding events in the history of music in New York—the series of recitals in which Artur Schnabel played all thirty-two of Beethoven's sonatas for piano. This series derived its importance both from the music and from the performer: the sonatas record a spiritual and artistic development which has led some to regard Beethoven not only as the greatest composer but as the greatest artist the world has known; and in Schnabel's playing, with its structural clarity, its intellectual and dramatic power, its intensity and elevation of

1935-36

feeling, they find their ideal medium of transmission. In the course of the series one realized again and again the absurdity of the notion of Schnabel as an over-intellectual and under-emotional pianist. There were sonatas, or movements in sonatas, in which his marvelous feeling for the shape of the phrase and for larger structure, for the coloring and timing of notes in a phrase, produced expressive subtleties that set him apart from all living pianists and caused the music to appear to take its natural, its inevitable course. But there were others in which crescendos were volcanic eruptions, *piano* was *forte*, and *fortissimo* more than the instrument could produce agreeably—in which Schnabel's emotion, in other words, was not contained within the musical structure—and one heard performances flawed, shaken, torn and even confused by excessive intensity of feeling.

In January also there began Toscanini's last concerts with the Philharmonic-Symphony, at which one experienced for the last time the distinctive qualities of his performances—the radiance and transparency of tone and texture, the perfection of phrasing, the supple continuity of tempo, the clarity and perfect proportion of structure, the new depth, spaciousness and power—and through these the distinctive purity of feeling, taste and attitude. The concerts were representative in more than the quality of the performances. In these last precious weeks, time that should have gone to matters like Beethoven's *Eroica* was devoted to matters like Cherubini's Symphony, Goldmark's *Rustic Wedding* and Saint-Saëns's *Danse Macabre*; and ensemble performances that should have had the participation of Schnabel, Hubermann and Szigeti had Casadesus and Heifetz.

Only the pianist Rudolf Serkin proved worthy of the honor of playing with Toscanini; and we have yet to hear what sort of pianist he really is, since we know him only from performances in which he has had to gear his operation with that of Busch or Toscanini. Thus, in the performances of Mozart's Concerto

1935-36 (1964)

K.595 and Beethoven's No. 4 his playing exhibited the same warm lyricism within the limits of delicacy and sensitiveness of tone and line as did the orchestral contexts provided by Toscanini, even where Beethoven called for something stronger.

[*Brooklyn Eagle*]

Postscript 1964 Within a year I was reporting that Serkin, "whose playing tends toward delicacy, sensitiveness and refinement ... has set himself to give it power and breadth—the result being ... occasional pounding of the piano to excess." This was the beginning of what soon was wowing audiences with its manifestation of intensity of feeling and involvement—the flailing arms battering the piano almost to the point of wrecking it. And the end was the playing which when it isn't violent is nerveless and without force, and which works in the empty bombast of a Brahms concerto, but which—with its tone that changes from a pallid *piano* only to an unpleasantly percussive *forte*, its melodic legato that is without continuity of dynamics, cohesive tension and outline—doesn't work in a concerto of Mozart.

As for Webster Aitken, a 1938 recording of his performance of Schubert's C-minor Sonata testifies to his distinction as pianist and musician (when I played part of it for Toscanini once, he said: "Is good—is good musician. Where is the rest?"). And the reasons why such distinction didn't win him a secure place in our musical life are worth noting. At that time the concert activity of the country was almost entirely controlled by the two big managements that trafficked in the celebrated virtuosos who dazzled the large musical public with displays of virtuosity, not in young American pianists who addressed sophisticated listeners with matters like the *Diabelli Variations*. And in obtaining even the few engagements available through a small management Aitken encountered an additional difficulty: that

1936–37

then as now a performer's engagements throughout the country depended on the review his New York recital got in the *Times*; and that although Noel Straus wrote high praise in the *Times* of Aitken's playing at his debut, his New York appearances thereafter brought him only Straus's disapproval (when Aitken played the *Diabelli Variations* again in 1945 Straus didn't wait to write the disapproval in the *Times* but kept proclaiming it at the concert loudly enough for people in the vicinity to hear). At the last of these appearances, in 1955, the *Times* reviewer was Harold C. Schonberg, then only an assistant to Downes, but already operating grandly in the consciousness of exercising the *Times* power. Aitken's performances that day had their eccentricities, which it was a reviewer's business to report; however it was his business to report also that they occurred in playing which revealed an impressive mastery in the handling of the piano and the music—mastery even when the operation made the music something one couldn't accept, and certainly when it produced something as wonderful as Aitken's statement of the opening of Schubert's Sonata Op. 78, one of the high points of the performer's art in my experience. But this mastery was something Schonberg had no ear for; and his review was a high-and-mighty rejection similar to the recent one—extreme in its vulgarity and offensiveness—of Glenn Gould's eccentric performance of Brahms's D-minor Concerto. Presumably this is why one hasn't heard of Aitken playing in public since then.

1936–37 The audience which occupied even part of the stage of Town Hall for Lotte Lehmann's recital on Saturday evening obviously was one that wanted what Mme. Lehmann has to give —charm of person, emotional intensity, a lovely voice; and she gave not only these things but a program of popular favorites.

1936-37 (1964)

Mme. Lehmann's way with *Lieder* is well known by now. She does well with quiet songs like Schubert's *An die Musik* and *Im Abendrot;* she is at her best in vivacious songs that employ her dramatic gifts but require no great emotional intensity, like Schumann's *An den Sonnenschein* and his humorous *Marienwürmchen* and *Die Kartenlegerin*, which her subtleties of phrasing and facial play on Saturday made a sheer delight. She is at her worst in a dramatic song like Schubert's *Der Doppelgänger*, in which her emotional intensity destroys the tonal and rhythmic framework of the song. The content of *Der Doppelgänger* is contained within the rhythm of its phrases; and these rhythms are framed by the chords of the piano; but on Saturday even a better pianist than Erno Balogh would have been unable to frame what Mme. Lehmann sang.

However, Mme. Lehmann was out to please her audience, not me; and it was pleased by *Der Doppelgänger* as mightily as by *Die Kartenlegerin*. [Brooklyn Eagle]

Postscript 1964 What Lehmann did in *Der Doppelgänger* was to load on the song an amount of personal emotion and expressive projection which destroyed its shape, but which in opera achieved the miracle one used to witness at the Metropolitan—of transforming dull Elisabeth, pallid Elsa, or the silent Sieglinde of the opening scene of *Die Walküre* into a radiant being who touched one's heart.

In the early forties the necessity of exercising care and skill in the use of an aging voice resulted not only in less constricted and more agreeable high notes but in refinement and subtilization of the singing, which now achieved expressive effect in a song through inflection of the continuous line of the phrase. For a few years Lehmann's Town Hall recitals offered unforgettable experiences of this perfected art; then the programs included more and more of the songs that lent themselves to the increasing

1 *January 1938*

archness and cuteness to which her adoring audiences responded ecstatically, and the concerts included goings-on that needed a stronger stomach than mine. I therefore stopped going to them; and thus I missed the climax of this public love affair—the celebrated scene of renunciation and farewell at the recital of 16 February 1951, which is immortalized by a recording that will enable future generations to hear Lehmann make her intermission speech, hear her say at the end of the concert that she will *try* to sing Schubert's *An die Musik*, and hear her, sure enough, break down dramatically in the last phrase. More important, future generations will be able to hear that she sang a good program with a still amazingly lovely voice and for the most part with beautiful art.

1 *January 1938*   The public will not read collections of newspaper or magazine articles on music, and least of all is it interested in reports of concerts and operas of fifty years ago—that was what American publishers said when I tried to get them to bring out Shaw's *Music in London 1890–1894*. If they were right, then the public will not read his reviews of musical events in *London Music in 1888–1889*; it will prefer to read Mr. Downes, Mr. Gilman, Mr. Chotzinoff on events of today. And if that is so, then the public is—to put it very mildly—making a great mistake. The performance of Boito's *Mefistofele* which Shaw wrote about on 29 May 1889 can be of no interest to anyone today; but it provided the occasion for Shaw to observe that Gounod's *Faust* was "a true musical creation, whereas Boito has only adapted the existing resources of orchestration and harmony very ably to his libretto. In short, Gounod has set music to Faust, and Boito has set Faust to music"; and that "the house likes Boito's prologue, in spite of the empty stage and the two ragged holes in

1 January 1938

a cloth which realize Mr. Harris's modest conception of hell and heaven." This is not the best example but merely the shortest; the fact is that the daily events of the musical season elicited from Shaw a flow of comment on music, on musical performance, on the entire musical scene, that is still among the most discerning, the most revealing, the most enjoyable one can read in any language.*

Read this comment, read the astounding article on a performance of *Il Trovatore* at the end of the book, the equally astounding article on Verdi; they will—or at least they should—kill your taste for the incompetent, the pretentious, the despicable critical performances of today. These are strong terms, but the terms I would like to use are unprintable; and if you suspect me of extravagance read Shaw, whose remarks about his colleagues are as timely as his remarks about *Il Trovatore*. Of one, disliked by the others, Shaw wrote:

He has the force to write individually, originally, making his mark with every opinion he delivers. Of how many critics in London is it possible to say as much? When one thinks of the average critic, with his feeble infusion of musical dictionary and analytical program, the man who has no opinion, and dare not express it if he had, who is afraid of his friends, of his enemies, of his editor, of his own ignorance, of committing an injustice (as if there were any question of abstract justice involved in the expression of a critic's tastes and distastes), it is impossible not to admire L. E., who, at an age at

---

* (1964) One should read the volumes in the complete edition of Shaw, not the Anchor volume, whose contents are selected, arranged, titled and introduced—all badly—by Eric Bentley. And one should add to these *How To Become a Musical Critic*, published here in 1961, with Shaw's very first reviews, written in 1876–77, which reveal that at twenty he operated without his later literary brilliance but already with the critical perception that enabled him, for example, to observe that Costa didn't have "that highest faculty of a conductor, which consists in the establishing of a magnetic influence under which an orchestra becomes as amenable to the *bâton* as a pianoforte to the fingers." The volume offers additional fine pieces from the 1888–94 period, and scattered writings from the later years which document the deterioration of his critical powers.

10 February 1940

which all ordinary journalists are hopelessly muzzled by the mere mass of their personal acquaintance, can still excite these wild animosities in the breasts of his colleagues.

And I would say of Shaw that what made him so great a critic was his integrity in relation to his material—by which I mean among other things that he used all his resources of knowledge, taste and wit in the process of dealing rigorously with the material as it required to be dealt with; whereas the others use the material to show their knowledge, taste and wit. Mr. Chotzinoff does anything to his subject to appear hard-boiled, blasé, wise to the things which the more naive and impressionable fall for; Mr. Gilman's act is different—he is the littérateur, the gentleman—but his subject suffers no less. Our musical life is the worse for a Barbirolli at the head of a New York Philharmonic, a Stokowski all over the place; it is the worse, then, for a criticism which helped to make these things possible; and to believe that Mr. Gilman believed what he wrote of Barbirolli's first appearance here, or of Stokowski's appearances during the past ten years, I would have to believe him to be without the understanding I know he possesses. Shaw created no such dilemma for his readers.

[*The Nation*]

10 February 1940 A commentator on the musical scene—on the music, and on the ideas, the activities, the institutions which music brings into existence—is, I pointed out a while ago, bound to concern himself with other men's comment, since this is itself a part of the scene and a part that in considerable degree determines the rest: criticism is one of the things that have interested me not only as a music-lover but as a critic; it is the thing I am interested in as I look back on the eighteen years in which, at intervals, I have written for the *Nation*.

10 February 1940

The critic has important functions: as a mere reporter, an appraiser of the particular musical event, he has the duty to give his reader not only an honest judgment but the basis of this judgment, the ideas about music and performance which will add up in the reader's mind to musical understanding, to a basis for his own judgment; the particular event gives the critic the occasion to consider the actual working of this organization or that institution in the light of what would be desirable; and events that determine the working of an institution, its structure, its very existence, are occasions for the critic to speak not only to his readers but for them. How, in those eighteen years, were these functions performed by the critics of important New York newspapers? Badly, I would say, recalling Olin Downes on the *Times,* Deems Taylor and Samuel Chotzinoff on the *World;* and this placed an even greater responsibility on men with the equipment, the position of W. J. Henderson of the *Sun* and Lawrence Gilman of the *Herald Tribune.*

Henderson's competence, honesty and vigor made him the only first-line critic one could read with respect. Yet Walter Damrosch's career led him to conclude that "a sound musician, who is also a man of energy, generous impulses, and broad outlook, can get well up toward the mountain tops without blowing his alp-horn every moment"—an appraisal which lent force to Shaw's contention that a critic should know no man, that "his hand should be against every man, and every man's hand against his." It is an appraisal, moreover, which I draw attention to because it was this sort of treatment, most of it less honest than Henderson's, that enabled Damrosch to do the damage he did.

Henderson not only was uncritical of a friend; he was, in his last years, a little crotchety. Irritated by the commotion over virtuoso conductors he insisted that the New York Philharmonic Orchestra and the music of Beethoven and Brahms would remain even without Toscanini and even with a conductor of lesser

10 February 1940

magnitude, though he must have known that orchestra and music would sound different under such a conductor; he cited the excellence which the Boston Symphony had achieved under a single permanent conductor as a reason for the New York Philharmonic to do likewise, though he must have known that the Boston orchestra owed its excellence at least as much to the competence as to the permanence of its conductors. Writing in this way, Henderson not only gave his readers incorrect ideas on conductors and orchestral performance but placed powerful arguments in the hands of the people who finally brought about the engagement of Barbirolli as single permanent conductor of the New York Philharmonic, which considerably reduced the orchestra's usefulness to the community.

More reprehensible, however, was Gilman's contribution to the same result. Henderson lived to hear the orchestra and Beethoven and Brahms as they sounded when conducted by Barbirolli, and disapproved. But Gilman, after Barbirolli's first appearance, wrote of a performance of Brahms's Fourth which had torn passion to tatters, that it had "set the seal of musical piety and eloquence upon Mr. Barbirolli's gifts as an interpreter"; the modest virtues of some other performances elicited the statement that "the whole magnificent orchestra, strings and wind alike, sang with a clarity and depth and lusciousness of tone, an imaginative choiceness of phrasing and of style"; and Barbirolli himself was elevated into "something better and rarer and finer than a conductor of power and sensibility. He permits us to think that he is akin to those uncommon interpreters who give us a measure of 'that inner standard of distinction, selection, refusal' which an incorruptible artist once defined: who have sifted from experience 'all that seemed beautiful and significant, and have treasured above all things those savings of fine gold.'" With this review Gilman was a great help to the influential people of the Philharmonic-Symphony Society who were out to put Barbirolli

10 February 1940

over—the help, perhaps, that an orchestra's program annotator should be; but he failed in his obligations to his position as critic, to his readers, to the community whose orchestra the Philharmonic was.

He failed in these obligations, though he helped the people on the Metropolitan board, when in 1932 he wrote of the low quality of the Metropolitan's repertory as something imposed on an unsubsidized company by the low taste of the opera-going public to which it had to cater, and saluted Gatti-Casazza for his "dauntless action" in giving *Elektra*, his "truly heroic idealism" with *Pelléas*. For the truth, which Gilman knew, was that after the courageous Hammerstein had given these two works in 1907, the timid Gatti had waited until 1925 for *Pelléas* and 1932 for *Elektra*, and that only his low taste and complacency had been responsible for the low level of repertory and performances even in the prosperous years when the opera-going public had eaten out of the Metropolitan's hand.*

But it was not only when he spoke that Gilman failed; as often the failure was in his silence. The ideas with which Taylor, Chotzinoff and Downes filled the heads of their readers ** demanded critical consideration no less than the sounds made by conductors and violinists; but Gilman observed the code of music critics that I described recently: he never mentioned a fellow-critic except to pay him a compliment. In all the years that

* (1964) Mr. Gilman, writing in 1932, knew it was not the Metropolitan's subscribers who had compelled Gatti-Casazza not to put on *Otello* since 1913, *Orfeo ed Euridice* since 1914, *Figaro* since 1918, *Don Giovanni* from 1908 to 1929; and not to engage a better orchestra than the one that disfigured the performances with, among other things, sour brass chords.
** (1964) Taylor wrote once of Walter Damrosch: "He never was a Karl Muck, and I don't believe he ever wanted to be one. He seems curiously impatient of ultra-subtle readings of the classics"—which converted the difference between Damrosch and Muck into the difference between healthy simplicity and ultra-subtlety, and Damrosch's inadequacy into a defect of Muck. This sort of thing flowed in a steady stream from Taylor's typewriter.

10 February 1940

Chotzinoff blew his penny trumpet on the *World* his performances did not draw a word of comment from Gilman; only when Chotzinoff published *Eroica* did Gilman break his silence, and then only to describe Chotzinoff as a critic with a "quick and warm responsiveness," a "guarding sense of measure and restraint," a style that was "spare, expressive, precise." Nor did Gilman find it necessary to comment on Downes until Downes published the talks he had given in the intermissions of the New York Philharmonic broadcasts. Then, referring to "the largely pretentious and semi-literate gush, rich in ignorance and error," with which Downes's predecessor had disfigured the broadcasts, Gilman quoted a passage by Downes: "In his scores he [Tchaikovsky] cries out, shakes his fist at the skies, remembers the agony of thwarted love, and the end of every man's desire. Admire such a man, such a neurotic, such a pessimist? I adore him, and rate him a thousand times higher than aesthetes who have never known Tchaikovsky's weakness and terror, who shudder at such emotional indecencies, and pull their skirts together at the sound of them." And of this Gilman wrote: "This is the right note, admirably skilful in its manner of insinuating information, yet never relapsing . . . from the plane of thought and feeling appropriate to a great subject."

Moreover, it was, as Gilman said, important that radio listeners who were hearing symphonic music for the first time be assisted with correct information and discriminating comment; yet this was the first time that he referred to the gush and ignorance with which Downes's predecessor had misled them for several years. The obligation of the music critic to concern himself with the broadcasting and recording of music, Gilman observed correctly on another occasion, was inescapable; yet he evaded it: he did not write a word about the program policies of the broadcasting stations, the rubbish that was spoken with the music, and he did not review records.

13 June 1942

Evidently, in the criticism of the past eighteen years there is little to recall with pleasure or respect. [*The Nation*]

Postscript 1964 I couldn't foresee that even worse was to come.

13 June 1942 New York's Metropolitan Museum of Art put on a special show of Rembrandt's paintings and etchings during the past winter; and the New York Philharmonic-Symphony Society, which has the same function in relation to music as the Metropolitan has to the plastic arts, put on a special six-concert show of Beethoven's nine symphonies, his *Missa Solemnis*, several of his overtures, and the Triple Concerto. Since a piece of music, unlike a painting, must be ever newly created as a form in living sound, the special character of the Philharmonic-Symphony Society's Beethoven show consisted partly in its choice of Toscanini to create the forms of Beethoven's works for the six concerts. And the choice was justified by the plastic beauty, the emotional significance and power of the forms he produced.

Though the concerts were interesting primarily for their presentations of Beethoven's works, they were interesting incidentally for other things. Involved in the presentations was the New York Philharmonic-Symphony Orchestra, to which, in the ten or more seasons that he had conducted it, Toscanini had given a discipline, a sound, a style as distinctive as those of the Philadelphia Orchestra when conducted by Stokowski, or of the Boston Symphony when conducted by Koussevitzky. This discipline, sound and style had departed from the orchestra when he had departed in 1936; and it was interesting to note their return with him at these Beethoven concerts. One would have supposed they had returned only after laborious inch-by-inch rehearsal; but

13 June 1942

actually nothing at the concerts was more breathtaking than what happened at the first moments of the first rehearsal, when Toscanini, with no preliminaries, simply began to conduct the orchestra for the first time after six years, and the orchestra began at once to play as though the interval had been only one day—when, that is, he began to convey his wishes through those largely molding movements of the right arm, those subtly inflecting movements of the left hand, and the orchestra began to produce the razor-edge attacks, the radiant and beautifully shaped sonorities, the sharply contoured phrases, the transparent textures of balanced sounds, that those movements had elicited in April 1936. For minutes at a time he continued to conduct and the orchestra continued to play in this way; only after such long stretches were there halts to go back and correct imperfections. And at the end of a later rehearsal he turned to the finale of the First Symphony and, leading the orchestra through it without interruption, produced the performance of six or seven years ago in all its marvelously perfected detail.

The explanation of this is to be found partly—but only partly—in the fact that Toscanini carries the specific gifts for conducting—the ear for orchestral precision and sonority, the personal force and technique with which to achieve what the ear demands—to the point of sheer virtuosity to which they are carried by only two other men, Stokowski and Koussevitzky; that at these rehearsals he was dealing with an orchestra which he had in ten years made as phenomenally sensitized to his direction as the Philadelphia to Stokowski's, the Boston Symphony to Koussevitzky's—so sensitized as to be able to respond again to this direction after an interval of six years; and that he was conducting this orchestra in works which they had rehearsed and performed together a number of times. But the explanation is to be found also in the nature of Toscanini's musical conceptions—the unfailing plastic continuity and coherence of the shapes he

13 June 1942

creates in sound moving in time. In such a progression the timing and force of one sound implies the timing and force of the next almost irresistibly; and it is the power of these implications, causing the many players in the orchestra to produce the next sound at the same point in time and with the right weight and color, that is partly responsible for the remarkable precision in Toscanini's performances, the extraordinary things the New York Philharmonic did at the first rehearsal.

Toscanini's feeling for the time element in the musical soundtime continuum is extraordinary; and its manifestations—in the choice of a tempo, in its subtle inflection, in its distention with increasing tension in the music, in the maintenance of proportion between successive tempos—are among the most distinctive characteristics of his performances. One hears, in the *Missa Solemnis*, the rightness of the pace of the *Benedictus* for the blessedness which the music is concerned with, and looking at the score one discovers that the pace is exactly the *Andante molto cantabile e non troppo mosso* which Beethoven prescribes; but Toscanini did not get his pace from this direction—he heard it in the music: with the same printed direction, but with not the same musical discernment, Koussevitzky causes the *Benedictus* to move at an *andante* so *troppo mosso* as to be an *allegretto*. Nor is it Beethoven's directions for the various parts of the *Gloria* or the *Credo* that give Toscanini the mutually related tempos which bind the parts into a continuous, coherent progression: with the same directions Koussevitzky produces awkward discontinuities. Again, though it is Beethoven who gives only one direction for the entire second movement of the Seventh Symphony, the entire Funeral March of the *Eroica*, it is the necessities of Toscanini's own understanding of the music that cause him alone to establish a single unifying tempo for the various sections of the movement. And with no directions at all from Beethoven it is such necessities that produce the subtle inflection of this single

7 November 1942

tempo, the distentions that build up the fugato section of the Funeral March to a climax of shattering power. [*The Nation*]

7 November 1942   "This man, is he a musician—or is he a musicologist?" was the way one great musician expressed his opinion not only of a statement in a book, and of the man who had written it, but incidentally of what musicologists feel and think and find to say about music. The musicologists' own opinion of the value of their activities was expressed in Dr. Paul Henry Lang's statement in the *American Scholar*—that the public would get the guidance it needed when newspapers opened their columns to the scholars. They do not contend merely that their investigations into matters like *Dissonance in Early Polyphony up to Tinctoris* establish valuable facts in the history of musical language and style, or that their investigations into the relation of a musical style to the other human activities of its period establish valuable facts in the history of culture; they contend instead that knowledge of such facts is indispensable for the complete experience and correct understanding of music as music. When they insist on our being aware of the relation between a piece of music and the other activities of its period, it is not merely to give us correct notions about history: we are, as I understand it, to take Mozart's G-minor or Beethoven's Op. 130 as a communication of the conditions, forces, tendencies of its period. Certainly it is possible to discover in a Cézanne still-life relations of its elements to what operated on Cézanne as he painted it—not only the work of other painters and their ideas about painting, but the general ideas and attitudes, the social and political conditions of his time. But it is possible also for a person with no notion of these relations to take the still-life for what it is and what it was intended to be—something exercising power on

7 November 1942

mind and emotions as an arrangement of pictorial elements. And so with one of Mozart's symphonies or Beethoven's last quartets.

Addressing a meeting of his fellows, Dr. Curt Sachs pointed out how they served music: "To music, elapsing in time and fading into oblivion, we give memory, permanence, and the dignity that history alone can yield." I have myself commented from time to time on the fact that while certain important works are played over and over again others are left unperformed; I have made this point about concertos of Mozart, sonatas, symphonies, quartets of Haydn, Berlioz's *Romeo and Juliet, The Infancy of Christ, The Trojans*. But it is not such music that the musicologists serve in the way Dr. Sachs described: for example, the unfamiliar music of Handel presented at a public concert of the International Congress of the American Musicological Society a few years ago turned out to be mere exercises in which the young Handel tried his hand in styles of his period. And Dr. Sachs had in mind the music of earlier centuries, about which the same thing can be said. Musicologists are concerned, rightly, about the idea many people have that nothing written before Bach is worth attention. "Music," wrote Dr. Lang in his article, "was a vital part of the culture of all ages and was affected by the same intellectual tendencies that animated the other arts and letters of the time"—his point being, I take it, that the intellectual tendencies in early centuries which produced great literature and painting and architecture must have produced equally great music. But this contention is refuted by our own century, which has produced the painting of Picasso, among others, but no music of comparable magnitude: it is possible, then, for the early centuries which produced great architecture and painting to have produced less great music, or music which satisfied their requirements but not ours. And the contention is made not only on behalf of the music of Lassus, Palestrina, Victoria, Monteverdi, Gesualdo, Byrd, the other English madrigalists, Purcell—which most music-

7 November 1942

lovers today do know and find beautiful and moving; it is often made on behalf of things like the inconsequential little keyboard pieces offered on some recent records with Dr. Sachs's comment that "the music in this album is not 'ancient music'; stale, dusty, and at best a curio for historically minded snobs. It is no more 'ancient' than Rembrandt's painting or Gothic cathedrals."

And almost inevitably the crying up of what is remote involves a crying down of what is immediate—which, as inevitably, lessens the guiding influence and authority that Dr. Lang explicitly demands for the musicologists and that Dr. Sachs apparently resents their not getting. The newspapers *have* opened their columns to communications from Dr. Lang which have elaborated some of the points in his *American Scholar* article, and which like that article have been curiously unscholarly in their intemperateness and confusion of thought and expression and in their misrepresentation of fact to make it fit into their conceptual patterns. And like Dr. Graf's concept of *the* musical theater with which he flogs everything after the Greek, and Dr. Sachs's concept of *the* dance with which he flogs modern "phenomena of a social degeneration from the primitive *typus*," is Dr. Lang's concept of *the* "fundamental approach to an understanding of music" with which he flogs the musical life of today as he creates it to fit into his argument. This approach is "the road of intimate choral music, chamber music, piano music, and songs" performed, as they were written to be performed in the seventeenth and eighteenth centuries, in the home. With it he attacks the transfer of this music to "a huge auditorium," where the chamber music "began to transgress its limits and assume certain orchestral characteristics ill-befitting its nature," where the songs were "bellowed . . . by an operatic prima donna intent on bringing down the house," and where music which had been something people "literally lived with" became instead something they "face . . . as exhibition." And with it

19 June 1943

he attacks also the music for large orchestra written expressly for the large concert hall. But a man who argues that because music once was written to be performed by small groups of instruments or voices in a home composers today must not write for a large orchestra and we must not listen to quartets or songs in Town Hall; who for this purpose misrepresents the Budapest Quartet's concerts of chamber music or Elisabeth Schumann's recitals of *Lieder*; who contends that we who listen to this music performed in a concert hall are affected by it less than an Esterhazy or a Lobkowitz who listened to it performed in his ballroom—such a man must be prepared to have us decline his guidance.

[*The Nation*]

19 June 1943 Mark Woods, president of the Blue Network, was reported by the *Times* to have said that in commissioning Roy Harris to write a Sixth Symphony he had "made no demands or even suggestions"—don't applaud yet—"other than to hope that since he is essentially a man of the soil and one of our own his Sixth Symphony will be dedicated to the American fighting forces, and that it will be a symbol of the struggle which our nation is making and has made throughout its eventful history for the freedom of mankind." Only a hope; and such a modest little hope, too; and right up the alley of the Shostakovitch of America, who on any occasion of blood and tears stands ready and eager to commune publicly with his soul in forty-five minutes of incoherently bombastic sound accompanied by several pages of program notes about why he did it and how he did it. In accepting the commission, reported the *Times*, "Mr. Harris said he would compose a 'major moral symphony' that would dwell on the Lincoln era, as significant today as were the trying times of Lincoln's presidency." I can hear it already; and I can hear Mr.

22 January 1944

Harris telling us what he did to make it moral, and what he did to make it Lincoln, and so on. My ears are still aching from the Fifth Symphony, in which Mr. Harris told a world that had to know how he had been affected by the heroism of the Russian people. [*The Nation*]

22 January 1944   A Chicago reader, who reports that the Chicago Public Library has many of the books of David Ewen and those of Sigmund Spaeth, Charles O'Connell, Deems Taylor etc., but does not have, among others, Tovey's *Essays in Musical Analysis* and some of Ernest Newman's books, goes on to make this comment: "But the influence of the first group is not permanent. I know; for I devoured all of them, adopted their opinions about music I hadn't heard often or at all, and discarded them just as quickly as I began to use my ears and intelligence." The comment establishes one rather important fact—that the critic is subject to check by his reader, or at any rate by the reader who, in the words of my correspondent, "listens to music with good ears and a sound mind." It is indeed from this check that the critic gets or fails to get his authority as a critic with his reader. One critic likes Toscanini and not Koussevitzky while another likes Koussevitzky and not Toscanini; the reader then listens for what, in the performances, each critic says he hears and likes or dislikes; he finds it or doesn't find it, agrees with the critic's reasons for liking or disliking it or doesn't agree; and he decides after a sufficient number of instances which critic has and which has not the perception, insight and understanding that are what give him authority.

When Virgil Thomson remarks that Mitropoulos has taken over the New York Philharmonic like an army of occupation, or that Stella Roman doesn't sing in phrases but only in single notes

22 January 1944

which she exploits with a spectacular technique of crooning and crescendo, a reader with ears and intelligence can listen to a Mitropoulos or Roman performance and hear what the statement describes; and he will feel pleasure and gratitude for the brilliantly expressed perception which has increased his own understanding. When Mr. Thomson says Toscanini's tempos are a shade fast, the reader can sometimes hear confirmation of that. But when Mr. Thomson works out a demonstration that Toscanini's performances have meter but not rhythm, the same reader will listen to a performance and hear the fact that contradicts the demonstration. Or when Mr. Thomson writes that Toscanini's performance of Beethoven's Seventh was a mere highly dramatized outline taken at too fast a pace for the orchestra to execute detail with clarity, and that in the performance of the *Missa Solemnis* "there was no continuity in dynamic gamut" but instead a constant "unsubtle contrasting of force with weakness," the reader will hear in the one performance the clearly executed detail, in the other the "continuity in dynamic gamut" wherever Beethoven asks for it. And having heard, the reader will decide that there is no profit for him in either the pat schematizations about Toscanini's work as it is in Mr. Thomson's imagination, or the reports of concerts at which Mr. Thomson hears not what happens in Toscanini's performances but what should happen to fit the pat schematizations.

But not all readers have good ears and strong minds; and there are occasions when even these are not enough. For example, Mr. Thomson makes the statement that the Boston Symphony, Philadelphia and New York Philharmonic Orchestras

are as different from one another as the cities that created them and forged them slowly into the image of each city's intellectual ideals. Conductors have been had in to aid this formation, and a few of these have left traces of their own taste on that of the cities they have worked for. But chiefly their function has been to care for a

22 January 1944

precious musical organism . . . and to allow it to mature according to its own nature and . . . its community's particular temperament. . . . [Of] Boston, the intellectually elegant and urbane, [the orchestra] makes thin sounds, like the Paris orchestras, thin and utterly precise, like golden wire and bright enamel.

To cope with and evaluate this statement a reader would have had to hear the completely different sounds, styles and characters of the 1917 Boston Symphony conducted by Muck, the post-1920 Boston Symphony created and conducted by Monteux, the post-1924 Boston Symphony re-created and conducted by Koussevitzky, or the New York Philharmonic conducted by Toscanini and the same orchestra the next week under another conductor; he would have had to understand from all this a great deal about the functioning and relations of orchestras and conductors; he would, then, have had to know that the 1917 orchestra of Boston did not make thin sounds like golden wire, and that the sounds it did make were dictated by the temperament not of Boston but of Karl Muck. And a reader would need such experience and understanding, in addition to good ears and mind, in the other instances where the general cultural and social background to which Mr. Thomson relates the musical phenomenon under discussion is a magician's hat into which he can put fact and perception, and out of which he then can pull the oddly, amusingly fantastic products of a mind at play that are suitable for tossing about in cocktail-hour chit-chat, or the serious conclusions—in the articles about the New York Philharmonic a couple of years ago, for example—that have no more relation to realities.

Into a discussion of things of this world as they exist and happen Mr. Thomson disconcertingly introduces, as though they were equally real, things from some private world as he would like them to exist and happen. Thus, he writes hard-headedly that the Metropolitan management is paralyzed by its fear of its intellectual inferiors instead of being animated by a fear of its intellectual betters; that the opera house is acoustically poor and inefficient and expensive to operate; but that first-class opera has been given there and can be given there again. But then he adds that first-class opera will be demanded by the nation-wide radio public after the war—this radio public demanding the first-rate being one that exists only in the Thomson world, in which there are American composers ready for a New York Philharmonic five-year plan to build an American repertory for an American audience, and other things of the sort. The mixture of real and unreal is disconcerting; but the worse trouble is that it often takes an experienced reader to be disconcerted. [*The Nation*]

12 February and 15 July 1944   One of the college-age readers of this column who amaze me constantly with revelations of how much better musical understanding and taste—to say nothing of better all-around perception—they have than I and my contemporaries had at the same age, remarked recently in a letter: "The end of *The Marriage of Figaro* has been running through my head. Just to think of this music—without even whistling it—sends chills down my back. Whatever happens to me, I can reflect that my life hasn't been wholly lost: I have had the opportunity to know that opera, and that part of it in particular."

I have had thoughts of that kind myself in the last two or three years—about pieces of music, about Toscanini's performances, about Markova's dancing. And one of the pieces of music, certainly, has been *The Marriage of Figaro*. I got to know it well only when the Glyndebourne Festival recording was issued here, and found it marvelous then; but each time that I listened to it again after an interval I heard new marvels for the first time, while the old ones struck me with enlarged or fresh significance and greater impact; and I can reflect that whatever else has hap-

12 February and 15 July 1944

pened to me, I have had the luck to achieve the heightened awareness that enabled me most recently to hear in *Figaro* one of the supreme wonders that have been produced on this earth by human powers.

As with the whole so with the part—the passage that my correspondent wrote about. Its effect, like that of any such passage, comes partly from its context—where it is placed, what it follows. Three hours have been filled with the poignant sorrow of the Countess's *Porgi amor* and *Dove sono*; the longing of Susanna's *Deh vieni, non tardar*; the amused tenderness of her *Venite, inginocchiatevi*; the confused adolescent emotions of Cherubino's *Non so più cosa son*; the ironic menace of Figaro's *Se vuol ballare*; the mock heroics of his *Non più andrai*; the pompousness and malice of Bartolo's *La vendetta*; the ear-ravishing loveliness of the *Letter Duet*; the humor and wit of the duets of Susanna and Figaro, Susanna and Marcellina, Susanna and the Count; the comedy of the first-act trio, the great finale of Act 2, the finale of Act 4. Three hours have been filled with the orchestra's running fire of gay, mocking, witty comment that has created the atmosphere of comedy in which even the serious things have happened. And this has continued to the very last: the music has exaggerated comically the pleas for forgiveness, the Count's stern refusals; and even in the hush of amazement and wonder produced by the Countess's entrance the violins have softly chattered their amusement. But then at last there has been an end to all this, and a moment's silence; and it is at this point, as the Count begins his *Contessa, perdono*, that we hear music which tells us of the sublimity of human forgiveness—music which, after what has come before, is overwhelming. And it becomes even more overwhelming when it is taken up softly by the others and is carried to a point of superearthly religious exaltation. Then, in the silence which follows, solemn octaves of the strings below distant wind chords gently ease us down to this

12 February and 15 July 1944

earth again—and to the bustle and fanfares of the final curtain of the operatic comedy. The passage lasts only a couple of minutes; but those two or three minutes, coming after the three hours, create the most wonderful, most impressive moment that I can recall in opera.

It is almost as though Mozart had decided to correct the notion we might have of him as being capable only of what he had given us in the first three hours of *Figaro*—or for that matter what he had given in the slow movement of the Piano Concerto K.467 and in other astounding pages of other great works—and had taken a couple of minutes to make us realize that he could, when he chose, reveal spiritual insights equal to the greatest we have known. That was as much time as he needed for the demonstration; and once it had been made it didn't matter whether he made it again. Those insights were there, in addition to everything else that he communicated through the medium which he used as no once else has ever done; and that use of the medium and what he expressed through it made him the most extraordinary musical artist that ever lived.

The Metropolitan's recent *Figaro* was one of the company's most brilliant performances in recent years. It is a long time since I have heard an opera sung so well throughout—even minor roles like Marcellina and Barberina by Irra Petina and Marita Farell; major ones by older singers like Pinza, Brownlee, Novotna and Baccaloni, who were in particularly good voice; and above all Susanna and the Countess by Bidu Sayao and Eleanor Steber. Sayao sang as beautifully this time as she had done many times before; but Steber's previous achievements had left me unprepared for singing that was the sensation of the afternoon. That is, she had used a fresh, agreeable voice with good musical taste; but she had begun every performance with a strong tremolo which sometimes had cleared up and sometimes had not. This time, however, the very first tones of *Porgi amor* were clear and

11 *March 1944*

lovely; and her technical security continued to produce such tones, which her musical taste molded into long, continuous and exquisite phrases. Moreover, arriving at the reprise of *Dove sono* she paused, lay back in her chair, and sang it pianissimo as though recalling a dream of past happiness—a stroke of dramatic imagination which brings me to the fact that her Countess was also the outstanding impersonation of the afternoon and one of the finest I have ever seen on the operatic stage. Nobody I have seen in the role has conveyed as Steber did the Countess's youth and beauty, her spirit, her wounded pride, her humiliation at having to call on her servants for help and involve herself with them in stratagems against her wayward husband.

The cavorting about of the other characters is easier to do, but it takes actors as good as Pinza, Baccaloni, Sayao, Novotna and the others to do it as well as they did. At moments in this performance, however, they did too much; and one piece of new business—Sayao's extravagant posturings in the Countess's cloak and hat, in the finale—Dr. Graf should eliminate. On the other hand there is one point—the V*enite, inginocchiatevi* scene—at which they do too little; and here Dr. Graf should make the sense of the words clear to the audience by having Susanna, who has measured herself against Cherubino, try one of her dresses on him.

The performance was excellently conducted by Bruno Walter.
[*The Nation*]

11 *March 1944* The Metropolitan has not accepted the contention that all its performances should be given in English so that the audiences may understand the words that are sung and know what the operas are about; but it has done so for operatic comedies, or rather for some of them—for Puccini's *Gianni Schicchi*, Mozart's *Magic Flute*, and now Verdi's *Falstaff*.

11 March 1944

It is true that an audience needs to know what an opera is about. But I question whether this is more true of the comedies than of the tragedies, or of the comedies I have just mentioned than of Mozart's *Marriage of Figaro* and *Don Giovanni* or Rossini's *Barber of Seville*. And I doubt that the knowledge is achieved by having the opera sung in English. If the advocates of opera in English were to attend a performance in Berlin or Vienna, where all operas are sung in German, they would see as many people reading librettos as are to be seen in the Metropolitan, and for the same reason—the fact that the words are difficult, and for the most part impossible, to hear and understand: often they have been distended to unintelligibility in the process of being fitted to the music; often they are drowned by the orchestra; and most of the audience are too far from the stage. Having been taken to *Falstaff* by a friend, I heard it from an excellent seat in row R of the Orchestra; moreover I was listening to a delicately orchestrated work; yet only very few of the words reached my ears, and I would have had no understanding of what was going on if I had had to get it from the words that I could hear. Even when the opera is sung in English, then, one must read the words in advance to know what it is about, precisely as one must for a performance in Italian or German. And if that is so the advance reading should be done for a performance in Italian or German. That is, when the only reason for English turns out to be without force, the force of the reasons against English and for the original language should be deferred to.

For one thing there is the fact—which I was made freshly aware of by the *Falstaff* performance—that when one strains to hear all the words one doesn't hear the music; and the music is the point of the whole business. One doesn't go to the Metropolitan for the play of *Norma* or *Aida* or *Salome* or *Tristan* or even *Falstaff*; one doesn't go for the words that Verdi ordered

11 March 1944

from his librettist by the pound or the ones that Wagner himself perpetrated. One goes for the music about that play, the music that is hung on those words, the music that has much the same relation to the action and words as Cézanne's still-life has to the apples and pears which he painted. Since action and words are there one wants to know what they are about, and indeed one has to know for the music itself to have its full significance and effect; but the following of the drama should be such as not to distract one's attention from the music—which is to say that it should be a recognition of what one already knows, not a straining to discover what one doesn't know.

Then there is the fact that a performance in English sacrifices the effect of the sound of the original language; and the loss is greatest where the greatest gain is claimed for English—in comedy. Even in the long stretches where words cannot be heard clearly enough to be understood, the loss of the mere sound of the Italian syllables is like the loss of an instrumental color in the orchestral part. But the argument for English is concerned with the places where the words come through clearly, and where, it is contended, the audience must understand them so that it may get the humorous points and laugh. But these are salient places which are planned for laughs; and because of the way they are contrived they are places which remain in the mind of anyone who reads the libretto, so that he recognizes and understands Dame Quickly's unctuous "*Revere-e-e-nza*" as she curtsies, her repeated exclamation "*Po-o-o-vera donna!*," her "*Siete un gran seduttore!*" as she pokes Falstaff in the ribs, and in addition he gets from these Italian statements something that is lost in "Oh most honored sir!" or "Unhappy lady!" or "You're a wicked seducer!" He understands Falstaff's argument with Ford over precedence at the end of the act, and enjoys the additional effect, with the delightful music, of the words "*Prima voi . . . Prima voi*" and "*Passate . . . Prego.*" [*The Nation*]

11 March 1944 (1964)

Postscript 1964 There can be damage, then, not only in what is lost in the translation but in what is added. I don't recall a performance of Mozart's *Figaro* or *Don Giovanni* or *Così Fan Tutte* in English that didn't repeatedly jar and distract me with the disharmony between the elegance of Mozart's music and the sound, the awkwardness and the lack of distinction of the English words. And not just lack of distinction: once it is decided to use English to make the performance amusing, further decisions follow inevitably—to make it even more amusing with colloquialisms, and then with horseplay, burlesque and clowning, which do bring additional laughs but also additional disharmony with the elegance of the music.

Nor is it as though actual experience had given the Metropolitan reason to fear that a performance of a Mozart comedy in Italian would only only half-fill the theater and cause those who did come to sit stony-faced and silent. I have never attended a performance of *Figaro* or *Don Giovanni* in Italian, either at the Metropolitan or at the City Center, at which the theater wasn't filled to capacity with an audience that gave plenty of audible evidence of being informed about what was going on and being amused by it. It is in the face of this reality—of audiences laughing at what they understand in the performances in Italian—that the opera-in-English cultist argues for translation to make the performance understandable and amusing.

And Mr. John Gutman of Mr. Bing's staff, who himself translates opera texts into English one would prefer not to hear and understand, doesn't argue: he decrees. Opera in English, he wrote once, was something to be accepted here as *Carmen* in German was accepted in Vienna. But *Carmen* in German is a monstrosity; and the fact that such monstrosities are accepted in Vienna is no reason for introducing them here, where—whatever else may have been wrong with opera at the Metropolitan before Mr. Bing took over—one thing that was right was that for the most

8 and 22 July 1944
part the works were given in their original languages. This practice began when the Metropolitan's singers were mostly foreigners; but the fact that they now include many Americans is no reason why it shouldn't continue. As between opera in the original Italian or French pronounced with slight defects by Americans, and opera in an English mangled beyond recognition by foreigners—e.g. the Germans who sang in Mr. Gutman's English *Alceste*—I would choose the first.

8 and 22 July 1944 In a recent article on modernism Virgil Thomson observed that "the leading masters of it, Arnold Schönberg and Igor Stravinsky, are now elderly gentlemen. Their precepts and practices are expounded at all the music schools and colleges; their followers constitute practically the whole pedagogical wing of contemporary composition. All this represents a consolidation of past gains for the modernist movement." And "since modern music itself has come to be a conservative and well entrenched institution, the opposition to it no longer represents an intellectual position of any strength at all"; which is like saying that since Alcoa has come to be a conservative and well entrenched institution the opposition to it no longer represents an intellectual position of any strength at all—the "intellectual" being an example of Thomson's use of language for much the same purpose, and with much the same result, as Father Divine's.

"The estimate of how much modernism, and in what degree of dilution, a given audience will take at a given time," he continued, "is purely a consideration of practicability. Few real disputes about aesthetics have been active since the modernists came into command of all the positions of intellectual eminence by winning, a full generation ago, all the chief arguments about aesthetics. That is why open compromises on practical policy are possible today without any loss of dignity to anybody. Etc., etc." What victories and so on those portentous-sounding words and phrases refer to I don't know; but the general music-loving public doesn't even care: it dislikes the music, and therefore objects to hearing it; being as strongly entrenched in the concert hall as the modernists are in the music schools and colleges, it can make its objection effective; and no amount of verbal abracadabra about its having lost the esthetic battle and about compromises without loss of dignity will fool it into doing anything else.

Not that the general public hasn't read about modern music. Others have had my experience: when, as a member of the general public, I began to listen to the music years ago with ears and mind that were open and receptive, I also began to read explanations and discussions of it in the hope that they would enable me to perceive the new artistic beauty or potency in what impressed me as hideous or feeble; but nothing I learned from reading about it changed the impression I got from listening to it. And in time what I heard made me increasingly impatient with what I read: the music was bad; but the talk about it was worse.

The kind of writing I mean is Paul Rosenfeld's statement—in contradiction to what one heard—that a Rhapsody for orchestra by Wallingford Riegger was "evidently ... magnificent in texture and consistent in idea, grateful to the ear and lucid in form." And, worse still, his subsequent statement about anyone who was prevented from hearing all this by the work's atonalism: "If indeed one is unable to hear the relation of note to note, freshly, and without past experience, in every composition, whether it be tonal, bitonal, or without any tonality whatsoever, what indeed can one be said actually to be hearing?" As though it were possible to approach anything—and above all a medium of com-

2 September 1944

munication—without one's past experience; as though any and every succession of sounds must convey a coherent, significant relation; and as though one's inability to perceive such a relation between any two sounds must set poor, perplexed Mr. Rosenfeld to wondering what indeed one could be said actually to be hearing.

Then there is Aaron Copland's equally wide-eyed, incredible-as-it-may-seem, how-can-such-things-be talk about the "fantastic notions" with which "newspaper writers and radio commentators who ought to know better" have, apparently for the sheer hell of it, misrepresented modern music and prejudiced the public against it—with which Copland tries to persuade us that we haven't ourselves heard the aridities, uglinesses and horrors of Hindemith, Bartók, Berg, Schönberg, Stravinsky and the rest. And his statement of correct notions about the music—with which he tries to get us to hear in those aridities, uglinesses and horrors an "enriched musical language" and a "new spirit of objectivity, attuned to our own times," that make the music "our music," as natural and acceptable to our ears, as interesting, significant and valuable to our minds, as people a hundred and two hundred years ago found *their* music.

From this it is only a step to Virgil Thomson trying with mirrors to get us to believe that the music of 150 years ago, which we are deeply affected by, is as incomprehensible to us as the the painting and literature of the past, since it was produced by men "whose modes of thought and attitudes of passion were . . . different from ours," and that we can understand only contemporary music, which we dislike, since it is the product of the thought and feeling of our time. [*The Nation*]

2 *September 1944*   A panel discussion of dance criticism last spring was an occasion to formulate my ideas on the critic's func-

2 September 1944

tion and his relation to artist and reader. Recently, I said, there had been people who thought themselves ideally equipped to write about music for the lay newspaper or magazine audience by the fact that they operated on a level of insight, judgment and taste no more professional or educated than their readers' own. But the idea used to be that the man who wrote about an art should be someone who could give his readers the benefit of an ability to see or hear more than they could. And that, I think, is the correct idea. The critic, properly, is someone with superior powers of perception who says to his reader: "This is what I have seen or heard"; after which the reader looks or listens, and says: "Why, yes—how true, how wonderful!" But of course he also may say: "But no—I don't see or hear that; I see or hear this."

I went on to point out that according to this conception of the critic's activity he writes for his reader, not for the artist. And I made this point because the artist has a tendency to think that the critic operates primarily for him. Aaron Copland, for example, has argued that it is the critic's duty to nurture the artist—to tell him what is good in his work and what is bad, and presumably what can be improved and how to improve it. That, I contend, is not correct. If we assume, as we should, that the artist works from inner necessities, then it is for him to produce whatever those necessities dictate, and for the critic only to report to his reader what they have dictated. It is true that in such a report the critic does have certain obligations to the artist—the obligation to bring an unprejudiced and receptive mind to the artist's work, to keep that mind entirely on that work, and to report honestly what it finds there; the obligation, in other words, to write a criticism of the work, not to misuse it and misrepresent it in an exhibition of the critic's own cleverness, his wit, his learning, his pet ideas, his amusing style. But the critic who operates with competence and with unself-conscious absorption in the work he is dealing with—this critic operates as he should, and with fairness to artist and reader.

2 September 1944

All of this could be elaborated; what I want to say a little more about right now is the reader's "But no—." As I have described the critic's activity it consists in using his powers of perception and evaluation to animate those of his reader. To animate—not to dictate: what the critic tells the reader about a piece of music the reader can accept as true for himself only if his own ears and mind verify it. But if the critic may not impose his greater insights on the reader, neither may the reader impose his lesser insights on the critic.

The reader who tries to do this, as I pointed out recently, is someone who, because he cannot hear something, doesn't believe anyone else can. One could say that he doesn't credit even the critic with insights greater than his own; but the truth is that he isn't aware of insights being involved. And this is only one of the misconceptions that add up to his ignorance about music and everything connected with it—composition, performance, criticism. He has no understanding of what sort of personal resources —of mind, emotion, character, experience—are involved, along with mere facility in sound, in the creation of good music; or of such personal resources being involved, along with mere facility of fingers, in good performance. And he has no understanding of the fact that an equipment of the same professional caliber—both in sensitiveness to the medium and in personal resources—is involved in good criticism. That is why he is shocked by the critic's disrespect for a composer or violinist, but feels free to be arrogant to the critic.

It is also why he is shocked by the critic's intensity about what he thinks good or bad. That is, he doesn't realize it is the intentensity of the professional who cares deeply about his art. Toscanini becomes enraged when a phrase is not as it should be, because that phrase is something he cares about. And Shaw once wrote: "People have pointed out evidences of personal feeling in my notices as if they were accusing me of a misdemeanor, not

14 July and 11 August 1945, 20 July 1946

knowing that a criticism written without personal feeling is not worth reading. It is the capacity for making good or bad art a personal matter that makes a man a critic." [*The Nation*]

14 July and 11 August 1945, 20 July 1946   The musicologists' attitude that I have been objecting to—the preoccupation not with the piece of music but with ideas about its style, period and tendency—turns up in unexpected places. It isn't only the New Friends of Music audience that, instead of listening to a quartet of Haydn or Mozart, reads in its program notes a history of chamber music by Dr. Curt Sachs, or a discussion of the style and tendency of the particular quartet (which is difficult to correlate with the details it refers to even when it has such real connection with the work). The Metropolitan Museum, which finds it possible to simply hang its pictures and let people look at them, cannot do the same thing with music: it must have a musicologist to construct programs and write program notes about styles and developments. And—most absurd of all—a record company which decides to reissue some outstanding recorded performances of jazz cannot offer them as something to be listened to and enjoyed: it must offer them as something to teach styles and developments, with the help of booklets containing the inventions, confusions, obscurities and sheer illiteracies of the "authorities" in this field.

And there is another attitude of the musicologists that turns up in jazz. They have a habit of establishing the original form of an art as the only legitimate form, of which the inevitable modifications and developments into new forms are sternly condemned as degenerations from the primitive *typus*. In the same way, the original New Orleans jazz—produced by "cornet lead, and clarinet and trombone countermovements, over a two-beat rhythm section," as one reader described it to me—has been set up as the only authentic form of jazz, with much the same result: any departure from New Orleans style is not jazz, and all the different departures are equally terrible. The reader I have mentioned went on to say that "all other methods wander out into the damnedest complications and methods having nothing but historical connection (if that) with the original jazz style." Thus the early Louis Armstrong Hot Five performances with "Armstrong's soloing," which were a "first break away from the sometimes less individually brilliant but always more collectively alive New Orleans style," were also a first step toward present-day "individual exhibitionism, powerhouse arrangements for 27 trumpets and 89 saxophones, and Duke Ellington," and toward the intervening performances of the Chicagoans that my correspondent disliked. So that while the early Hot Five with Dodds and Ory played jazz, even the slightly later Armstrong-Hines-Robinson combination only played *"like* jazz."

But another reader with a more rigorously systematizing mind contended that the term 'jazz' was correctly applicable only to the New Orleans type of ensemble performance to which it had been applied originally; and that performances which emphasized solos rather than ensemble—even performances as good as those of the Armstrong Hot Five, the Dodds Black Bottom Stompers, the Chicago "jazz imitators like Beiderbecke, Teschmacher and Spanier"—were not "jazz in the strict sense." And he too pointed out that they were the first step toward the later Armstrongs and the performances redeemed only by a solo by Buck Clayton or Bix; and that "from there it is only another short step to Glenn Miller and Tin Pan Alley."

This is of course all nonsense. Jazz couldn't stop with the New Orleans style; and among the departures and developments we have to distinguish those, like the Chicago style, that are jazz, from those, like the "powerhouse arrangements," that are not.

14 July and 11 August 1945, 20 July 1946

Moreover we have to recognize value in whatever style it appears —to recognize that a particular Chicago performance happens to be better than a particular New Orleans. And I object to the "only-a-step" argument. If the Dodds *Wild Man Blues* or the Chicagoans *Shim-Me-Sha-Wabble* is good, it doesn't become less good because something bad has followed from it: only the bad thing that followed is bad; and the argument leaves out of consideration the good things that have followed. My reader's letters have made me feel more strongly about the preoccupation with developments and tendencies: it is the individual work of art that is important and that is good or bad, not by its relation to developments and tendencies, but by its own particular qualities as a work of art.

My idea of what is jazz and what is not I described in an answer to a further letter from my systematizing correspondent, in which he argued that to insist that the music produced by the Armstrong Hot Five is the same as the obviously different music produced by the later Armstrong Savoy Ballroom Five "leads to hopeless confusion," and therefore he did not see "what is gained by insisting that both must be called jazz." I wrote: "I have considered jazz to be the performances of small groups of musicians—performances spontaneously, freely creative in the traditional language and style described by Wilder Hobson in *American Jazz Music*, and exhibiting the integration, the immediacy of relation of ensemble performance in both the ensemble and the solo passages. Against these I have set the well-oiled performances of written-out arrangements by large bands. And I have taken into account the in-between types like the various Ellingtons, ranging from the early ones nearest jazz, in which the soloists operate with considerable freedom, to the later ones that are nearly all arranged gilt-and-plush. But the New Orleans performances, the Armstrong Hot Fives and Hot Sevens and Savoy Ballroom Fives, the Chicago performances—these I have regarded as

6 October 1946

different ways of doing what I have described as jazz.... The same thing is gained by calling a Hot Five and a Savoy Ballroom Five both jazz as is gained by calling a work of Mozart and a work of Beethoven both symphony; and confusion is created by giving them two names."

I should add that from some of the material sent by my systematizing correspondent I discovered that it wasn't only the attitudes of the musicologist that were turning up in jazz, but the musicologists themselves who had moved in on jazz, finding in it, as usual, not something to enjoy but an additional material for their categorizing and system-grinding. This was something I hadn't realized when I had encountered in the *Herald Tribune* an article on *Jazz Purism* by Rudi Blesh, which used the same method of falsifying schematization as did the monstrosity on chamber music in the nineteenth century that Professor Paul Henry Lang contributed to a New Friends of Music booklet. [*The Nation*]

6 October 1946 The first singing that Maggie Teyte did in this country a year ago, after many years' absence, was for the *Telephone Hour*; and that in itself was extraordinary, since the *Telephone Hour* normally presents only the singers and instrumentalists who are well known to the mass public, and Miss Teyte was known only to the comparatively few and sophisticated thousands who had bought her recordings of French songs. Also, the *Telephone Hour* normally pays those celebrated musicians its handsome fees to sing or play the music it thinks the mass public likes to hear; and another extraordinary thing about that first broadcast was that Miss Teyte sang the kind of music she was accustomed to sing in recital and on records: she began with

6 October 1946

Berlioz's *L'Absence*, went on with *Voi che sapete* from *The Marriage of Figaro,* and ended with *Oft in the Stilly Night.*

As soon as the broadcast was over, telephone calls began to come in—not in protest but in approval, and the total response was such as to cause the *Telephone Hour* to present Miss Teyte again. The incident should have corrected the ideas of the producers of the broadcast about the kind of music the mass public is willing and not willing to hear; but these ideas are beyond correction by such rational processes; and when I heard Miss Teyte on the *Telephone Hour* recently it was interesting to note that this time she sang popular pieces like *Adieu, notre petite table* from *Manon* and Noel Coward's *I'll Follow My Secret Heart,* with only Chausson's *Le Temps des Lilas* from her recital repertory.

It was interesting also to see how the Coward and Chausson songs were introduced and justified. For the Coward song Miss Teyte was asked to say something; and she informed the radio audience that she and Noel were good friends and she had always liked his music and enjoyed singing it, and this particular song was one of her favorites. Maybe so, but it hadn't caused her to sing the song in Town Hall—at least whenever I was looking. Concerning the Chausson, the producers of the broadcast thought it necessary first to awe the audience with the information that it was a great French art song, then to reassure it against the presumed boredom of Art with the information that it was "simple and nostalgic, yet fervent, telling of love that is faded and gone."

But before the verbal introduction to each piece of music there was an orchestral introduction that calls for comment. That comment was provided by a sharp-eared youngster who wrote me once about what he had heard during a nightmarish couple of hours in barracks with someone's radio going full blast. "The worst single item," he wrote, "is those fanfares that begin variety

6 October 1946

shows—each blatant, pompous and stupid enough to sink a battleship. And one isn't enough; we have to have about four of them before the program can start. Thus—Fanfare: 'Rapid Hairgrow presents'—Fanfare: 'Tommy Bingle, his basset horn and his Kansas Kretins'—Double fanfare: 'Frankie Kopak, that sterile entertainer of stage, screen and radio'—Triple fanfare: 'With a great supporting company of faded favorites'—Theme up, *tutti, fortissimo:* 'What Rapid Hairgrow will do for your hair' —and so on." He was describing one of the features of American broadcasting style not only for variety shows but for other programs: a flourish of orchestral bombast introduced the announcement of every piece of music on the *Telephone Hour,* whether it was the show song of Noel Coward or the great French art song of Chausson.

Fifteen years ago, when I first acquired a radio and began to be interested in what was being broadcast, the people in charge of studio programs were insisting that the mass public had to be led up to great music very gradually—by the programs in which a Metropolitan Opera soprano sang the *Habanera* from *Carmen* or the *Hymn to the Sun* from *Le Coq d'Or* along with things like *Somewhere in Your Heart, A Dream* and *The Rosary.* After fifteen years these people are still thinking of that public as a "huge audience to whom good music is . . . foreign" and who "must be attracted to good music by way of the familiar and popular" (I am quoting from an interview with Sylvan Levin, musical director of the Mutual Broadcasting System, in the *Times* of May 5); they are still developing the public's taste for Mozart and Schubert by feeding it not Mozart and Schubert but Massenet and Noel Coward; they are educating in this way a public which in fifteen years has grown thoroughly familiar with the music of the great composers through the broadcasts of symphony concerts and opera performances; and they continue this method of education, as I said before, in disregard of the re-

6 October 1946

sponse to Maggie Teyte's first broadcast, which should have taught them that the way to develop the public's taste for Berlioz is to let it hear not Massenet or Noel Coward but Berlioz.

Most of the studio programs featuring big-name performers, therefore, are still like the *Firestone Hour* that preceded the recent Teyte broadcast—with Eleanor Steber singing *Depuis le jour* from *Louise* along with *I'm Falling in Love with Someone, In the Gloaming* and *My Hero*. Or the recent *Prudential Family Hour* in which Patrice Munsel sang in a chiffon-and-rhinestone arrangement of *Oche Chornye* with male chorus and Al Goodman's Orchestra (first slow and sentimental, then fast, then in waltz time), later sang the *Hymn to the Sun* (re-orchestrated in the Al Goodman style, speeded up, cut, and with an additional high note tacked on at the end for Patrice), and finished with *O soave fanciulla* from *La Bohème*—these in alternation with *Torna a Surriento* sung by Nino Martini, *Why Does It Get So Late So Early*, sung by Jack Smith, and the *Whiffenpoof Song*, sung by Smith and the chorus.

Fifteen years ago a performance of Handel's *Water Music* was incidental to a dramatization of the story of his reconciliation with George I ("King: 'Tis the spirit and soul of water. . . . Like fountains, with the theme of a bird's song woven through the slender spray . . ."). Or Rachmaninov's *Silence of the Night* had to be led up to with fancy language ("Once more does night, with magic minstrelsy, bring forth the music of the glamorous past, stirring the soul of Don Juan to awake and leave its dreams for visions 'neath the moon"). And today *Oche Chornye* cannot be sung without some introductory whimsy about September being, to Miss Munsel, "a gypsy that comes when summer's gone and stays a little while . . . brightening the days with a wild palette of reds and golds and the soft blue-gray of far-away

13 October 1946

smoke," and about how "if September were truly a gypsy there is a song she might sing." [*Herald Tribune*]

13 October 1946 As I was reading the article on radio music on the music page last Sunday, my eye caught the advertisement of the Prince Matchabelli broadcast of the Stradivari Orchestra that afternoon: "The ONLY orchestra with a string section of priceless Stradivari violins!" Looking to see what these priceless Stradivari were going to play, I found it to be the usual half-hour jumble—the Polka from *The Bartered Bride, Surrender, Yours Is My Heart Alone,* the *Blue Danube Waltz, Caprice Viennois, Arkansas Traveler, Just a-Wearyin' for You* and a group of gypsy airs—which even the Stradivari couldn't tempt me to listen to. What I did tune in for at 11 o'clock that night was the performance of Schubert's *Death and the Maiden* Quartet announced in the American Broadcasting Company's bulletin; but this was not the first time that a quartet announced by ABC didn't materialize. And so I didn't discover how ABC got a work that lasts about forty minutes to fit into the assigned half-hour. Not that I didn't have an idea of how it would have been done: part of the quartet would have been sliced out in the middle or chopped off at the end.

This is one major consequence of the division of American broadcasting time into salable hours and half-hours which, rigidly maintained in week-after-week scheduling, create difficulties with the works whose composers didn't plan them to fit exactly into half-hours and hours. And it has given us not only mangled quartets of Beethoven and Schubert, but the Boston Symphony performance of Beethoven's Ninth without its first movement, only half of the New York Philharmonic's performance of Bach's *St. Matthew Passion,* the *Telephone Hour* performances of

17 November 1946

concerto first movements exemplified by the recent one in which the first movement of Beethoven's *Emperor* jumped from the introductory flourishes to the recapitulation.

The non-commercial British Broadcasting Corporation, which can assign to each work whatever amount of time it requires, doesn't perpetrate butcheries like those I have cited.

[*Herald Tribune*]

17 November 1946 Berlioz's Overture to *The Trojans*, broadcast by WQXR a couple of weeks ago, turned out to be a brief prelude; and as WQXR presented it, it became, in effect, a prelude to Rachmaninov's Rhapsody on a theme of Paganini. I find it difficult to think of two pieces of music less suited to each other in feeling and style, or of any one interested in the Berlioz wanting to hear the Rachmaninov and vice-versa. But the WQXR and WNYC program booklets are full of such combinations thrown together with no apparent regard for what can suitably precede or follow what, or for what a person will want to hear before or after what.

A Corelli sonata is followed by Liszt's *Mephisto Waltz* and the *Drinking Song* from Thomas's *Hamlet*; a Mozart overture and a Handel concerto grosso by a Wieniawski violin concerto; Debussy's *Après-midi d'un Faune* by Tchaikovsky's *Francesca da Rimini*; and one *Breakfast Symphony* hodgepodge comprises a Vivaldi concerto grosso, the Bacchanale from *Tannhäuser*, Rachmaninov's Piano Concerto No. 4, Cherubini's Overture to *Anacreon*, Saint-Saëns's *Havanaise*, and the *Wooden Shoe Dance* from Lortzing's *Tsar und Zimmermann*. These are all from WQXR; as for WNYC, it offers Roy Harris's Symphony No. 3 stuck in among three works of Saint-Saëns, and a Saint-Saëns piano cencerto between excerpts form *Parsifal* and Strauss's *Don*

1 *December 1946*

Quixote; and for a couple of months it ran a Berlioz-Tchaikovsky cycle and a Debussy-Rachmaninov cycle, among others. But no doubt such combinations seem wholly natural to the listeners who have learned to know music through the radio and its programs, and have absorbed its underlying attitude—that everything made of musical sound is equally music, and nothing is different, better or worse than anything else. [*Herald Tribune*]

1 *December 1946* I imagine that some people must be vastly annoyed by NBC's reiteration, at each NBC Symphony broadcast, of how its revenue from sponsored programs pays for these concerts, and how the "sound American plan of financing broadcasting by advertising" gives American listeners the finest programs in the world. And I imagine that they must be even more annoyed if they have read how the British plan of having broadcasting financed by the listeners themselves has enabled the BBC recently to devote the evening time of one of its three wave lengths entirely to the best in the arts for the part of the radio public that is interested in it—the music during the first week of this *Third Program* including Bach's *Goldberg Variations* and a choral and orchestral concert Sunday, a full-length chamber music concert Monday, short programs—including a recital by Szigeti—between acts of Shaw's *Man and Superman* Tuesday and Wednesday, a program of Kodály's music and a concert by the Paris Conservatoire Orchestra Thursday, *Don Pasquale* and Beethoven's *Hammerklavier* Sonata (the Schnabel recorded performance) Friday, an orchestral concert Saturday.

Not that any one here would ask NBC or CBS to devote all its evening time to the best in the arts that a minority of the radio public cares about. BBC itself has done this only now when it has acquired a third wave length. But even when it had

1 December 1946 (1964)

only two wave lengths it gave fair shares of desirable evening time to both minority and majority. And the large number of people who constitute the minority here want that way of dividing the time adopted in place of the American way, which is to give all the desirable time to the majority and a half-hour at 11:30 to the minority. [*Herald Tribune*]

Postscript 1964 Worth noting here is the curious performance of John Crosby. Even in the first years of his radio column his critical intelligence seemed to stop working whenever he ventured to discuss a musical program: one would have expected that intelligence to perceive what called for criticism in the *Telephone Hour's* operation, the goings-on in the intermissions of the Metropolitan Opera broadcasts, or Deems Taylor's and Benny Goodman's disc jockeying; however they received only Crosby's praise. But in an article, *In Defense of Sponsored Radio*, that he contributed to the *Manchester Guardian* in 1951 Crosby seemed to be trying to get British readers to believe black was white in other matters besides music.

Thus, the money from advertising, in American broadcasting, went into programs that were monstrosities of vulgarity; but, said Crosby, it also paid for the variety of programs required by "a very large country with far greater divergence in temperament, racial origin, and local custom among its people than in Great Britain"; whereas actually what he described as available to a New Yorker—"concert music, popular music, soap opera, hints to the housewives, lectures, discussion programs, comedy"— was carried by the sponsored network programs to everyone everywhere in the country, whatever his racial origin or its local customs. And actually much the same programs went out to the British on their non-commercial radio, with additional programs adapted to local interests.

As for music, without the money from advertisers, said Crosby,

1 December 1946 (1964)

the NBC Symphony wouldn't have existed and Toscanini mightn't have been lured back to America; without their income from broadcasting—i.e. directly or indirectly from advertisers— the New York Philharmonic, the Boston Symphony and the Metropolitan Opera would find it even harder to keep going than they did. He said this to readers in a position to know that their BBC had (at least ten years before NBC, let me point out) used money from the license fees on radio sets to establish its own symphony orchestra, to engage for it the world's foremost conductors including Toscanini, and to broadcast the performances of other British orchestras and opera from Covent Garden. But these British readers were not in a position to know what Crosby had written a few months earlier in the *Herald Tribune* about the way the NBC Symphony and the Philharmonic had been kicked around, and the Boston Symphony kicked off the air entirely. Nor could they know that the networks had dropped a number of other musical programs (CBS the Philadelphia Orchestra, *Invitation to Music* and the CBS Symphony summer series; ABC the summer series of its ABC Symphony) that Crosby hadn't mentioned even in his *Herald Tribune* column; and that at the time he was telling the British readers what the American system had done for music, the American system had reduced music on the networks to the NBC Symphony, the New York Philharmonic, the Metropolitan Opera and the Biggs organ recital; whereas the BBC was continuing its program undiminished. Nor could British readers know that this program was one that American radio music even at its highest point had never approximated. The American networks, exploiting names that had prestige for the mass public, had presented the great orchestras and the Metropolitan, and had come to see music almost entirely as the standard orchestral and operatic repertory; whereas the BBC had systematically explored the entire musical literature—the literature not only of opera and the orchestra

1 December 1946 (1964)

but of solo instruments, the voice and chamber groups, the unfamiliar music of the past, the new music of today.

Moreover, a couple of years after giving the British an incorrect idea of American broadcasting, Crosby gave Americans an incorrect idea of British broadcasting—or rather confirmed the incorrect idea they had been given for many years. In a column from London Crosby wrote that "a small group of—let's face it—highbrows determine what the British shall and shall not see and hear. It is a tyranny of good taste which in many ways is as inherently dangerous as our own tyranny of the rating systems or popular demand." And this confirmed the idea Americans had that the highbrows who ran the BBC allowed the British public nothing but programs in Sanskrit.

Twenty-five or thirty years earlier one might talk about inherent dangers; by now one had to talk not about the inherent but about the actual. And actually—as Crosby was in a position to observe in London, and as anyone can discover here by looking at the weekly programs in the files of the BBC's *Radio Times* in its New York office—there is no tyranny of the highbrow in England analogous to the tyranny of the lowbrow here. Only one of the BBC's three wave lengths carries the highbrow *Third Program*; the other two carry the *Home Service* and *Light Program* that satisfy the interests and tastes of the general public.

This is in accordance with the BBC's guiding principle, that it has an obligation, in the words of its former director general, Sir William Haley, to "provide for all classes of its listeners," and "in the course of the limited peak listening hours every evening to give some service to every possible taste." And the BBC adhered to this principle even before the *Third Program*: when it had only two wave lengths it gave the highbrow an hour or two every evening, the rest of the time to the general public; and with a program of serious music on one wave length for the highbrow

5 January 1947

there was always something for the general public on the other wave length.

A lowbrow tyranny on the American networks that considered itself obligated "in the course of the limited peak listening hours every evening to give some service to every possible taste" including our own would be something we highbrows would be glad to settle for.

5 January 1947   Opera, I have observed, is the subject Mr. Thomson's readers seem to be most intensely interested in to the point of writing him about. And the opera broadcasts are a subject which readers of this column seem to be concerned about in the same way. Their continuing letters are my reason for returning to the subject; and I think it worth while to begin with a description of a broadcast of an opera from the Salzburg Festspielhaus that I heard in Salzburg in 1937—not, of course, every detail, but some of the essentials that I still remember.

The broadcast began with an anonymous announcer's statement, in simple conversational style, that this was a broadcast from the Salzburg Festival, and that Mozart's *Don Giovanni* would be performed by the cast which he then gave. He made this announcement first in German, then in French, Italian and English. That was all he said before the performance: if there was an interval of a couple of minutes before it began—which I don't remember—it was not filled in (I can see American broadcasters fainting in all directions at the thought) by a star announcer's adenoidally rapturous description of the wonderful scene in the world-famous Festspielhaus and build-up of the great composer, opera and performing artists. After the first act there was a repetition, in the various languages, of the information that had been given earlier; for the rest of the intermission

5 January 1947

there was only the ticking of a metronome in the silence in which one was free to think, to read, to talk; at the end of the intermission the information about the performance was repeated again. And that was all.

It was all, because for people interested in *Don Giovanni* it was enough, and because the performance was being broadcast for the people all over Europe who were interested in *Don Giovanni*. If *Don Giovanni* were broadcast in this country for such people, no more would be done here. Actually, though such people may listen too, *Don Giovanni* is broadcast in this country for the people who are assumed not to be sufficiently interested to listen without the inducement of other entertainment; and that is why it is broadcast with a six-ring circus in the intermission. Recently I thought it "fair to assume that if they didn't get the circus . . . those 12,000,000 people would not snap off their radios and stop listening to the opera." Sigmund Spaeth represents the broadcasters' viewpoint when he writes: "I still insist that without some entertaining material during intermissions most listeners *would* turn off their radios"—to which he adds "just as I and millions of others do for those frightfully dull talks that are handicapping the U. S. Rubber Company broadcasts of the New York Philharmonic."

Sternly putting aside thoughts of the logical progression in Dr. Spaeth's sentence, which has fascinated me, and its unintended humor, which has delighted me, I venture to observe—for a few other music-lovers besides myself—that I would leave the radio on during the opera intermissions if there were no quizzes and round-table discussions, but that I shut it off during the intermissions to avoid the painfully embarrassing business of three or four people making fools of themselves, which is worse than a talk on astronomy. [*Herald Tribune*]

6 April 1947

30 March 1947 Strauss's new work, *Metamorphosen*—performed by Stokowski and the CBS Symphony on CBS's March 19 *Invitation to Music*—was half over by the time I was able to get to a radio; but I am sure that what I missed was only more of what I heard—an endless manipulation of a couple of themes in an apparent progression that never really moved an inch. The works after Strauss's masterpiece, *Don Quixote*, revealed the operation of undiminished technical powers in the service of steadily and appallingly deteriorating musical ideas and eventually no ideas at all. These powers could produce even in what was completely synthetic the spurious appearance of coherent progression; but what they have produced in *Metamorphosen* is the musical counterpart of an old man's mumblings into his beard. [*Herald Tribune*]

6 April 1947 If the Lily Pons style is easier to take with the *Telephone Hour* than in a performance of *Rigoletto*, the *Telephone Hour* style is easier to take with Lily Pons than with Marian Anderson. A reader contended last fall that the orchestral flourishes provided the listener's mind with necessary transitions between pieces of music on different emotional levels; but actually those flourishes are all in the same movie palace style and have no relation with what precedes and follows—none, certainly, with the Schubert song, the Negro spirituals, the Debussy aria that Miss Anderson sang last Monday.

But it wasn't only those flourishes that were offensively unsuitable. A few weeks earlier Heifetz had played a movement of a sonata for violin and piano—not an arrangement for violin and orchestra, but the original piece of chamber music for violin and piano, which he had played with his pianist. Now the songs of Schubert, Schumann and Wolf are also pieces of chamber music for voice and piano; and as it happens Miss Anderson sings them

29 November 1947

in her recitals with Franz Rupp, who has long been famous in the musical world as an ensemble pianist (with whom Kreisler, for example, recorded all the Beethoven violin sonatas for His Master's Voice). But on the *Telephone Hour* she must sing them with orchestral transcriptions of the piano parts—and transcriptions which translate the piano terms not into the closest orchestral equivalents, but into the glitter and luxuriance of the *Telephone Hour* style. Last Monday the simple accompaniment of Schubert's *Ständchen* was amplified with newly composed bits of orchestral counterpoint; the accompaniment of the gravely poignant spiritual *Poor Me* was enriched with chiffon-string countermelodies, its concluding chords with notes of the celesta.

But even this was as nothing compared with the lurid details of an orchestral transcription of Liszt's Etude in D-flat and its frenzied performance. In all a staggering amount of bad taste and artistic outrage was sponsored by the genteel Bell Telephone Company in that half-hour.

Apart from the bad taste involved in all this, there is the notion that music means an orchestra. It is time the people in radio got rid of that notion—time they began to make the radio public as well acquainted with the literature of the sonata, the trio, the song, as it is with that of the symphony, the opera. Let there be nation-wide broadcasts of the violin-and-piano sonatas of Mozart and Beethoven by Szigeti and Balsam, of Schubert's *Winterreise* and Schumann's *Dichterliebe* cycles by Harrell and Rupp, instead of additional nation-wide broadcasts of Beethoven's *Pastoral* Symphony and Schubert's *Unfinished*.

[*Herald Tribune*]

29 November 1947 Some of the kind of music by Stravinsky in which I used to hear only "expertly contrived aridity and ugliness" I have recently begun to find interesting and enjoyable

29 November 1947

—and nobody could be more surprised at this than myself. Trying to account for it I think that one of the factors was the Balanchine choreography for *Danses Concertantes*, which was like the additional line of counterpoint that completes a musical texture and gives it the significance it lacked without such completion: * when I heard another work I heard it with what such a Balanchine counterpoint would have imparted to it. Another factor was the score of *Le Baiser de la Fée*, which, even without what Balanchine imparted to it, had seemed to me years ago to be an unusually beautiful result of Stravinskyan manipulation of materials borrowed from other composers: now I was struck not only by the beauty of what Stravinsky contrived with Tchaikovsky's materials, but with its direct expressiveness, something almost unique in Stravinsky's music, which I could recall in only one other work, *The Firebird*; and I was fascinated by the way the beautiful and expressive details were contrived—which is to say, by the operation of Stravinsky's mind. It was this operation of his mind that I began to be aware of, interested, fascinated, and amused by, in the ostinato figures and rhythms, the perverse accents, the distorted melodies, the strident harmonies and sonorities in *Danses Concertantes*, the *Symphony in Three Movements* and the *Dumbarton Oaks Concerto*. [*The Nation*]

* (1964) It had taken me that long to perceive the nature of the relation of Balanchine's choreography to music. What his feeling for a piece of music produced was not movement that expressed or interpreted it, but movement that was contrived to go with it effectively ("I had learned to dance, to move; I loved music," he recalled a few years ago, "and suddenly I wanted to move people to music, to arrange dances."). The movement interacts with the music like an added line of counterpoint—movement and music enlarging and intensifying each other's effect and significance. One of the greatest examples of this is the slow movement of *Concerto Barocco*, in which the seemingly endless flow of Bach's lovely melody and the never-pausing flow of Balanchine's fascinating invention—each building up and releasing its phraseological tensions—work together with mutual enrichment and intensification, and with a cumulative impact, in the end, like that of the long flow of calm melody over agitated accompaniment in the Andante of Mozart's Piano Concerto K.467.

14 December 1947

14 December 1947 No doubt we shall hear effective performances of Verdi's *Otello;* but I think it improbable that we shall ever again hear the *Otello* that Toscanini produced for his NBC Symphony broadcasts of the last two Saturdays (I am writing this after the first one, on assumptions I think safe to make). What was so extraordinary about this performance was best stated by the most distinguished music critic of our generation, the late W. J. Turner, on the occasion when Toscanini conducted four concerts of the British Broadcasting Corporation's London Music Festival in 1935.

Writing in *The New Statesman and Nation,* Turner asked his readers to suppose "that in reading poetry one were used to see poems only in a very poor print upon inferior-quality paper; imagine, for example, having only been able to procure Keats's Ode to a Nightingale printed in smudged ink on a piece of blotting paper with the stanzas scattered haphazard all over the sheet and either no punctuation or all the punctuation wrong." This, he continued, was how music was very often performed, "and the first distinction between a good reproducing artist and an inferior one is that from the good artist we get an orderly, correct, audible impression." Or, better still, "we may compare one conductor's performance of a symphony with another's as we may compare a poor photograph taken with a mediocre camera by a not highly capable person with a first-class print taken by an expert using the finest materials." And for Turner "the musical impression made by Toscanini when he conducts a work is incredibly clearer in detail, better proportioned as to parts, and more vivid as a whole, than those made by any other conductor."

It is this extraordinary clarity and rightness of proportion described by Turner that are largely responsible for the impression of revelation that Toscanini's performances give (Turner spoke of the performance of Debussy's *La Mer* as "a revelation of its musical qualities," the most conspicuous fact about it being "how

1944-47

much more lucid and well-defined are Toscanini's reproductions of the music than those of other conductors"). It is literally true that one hears the work as one has never heard it before. And that was true of the *Otello*. Never had one heard the orchestral part stated with such accuracy, such clarity, such precision and refinement of execution, sonority and style (one had, after all, never heard it performed by a virtuoso orchestra like the NBC Symphony); never had one heard the vocal parts sung with similar accuracy and refinement; never had one heard vocal and orchestral parts fitted together with such precision; never, therefore, had one heard what all this accuracy and refinement revealed. And never, in all probability, would one hear it again. Even if there were assembled an orchestra like the NBC, singers with the youthful soprano of Herva Nelli, the ringing tenor of Ramon Vinay, the subtle baritone of the amazing Giuseppe Valdengo, it was unlikely that there would be a conductor who could get them to operate as Toscanini got them to do.

For myself, as someone who was surprised constantly by how much more marvelous the work was even than I had remembered, I must report one surprise of a different sort: the fact that among all the successes there was—for me—one failure: the *Credo*, which is a lot of things, but—again I say for me—not what it sets out to be, namely a musical embodiment of the ideas of the text. But that still leaves me a considerable distance from one of the Ninth Floor notables at the broadcast, who was overheard saying afterwards: "Ah, oui, c'était incontestablement magnifique, mais c'était quand-même Verdi!" [*Herald Tribune*]

1944-47 (*From Articles on the Ballet*)   Balanchine, for me, stands out among choreographers in the way Picasso stands out among even the best painters: by the mere power in manipulation of his medium; the additional powers of the mind and imagination that reveal themselves in the constant development and originality of his invention; its inexhaustible fertility; and in Balanchine's case the additional powers which this invention reveals in relation to music, drama and theater. They make Balanchine, it seems to me, an artist of the same magnitude as Picasso, the only one I can think of now working in any of the arts. He is, I would say, even more disciplined in the exercise of his powers than Picasso: the originality, no matter how astounding, always operates within the continuous development; a work as singular as *Danses Concertantes* is only a special use of the permanent but developing elements of the idiom and style of all the works.

There are people who object that the movements of classical ballet don't mean anything. Certainly those ballet movements, like any other plastic materials—for example, the materials of formal music—can be made to mean nothing. But as certainly they can be made to have the "eloquence of pure form." And some of the most exciting experiences of this eloquence that I have had have been those offered by the classical ballets which Balanchine has created in recent years: *Concerto Barocco, Ballet Imperial, Danses Concertantes, Mozartiana, The Four Temperaments*. This series is like the series of Mozart's piano concertos: the creative mind and personality, the language and style in which these express themselves, the formula which they fill out with the language and style—these are always the same; but the completed forms are constantly new and fascinating; and like Mozart's musical forms they fascinate and delight one with the play of mind and wit in the endlessly inventive manipulation of the formal elements.

No less fascinating, on the other hand, are the works in which Balanchine's choreographic invention is the medium for his extraordinary dramatic imagination and feeling for the theater. In *Le Bourgeois Gentilhomme* that imagination and theatrical sense produce delightful comedy; in *Le Baiser de la Fée* we get their full range—in scenes which begin with radiant gaiety and humor and end with dark, terrifying violence. We also get wonderful examples of how that imagination uses traditional ballet materials and situations. I have spoken more than once of the new thing that Balanchine makes in each ballet of the movements and poses of the *pas de deux* of ballerina and male dancer: the seduction in *Le Fils Prodigue*; the strange, ominous, menacing *Hand of Fate* episode in *Cotillon*; the exquisite, touching expression of the emotions of youthful love in *Le Bourgeois Gentilhomme*. In *Le Baiser de la Fée* there is the tender, playful *pas de deux* of the boy and his bride; there is, on the other hand, the terrifyingly violent *pas de deux* in which the fairy takes possession of the boy at the end of the village scene. And this one is followed by a powerful stroke of the *fantaisie Balanchine* that is a further manifestation of Balanchine's dramatic imagination and theatrical sense: the fairy stands behind the limp body of the boy, her right arm extended over his shoulder and pointing forward, and with her left hand gives him a push that impels him a few steps; moving up behind him with her extended right arm still pointing forward, she gives him another push that impels him another few steps; again she moves up behind him with her extended right arm pointing forward and gives him a push that impels him off the stage; and with her extended right arm still pointing forward she follows him off as the curtain falls.

And the climax of *The Night Shadow* is a supreme stroke of *fantaisie Balanchine*—the *pas de deux* of the poet's encounter with the somnambulist, in which his way first of expressing his wonder, then of attempting to establish contact with her mind, is to experiment with her moving body, to control its motion—to stop it, to send it now in this direction, now in that, to spin it, to grasp the candle in her hand and swing her now this way, now that. The episode has terrific impact—from its originality both as dance and as theater invention, from the sudden simplicity and

28 March 1948

quiet after all the animated intricacy, from Danilova's concentration and intensity in her exquisitely limpid flow of movement.

In these new works the Monte Carlo offers one group of the greatest things one can see in ballet; and another group is the performances of old classics in which Danilova appears: the performance of *Coppelia*, which she makes enchanting; the performances of *The Nutcracker* and *Swan Lake*, which she enriches with an art that grows ever more wonderful—this developing art being what age gives her while it takes away mere stamina. It is the same thing as has happened in the singing of Lotte Lehmann; and this suggests a further analogy: Danilova's classical dancing is, in relation to Markova's, as Lehmann's *Lieder*-singing is in relation to Elisabeth Schumann's. That is, the line that is so pure in Markova's *Swan Lake* or *Nutcracker* performance is suffused with personal warmth and radiance and graciousness in Danilova's.

And still another musical analogy suggests itself. In addition to the expressive force, the poignancy, the loveliness, and everything else that makes a work of Mozart wonderful, there are the ways the things happen, the ways they come into existence, the precise way, for example, a woodwind adds itself to strings at a certain point. These are the unobtrusive, effortless, inevitable manifestations of extraordinary human powers; and under the impact of their succession it is sometimes difficult to keep from crying out in excitement and delight. The same thing is true of the succession of movements in the slow movement of Balanchine's *Concerto Barocco*. And it is true of the succession of movements in Danilova's *Nutcracker* performance. [*The Nation*]

28 March 1948 The last step has been taken: one can now, sitting at home, not only hear a performance by Toscanini and the NBC Symphony but see them producing the performance

28 March 1948

one is listening to. It is a new and strange experience to be in agreement with David Sarnoff; but I do share the gratification he expressed—at the first NBC Symphony telecast on March 20—over the fact that people in remote parts of the country who would never have seen Toscanini working with an orchestra may now be able to do so (I say "may" rather than "will" because that is as much as one can say: even the ordinary broadcasts of the NBC Symphony and other great orchestras are, after all these years, not carried by local stations everywhere in the country, as Mr. Sarnoff no doubt said they would be).

I feel this gratification because the process of a Toscanini performance is as special as its result. What is special about the result—apart from its expressive and imaginative power—is its continuity. Continuity, first, of impetus: once the progression is set going it never sags or breaks, but carries over from each sound to the next. And, second, plastic continuity: the continuum of sound moving in time is a plastic medium; and in the changes of sonority and pace which inflect the contour of the melodic line and shape the tonal mass in a Toscanini performance, one hears the operation of an unerring plastic sense on that medium—a plastic sense which makes each change of sonority or pace proportional to what precedes and follows, thus gives the developing form in sound coherence, and causes each sound in this coherent progression to imply, by its timing and force, the timing and force of the next, so that the successive sounds fall into place with inevitability and ease.

This continuity in the moment-to-moment flow of the performance is produced by a continuous activity—a moment-to-moment exercise of the utmost attentiveness, concentration and control. Once he has set the progression going, Toscanini marshals it along, watches over it, controls it to make it come out as he planned. The marshaling is done mostly with those large, plastic, sensitive movements of his right arm (extended to the point of

28 March 1948

his baton), which delineate for the orchestra the flow of sound in much of its subtly inflected detail and literally conduct the orchestra from one sound to the next in that flow—the effectiveness of these movements being due to their extraordinary explicitness in conveying his wish at every moment to the players, and to the compelling personal force which they also convey. The left hand, meanwhile, is in constant and fascinating activity as the instrument of the watchfulness that shows itself on Toscanini's face—now exhorting, now quieting, now warning, now suppressing.

The relation of these two geared continuities of activity and sound is fascinating and moving to watch as the unself-conscious operation—in response to each momentary situation—of a combination of powers beyond anything we have known or are likely to encounter again. And I find it moving for an additional reason: not only is every movement equal to the situation but it never is more than equal to it; those extraordinary powers operate, then, with an economy that is a form of honesty in relation to the situation and material; and in this way the performance is, in addition to everything else, a moral experience which I find intensely moving.

It is those two geared continuities of activity and sound, then, that television can let people everywhere see and hear. The March 20 telecast did this—but only for short periods. That is, taking over the technique used in films of orchestral performances (for example, the Toscanini film *Hymn of the Nations*)—of shifting back and forth between conductor and players of the orchestra—the telecast presented a number of close-range and long-range sequences of Toscanini in action—but each broken off after a few moments to show the blowing of the woodwinds or the plucking of the harps. The Toscanini moments were impressive and exciting; the goings-on in the orchestra interesting; but I would like to see the effect of maintaining the continuity of Toscanini's activity unbroken by keeping him in uninterrupted

20 June 1948

view throughout each performance, establishing his momentary relation to members of the orchestra either by changing the direction of the camera to include them or by combining their image with his, as was done at the end of the telecast. [*Herald Tribune*]

20 June 1948 "When we read the criticism of any past age," wrote Randall Jarrell in the *Nation* of June 12, "we see immediately that the main thing wrong with it is an astonishing amount of what Eliot calls 'fools' approval': most of the thousands of poets were bad, most of the thousands of critics were bad, and they loved each other. Our age is no different." I mention his statement in a column on radio music because most people understand some things about literature and its criticism which they don't understand about music. One thing they understand is that poets have been bad in the past and can be bad today, and that this is something critics may say; whereas they have been led to believe that only good music has been and is being composed, and that only this may be said by a critic. Radio has contributed most to this belief; and another contribution has been that of the musicologists (may their tribe decrease) who, to prove the value of their explorations and excavations, and reasoning in a world of concept millions of miles removed from fact, have produced one of their pat schematizations: that each period has had *its* music, which represented *its* creative energies and satisfied *its* esthetic needs; that the creative energies of early centuries which produced valuable painting and architecture produced equally valuable music; and that this music was as valuable as that of the eighteenth and nineteenth centuries, since creative energies have been equal in all periods. And the composers of today have adopted this reasoning: they are producing the music of *our* period, which represents *its* creative energies and satisfies *its* esthetic needs as the

22 August 1948

painting of today does, and as the music of Haydn, Mozart and Beethoven did the creative energies and esthetic needs of their periods.

Actually art is produced by the particular creative energies of particular artists, which are not equal even in one period and even in one art of that period. The musicologists haven't understood this fact, and the further fact that what Jarrell said of the poetry of past periods is true also of the music: most of it has been bad. The keyboard pieces from 1350 to 1700 that Dr. Curt Sachs wrote about on one occasion—insignificant in ideas, in structure and in mere size—were not, as he contended, the musical equivalents of Rembrandt paintings and Gothic cathedrals, or—one might add—of the keyboard works of Haydn, Mozart or Beethoven. The music produced by most of Haydn's, Mozart's or Beethoven's contemporaries was not of the stature of theirs. And today the ballets of Copland and operas of Virgil Thomson on the one hand, and *Odes to Truth* of Roy Harris and *Prayers in Time of War* of William Schuman on the other hand, are equally music of our period, but they are not equally good music.

That is something the critic must say if he thinks it—without regard for what anyone else thinks today or may think fifty years from now. It certainly is true that some of us may be making fools of ourselves in the eyes of the future by thinking as little as we do of the talents and achievements of our Harrises and Schumans; but it is also possible that it is the approvers of today who will turn out to be the fools of the future. [*Herald Tribune*]

22 *August 1948*   Kurt Weill's *Down in the Valley*, which was given its radio première by NBC August 7, is a work similar to Duke Ellington's *Black, Brown and Beige*, which represented the idea that, since the Negro had produced jazz, jazz was the me-

25 September 1948

dium in which to tell in musical terms everything that had happened to the Negro in America from his arrival in slave ships to his participation in World War II. Or to Gershwin's *Porgy and Bess*, behind which was the idea that, since the Negro had contributed to the amalgam of Broadway show music, Broadway show tunes were the right musical medium for a comedy-melodrama about Negroes in Charleston, S. C. Or, most of all, to the work produced by the American Lyric Theater in 1939, in which anything and everything that happened in an operatic romance about the mid-nineteenth-century mid-South was tacked on to a melody by Stephen Foster.

Down in the Valley, that is, is described as a folk opera because its rural-folk characters sing their anguish and terror and other powerful emotions in completely irrelevant American folk melodies divorced from their own texts. And there is additional irrelevance in the style in which the melodies are used: Weill's adaptation to the American scene has had the result that when the man about to be hanged for murder thinks with desperate longing about his girl, or she thinks similarly about him, each breaks into what is in actual style a leading tenor's or soprano's number in a Broadway musical, complete with Robert Russell Bennett orchestration. Obviously that doesn't work—except for the confused minds that are responsible for the eighty or so productions the work has had. [*Herald Tribune*]

25 September 1948 In *The Schubert Reader: A Life of Franz Schubert in Letters and Documents* by Otto Erich Deutsch, translated by Eric Blom, we are given every known document—letters, diaries, publishers' announcements, programs, press reviews, government records—concerned with Schubert, and notes after each document supplying necessary information about

25 September 1948

its contents. The book contains some of the material out of which any biography would have to be made; but that material is so full and continuous as to constitute in itself a biography that is illuminating and touching.

Illuminating, for example, is the material which shows that what has been inferred from Schubert's poverty and early death—that he was another illustration of the melancholy fact that great composers are not recognized by their contemporaries—is as incorrect in his case as in those of other great composers. Professor Deutsch contends in a note that Beethoven's last quartets "were at that time [1828] appreciated by few even of the master's admirers"; but we read of their being performed and published at that time—which is evidence that Beethoven's greatness was recognized. And Mozart did die at thirty-five of sheer exhaustion from poverty and overwork; but these resulted not from the public's failure to recognize his greatness, but rather from his own lack of skill—whether he was dealing with a French duke who didn't pay him for his daughter's lessons, or an Austrian emperor who paid him only half the salary he had paid Gluck, or a manager who paid him only half the customary fee for an opera, or a publisher who paid him nothing for some quartets—in manipulating the musico-economic machinery of the period to convert the public's appreciation into the money that would have kept him from dying wretchedly at thirty-five.

Schubert was poor all his life, and especially hard-pressed the few months preceding his death; but he never suffered privation; and if his body was weakened in its resistance to the typhus of which he died it was by the venereal disease of a few years before. Nor was his poverty caused by lack of appreciation of his work. From the start his songs and piano pieces were admired by a group of devoted personal friends, in whose homes there were given, throughout his life, the private concerts of his music called *Schubertiaden*. The celebrated singer Vogl, who took part

25 September 1948

in these concerts, also made the songs known to the general public, as did other singers; and while one of them, Anna Milder, might regret that these beautiful songs were not suitable for the crowd that "wants only treats for the ear," they evidently had enough appeal for publishers to publish them—this being more significant than the fact that they paid Schubert too little for them. His Piano Sonata Op. 42, in 1826, and his Sonata Op. 78, in 1827, were reviewed at length and with admiration of his powers in the Leipzig *Allgemeine Musikzeitung*; by 1825 it was worth while for a publisher to put on sale an engraving of one whom he described as "the composer of genius, sufficiently well known to the musical world"; in 1828 the Vienna correspondent of the Dresden *Abendzeitung* referred to "the inspired Schubert" whose "name already resounds from all lips." By that time publishers whom he had approached earlier with little or no success were asking him for works. True, they didn't pay him enough for them; but he was only thirty-one, still at the beginning of his career, and beginning also to produce works of a new stature and power like the C-major String Quintet and Symphony; and it seems probable that if he had lived to continue the career that was barely picking up momentum and to produce additional works of that stature and power, he would in a few years have reached the point of being able, like Beethoven, to command proper compensation from publishers.

Touching are some of Schubert's own statements in his letters and diary. For example, his description of the unhappiness of "a man whose health will never be right again . . . whose most brilliant hopes have perished, to whom the felicity of love and friendship have nothing to offer but pain, whom enthusiasm . . . for all things beautiful threatens to forsake," in a letter written at the time of the venereal sickness that may have been one of the reasons for the melancholy which clouded his normal cheerfulness in the remaining years of his life. Or his statement after

25 December 1948

a visit to Graz that he "cannot as yet get accustomed to Vienna," which is "empty of cordiality, candor, genuine thought, reasonable words, and especially of intelligent deeds. There is so much confused chatter that one hardly knows whether one is on one's head or one's heels, and one rarely or never achieves any inward contentment." Or the very last note: "I am ill. I have eaten nothing for eleven days and drunk nothing, and I totter feebly and shakily from my chair to bed and back again.... If I ever take anything, I bring it up again at once. Be so kind then, as to assist me in this desperate situation by means of literature"— that is, of Cooper's novels, which he was reading.

Touching also is the picture of him created by all the material in the book—of a man of childlike affection, candor and loyalty, sociable, modest about his achievements, incapable of envy or bitterness. Only one letter describes him as something more: Anton Ottenwalt, whom he visited in Linz, wrote afterwards of a conversation one night in which "I have never seen him like this, nor heard: serious, profound, and as though inspired. How he talked of art, of poetry, of his youth, of friends and other people who matter, of the relationship of ideas to life, etc.! I was more and more amazed at such a mind, of which it has been said that its artistic achievement is so unconscious, hardly revealed to and understood by himself, and so on." Ottenwalt did not quote any of Schubert's statements on this occasion; and no statement attributed to him in all the other documents of this book gives any indication of the powers and insights we know he possessed only through the evidence of his last great works. [*The Nation*]

25 December 1948 Rimsky-Korsakov's injury to Musorgsky was not merely that he made Musorgsky's works known to the world in outrageously altered versions, but that he got the world

25 December 1948

to accept the idea which justified not only his falsifications but anyone else's—the idea of Musorgsky as a clumsy dilettante whose insufficient technical equipment prevented him from achieving more than partial realizations of his conceptions, which other people were, therefore, and still are justified in helping him to complete. And exposure of Rimsky's falsification of the music has had only this result—that a Stokowski will give his own falsification legitimacy by telling us it is based on the original Musorgsky score and only fulfills what is no more than implied in, say, the mere sketch that Musorgsky left of *Pictures at an Exhibition*. Actually there is no sense in a claim that one has gone back to the original score if one has done so only to depart from it again as far as Stokowski does; and anyone who does go back to the original score of *Pictures* should be able to hear that it is not a mere sketch but something completely achieved—that, as I said in this column several years ago after someone had played it for me, Musorgsky "writes at every point, in every detail of melody, harmony, figuration, with the unfaltering sureness of a man who is absolute master of his style." For he was a pianist, and the *Musorgsky Reader* is filled with testimony concerning his extraordinary command of his instrument. Certainly it is not without significance that even Rimsky-Korsakov left this work almost untouched. But not Stokowski. And, now, not Horowitz, who has recorded his version for RCA Victor.

We are assured by Olin Downes, as Horowitz's spokesman, that the version does not "introduce any extraneous elements into the music as Musorgsky wrote it," but "is a return to the original text . . . in the Lamm edition. . . . Following it carefully, Mr. Horowitz has done a little 'piano orchestration' in ways confined to octave doublings, redistribution of passage work between the hands, transpositions of brief passages an octave below or above the original pitch, etc. The effort has been solely to realize the intention of the composer, and to refrain from gratuitous

13 February 1949

ornamentation or officious 'correction' of any detail of his text as it stands." But if Horowitz wanted "solely to realize the intention of the composer" all he needed to do was play what Musorgsky wrote, which realizes his intention completely. And listening to the recorded performance up to *Baba Yaga* with the Lamm edition before me I have heard such "extraneous elements" and "gratuitous ornamentation" and "officious 'correction' " as the completely new figuration in measures 12 to 24 of *Limoges*, which realizes the intention not of the composer of *Pictures at an Exhibition* but of the composer of the Fantasy on themes of *Carmen*; the changing of the rhythmless octave tremolo in *Con mortuis in lingua morta* to a rhythmed figuration, with different effect, of two upper notes, two lower, two upper, two lower; the insertion, in the last ten measures of this episode, of a reiterated off-beat F-sharp in the bass, which introduces rhythmic, pedal and other effects not intended by Musorgsky; the substitution of a crescendo for the diminuendo in the four measures before the last two of *Catacombs*; the insertion of measures 4 to 7 of the opening statement of *Gnomus* into the repetition of the statement in which Musorgsky chose to omit them; the substitution of rich chords for bare octaves; the cut in *The Old Castle*, the omission of the *Promenade* before *Limoges*, etc.

In addition there is the falsification of almost every phrase of the work through the affected, sentimentalizing style of performance. [*The Nation*]

13 February 1949 Listening to Toscanini's performances in recent years and marveling at his continuing powers, one has realized that some day there would nevertheless be an end, and has wondered if there would be again the accidental coming together in one man of the particular musical insight and taste,

13 February 1949

technical capacities and personal characteristics which in combination have produced this unique way of functioning as a conductor and its unique results. A couple of years ago I was excited by a performance of Mozart's *Requiem* recorded by De Sabata in which there was evidence of similar powers in the similar sustained impetus and continuous control of the beautifully contoured progression—only to discover in a performance of Beethoven's *Eroica* that he could be erratic and perverse. But with young Guido Cantelli, recent guest conductor of the NBC Symphony, the exciting thing is not only that his attitude and method and results are similar to Toscanini's, but that they are consistent—or were, at any rate, in the three broadcasts I can speak of.

His performance, like Toscanini's, shapes the work strictly on the lines laid out by the composer's directions about tempo and dynamics in the score; and the shaped progression has the same steadiness, continuity and organic coherence, the same clarity of outline, texture and structure. In addition it has the same precision of execution and sonority; and the performances I heard were of breathtaking virtuoso caliber and brilliance. If any one points out that Cantelli was, after all, conducting a virtuoso orchestra, the answer is that such an orchestra plays in that way only for a virtuoso conductor. In the playing as it came over the air one could hear the authority of directing mind and hand that was evident in the conducting in the studio—the authority of the kind of knowledge of everything in the score and everything going on in the orchestra, of one's purpose and the means of achieving this purpose, that commands the respect and response of an orchestra like the NBC Symphony.

Inevitably he too, like Toscanini, plays music by Italians that seems worthless to us—though no worse to me than some of the music by Soviet Russians that other conductors play. But he also gave us Bartók and Hindemith of the moderns, Wagner, Tchaikovsky, Franck, Ravel and Haydn of the standard repertory. What we have yet to hear from him are the other great German masters, the best of the French composers, the old Italians: Mozart, Beethoven and Schubert, Berlioz and Debussy, Vivaldi and Corelli.

In any case, on the basis of what we have heard already, he is the real thing, and the most remarkable and exciting real thing in many years. [*Herald Tribune*]

15 May 1949 The sixth and last broadcast of ABC's *Music of Today* series offered the radio première of Schönberg's String Trio, which was preceded by a brief talk by Schönberg. He began by telling of a musician who noted in the score of a piece of music the mistakes that were being made in a performance he was listening to, and who afterwards showed them to the performer, only to be answered with "Maybe; but nobody noticed them." To someone who did notice them, said Schönberg, this was a strange answer—like saying a crime could not be proved; and in his elaboration of this he remarked: "Imperfection [in performance] can spoil much more than perfection can create." He was acquainted with the preference of concert-goers for easily digested entertainment; and contrasted these people with those "who want to be elated if it hurts." His trio, he said finally, would be played by three musicians—Adolph Koldofsky, Cecil Figelsky, Kurt Reher —who had studied it and played it to people who noticed. And it was a good thing that he provided this assurance, for otherwise one might have thought every note in the work was a mistake of the performance.

All that the music conveyed to me was an extreme of the exacerbation one feels in Schönberg's statements. Not only that; but I was aware that tremendous powers were operating in the music,

26 June 1949

including the mental power and personal force which are evident in his statements; but that these powers operated in the service of an extreme eccentricity and perversity in the music as in the statements. The statement, for example, establishing only two categories of the concert-goers who want easily digested entertainment (and who don't like his music) and those "who want to be elated if it hurts" (and who do like his music), and omitting the more important category of people who don't want easily digested entertainment and are willing to work for their elation from music, but whose work brings them no elation from music like Schönberg's String Trio. [*Herald Tribune*]

26 June 1949 Samuel Barber's *Knoxville: Summer of 1915*, a setting of a prose piece by James Agee, was given its first radio performance on June 19 by Bernard Herrman and the CBS Symphony, with Eileen Farrell as soprano soloist. And the right comment on the work was provided by Bernard Shaw more than fifty years ago. Writing about Parry's *Job*, Shaw observed that there was "not one bar in it that comes within 50,000 miles of the tamest line in the poem," and amplified this by pointing out that the poem was one to tax "the highest powers of Bach, Handel, Mozart, Beethoven, or Wagner," but the composer was not Bach nor Handel nor Wagner, "not even Mendelssohn or Schumann, but Dr. Parry."

Mr. Agee's prose piece makes less taxing demands than *Job*; nevertheless it does make demands—demands which Mr. Barber, talking with James Fassett in the intermission Green Room, seemed to be sensitive to. He had, he said, always admired Mr. Agee's poetry, and had been particularly struck by this piece because it created an atmosphere which he could recall from his own childhood. Then he and Mr. Fassett read lines from the

18 March 1950

piece which had impressed Mr. Barber especially and, one gathered, had affected his imagination most in the writing of his work; and he read them in a way that seemed to indicate awareness of the understatement with which they achieved their intensity. And so it was astonishing, later, to hear the melody fussing or curving luxuriantly around words of the utmost quiet ("We all lie there, my mother, my uncle, my aunt, and I too am lying there"); or to hear violent outbursts or build-ups to points of climax in the music where there were none in the words ("One is an artist, he is living at home. One is a musician, she is living at home. One is my mother who is good to me. One is my father who is good to me."). Agee's prose had stimulated Barber's musical imagination—but had set this imagination operating in its own way and its own terms, which were irrelevant and even contradictory to the Agee way and terms.

Nor was the music impressive even considered by and for itself, providing as it did an illustration of the distinction Virgil Thomson once made between being a composer and being a creator. Barber had fitted musical sounds together into a progression that went coherently from a beginning to an end—which made it the work of a composer; but one heard nothing in this progression, from beginning to end, that was the fresh or individual statement of a creator and as such worth one's attention. Instead there were only familiar materials of various kinds that were not first-class and not used with any attractiveness. [*Herald Tribune*]

18 March 1950 In the course of the intermission interview following the New York Philharmonic broadcast of his new symphony, *The Age of Anxiety*, Leonard Bernstein described the conflict which goes on in the life of someone who is both a composer and a conductor. The composer, he said, is an intro-

18 March 1950

verted person with a strong inner life; the conductor a performer always dealing with various large groups of people, and thus leading a mostly external life. I found it difficult to imagine the composer of the work I had just heard as an introverted person with a strong inner life; like his other works it had given me the impression of the composer in Mr. Bernstein being as much an extrovert as the conductor; and it seemed to me that composer and conductor had the same fault—a lack of inner discipline. The Philharmonic performance of *The Age of Anxiety* and the one later in the same day in connection with Jerome Robbins's new ballet—given by the New York City Ballet Company—confirmed for me some of the observations of Virgil Thomson based on greater knowledge of the work from a reading as well as a hearing of the score: that the expressive content was banal and derivative in feeling, the form improvisatory. And it seemed to me that even the poor quality of the musical ideas, and certainly the sprawling form, were the result of a lack of discipline which left the creative process one of everything going out with nothing held back.

The Robbins *Age of Anxiety* was more impressive, at least in part. It is again a ballet about lonely people—four this time, as against *Facsimile's* three; and much of the Martha-Graham-esque movement in which they define their loneliness is again like an exhibition of personal privacies that one is embarrassed to look at. But this time the four get involved with a lot of other people; and it is in some of these episodes that Robbins's powers of observation and imaginative invention achieve exciting images and large-scale orchestrations of movement. One of these is the frenetic close of the first part; but the best, I think, is the Masque in which the four "attempt to become or to appear carefree"—an episode danced to what I think is also the best music of Bernstein's score, the section of piano jazz (with percussion). It is another example of what happens when Robbins's sharp eye and satiric sense concern themselves with American lowbrow dancing; and it makes one wish that if he feels that as a serious artist he must deal with serious subjects he would deal with them in comedy, of which he is so brilliant a master. [*The Nation*]

Postscript 1964 Robbins continued, of course, to please himself, not me, with further serious ballets embodying his thought on the human condition. But on one occasion he pleased both of us with *Afternoon of a Faun*, a masterly embodiment—in movement keyed to the scale and tone of Debussy's music—of a keen and wry perception about the young people of the world bounded by the walls and mirrors of the dance studio: a movement which begins as personal involvement ends with the two dancers turning to see how they look in the mirror, and what begins as something they look at in the mirror ends as personal involvement.

3 June 1950 Much of the discussion of Menotti's *The Consul* has been concerned with this "musical drama," as he calls it, being not an opera but in fact a new kind of musical drama; and its new form has been thought to account for its unprecedented popular success. But I would say that whatever the reasons for its popular success there is nothing new about its form. Opera *is* musical drama; and Menotti's musical drama is an opera. It is a modern opera, which carries the continuous action and dialogue in continuous orchestra-supported declamation and recitative to points where action stops for emotional expansion in the extended melody of aria, duet, or some other concerted number. And the orchestra-supported declamation and recitative are in a skilfully contrived modern style; but—and this was for me the most striking fact about the work as I listened to it—the melody

3 June 1950

which takes off at the momentary climax of the action to expand this climax relapses into the mellifluous pre-modern style which is apparently the one melodic style Menotti has for all expressive requirements, and which is inadequate for these requirements—shockingly inadequate for something like *To this we've come*. The facile third-rate tunefulness seemed to me even worse this time than in previous works; the eclecticism this time reached the point of producing—in the Italian woman's lament over her *bambina*—not just something reminiscent of a Puccini aria but something which *is* a Puccini aria complete even to the last orchestral detail. This column's award for the understatement of the year goes, therefore, to Virgil Thomson for the observation that *The Consul* is "melodically . . . a shade undistinguished."

The music, then, is of a kind to satisfy and please the listener who is satisfied and pleased by Puccini in the opera house, and also the members of the wider public in the Barrymore Theater; and it is therefore one of the reasons for the success of the work. But the chief reason for this success, in my opinion, is the dramatic idea, which powerfully engages the audience's interest and emotions as it is spaced out and filled out in time by the activity of the music (in place of the words and incidents that would space and fill it out in a spoken play). So powerfully in fact as to mislead the audience into ascribing to the trashy music the impressive qualities it is being moved by in the dramatic idea.

The Consul, to sum up, is not a new kind of musical drama which had to be performed in a Broadway theater instead of an opera house: it is an opera which could have been performed at the Metropolitan, and which would have been as successful there as at the Barrymore, but not for the reasons alleged by Winthrop Sargeant in his article in *Life*. Confirming the notions of his *Life* readers with a picture of "patient opera-goers" who "had almost resigned themselves to the idea that opera was a dead art form—something that could be seen at its best only in aged master-

7 October 1950

pieces ritualistically performed in such museum-like institutions as the Metropolitan," Sargeant had these opera-goers beginning "to breathe more easily" as they listened to *The Consul*, which he declared "undeniably has all the attributes of a first-class opera" and "meets the high-brow's most exacting specifications." What Sargeant pronounces undeniable I deny: *The Consul* lacks the indispensable attribute of a first-class opera—of works like *Figaro, Don Giovanni, The Barber of Seville, Carmen, Otello, Falstaff, Tristan, Die Meistersinger, Boris Godunov* and other "aged, ritualistically performed masterpieces"—namely, first-class music. And thus it fails to meet even the highbrow's minimum specification.

But producing *The Consul* as a new kind of musical drama in the Barrymore Theater had these important results: that the publicity material—about its being a new form of musical drama—appeared on the newspaper theater pages; that it was reviewed—and described as a new form of musical drama—by the newspaper drama critics; that in these ways it was brought to the attention of the wider public which reads the theater page and drama reviews and not the music page and music reviews; and that its success, therefore, was magnified enormously beyond what it would have achieved if it had been produced as an opera at the Metropolitan. There comes to mind Professor George F. Whicher's remark in a recent review—about "how much goes into the making of an established poet besides the mere writing of poetry." [*The Nation*]

7 October 1950 * My reading here and there in the Barzun *Berlioz* has been a process of, say, encountering with surprise, on

* (1964) Barzun's enormous *Berlioz and the Romantic Century* included a great deal that was outside of my interest and competence, and was

7 October 1950

p. 12, the name of Herbert Weinstock among those of the writers of the "new Berlioz criticism" of the last twenty-five years, of looking in the index, turning to the statement of Weinstock quoted on p. 19, being directed by the footnote "1308, art. Berlioz" to the bibliography, and discovering there that the "art. Berlioz" is the paragraph introducing the Berlioz recordings in the 1942 Gramophone Shop Encyclopedia—this being as far as I know the total Weinstock contribution to the "new Berlioz criticism." (Understandably, Weinstock found Barzun's book to be one deserving high admiration at length in the *Herald Tribune*.)

This kind of thing arouses incredulous amazement right from the start. One is dumbfounded when the "thoughtful critic" on the first page turns out to be Olin Downes (he said something good about Berlioz for once); when someone with as little critical gift and experience as Mark Schubart is, on p. 9, an "experienced practitioner" who "has declared that nothing too harsh can be said against music criticism as we find it" (critics have said bad things about Berlioz); when Schubart's opinion is "confirmed at the two recent conferences where music criticism was treated as an element of general culture." (The confirmation at the Harvard Symposium was the address by Professor Lang which Henry David Aiken, in his *Nation* review of the proceedings, correctly described as "a confused and vindictive diatribe" and an example of "the failure to distinguish between understanding of music and knowledge about music"—concerning which Barzun himself once pointed out that the "secret of talk-

---

therefore reviewed in the *Nation* by Robert E. Garis. My interest led me only to read the introductory chapter, to look up what Barzun had to say about a few particular works of Berlioz, and to investigate further some of the statements encountered in this way; and my comments in this article were concerned with what I had read. To discuss the few matters I dealt with didn't require acquaintance with everything else in the book; and such acquaintance wouldn't have altered what I said about them.

7 October 1950

ing about music is to describe [it] . . . as something which hits our senses and is experienced," and that "any other treatment, from the pseudo-poetical to the . . . historico-academic, is beside the point." But even more remarkable are Barzun's explicit references to Lang, a Columbia University colleague and editor of *The Musical Quarterly*, which published a section of the book. One finds an acknowledgment of indebtedness for conversations, a mention of Lang's articles on Wagner, but complete and unexpected silence about Lang's disparagement of Berlioz's music.)

Then there is that list of writers of the "new Berlioz criticism" —an indiscriminate jumble of anybody and everybody, including some nobodies, who has written anything favorable about Berlioz, whether the large-scale writing of men like Newman, Turner and Wotton, or the occasional review of men like myself, or the mere paragraph in a record encyclopedia. It includes Paul Rosenfeld—his contribution being the essay in *Musical Portraits*; and further investigation turns up a Barzun statement about the new Berlioz criticism in this country (II, 311) which has "Mr. B. H. Haggin taking up the tradition which Paul Rosenfeld had inaugurated amid general indifference in the previous decade." It sounds very grand and should make me feel as happy as Weinstock; but it happened that way only in the Barzun world of graciously grandiose inventions which collapse in absurdity: in the real world Rosenfeld's essay did not initiate the cohesive or continuous Berlioz criticism that was not written in the twenties and that I did not take off from in the thirties.

Even peripheral reading, then, reveals the spinning of fancy invention in this work of ostentatious scholarship. And so it isn't surprising that the scholarship itself is sometimes flawed. One of Barzun's major lines of thought is to demonstrate that after 1830 "the one seminal mind was Berlioz," and in particular how much was derived from him by Wagner who "emerged in the seventies" (all characteristically excessive and grossly inaccurate: Wag-

7 October 1950

ner had "emerged" even before *Tannhäuser* in 1845; and neither in his music nor in anyone else's does one hear the very language and thought of Berlioz in the way one hears Wagner's in most of the music after his). In support of his contention Barzun quotes from a 1924 article on Berlioz and Wagner by Gerald Abraham, and ignores Abraham's later estimate of their relation in his book *A Hundred Years of Music* (1938, 1949). "In Wagner's earlier operas," says Abraham *now*, "a style originally derived from Beethoven and Weber . . . Marschner, Spontini and Bellini, with harmonic hints probably from Chopin and Spohr, and orchestral ones (with a few melodic ones as well) from Berlioz, had been gradually forged by the force of his genius into the perfectly original medium of . . . 'Lohengrin.' " And accounting for the radical changes in this medium in the later Wagner music dramas, Abraham mentions only the influence of Beethoven's Quartet Op. 131 on rhythm and structure, of Liszt on harmony.

Nor is it because Barzun doesn't know of the Abraham book. In the course of a very fancy discussion of Berlioz's elevated aim in the *Symphonie Fantastique*—which, says Barzun, was to produce not a piece of program music but, like Beethoven, "a large-scale piece which should be *une oeuvre*—One Work"—i.e. a unified musical work—Barzun quotes from Abraham's book the statement that "for the first movement. . . . Berlioz cast his 'reveries and passions' in the shape of a perfectly comprehensible modification of classical first movement form," but doesn't mention Abraham's preceding statement that Berlioz "had three or four orchestral pieces, from the derelict 'Faust' ballet of 1828 and the 'Francs Juges' opera, on his hands; cast about for some central literary idea to bind them together; and, having found it, composed the first movement and revised and rearranged the remainder to fit into the scheme. . . . One's first reflection is that

21 October 1950

Beethoven would never have thought of sticking several unrelated pieces together and calling them a symphony...."

But the most revealing of the astonishing things I have encountered in the book is the footnote (I, 324) in which, having described *his* way of correcting an error in the score of *Romeo and Juliet*, Barzun reports Toscanini's different way, which Toscanini once explained to him "during a conversation"—Barzun must let the world know—"sought by him [Toscanini]." What produced that, produced the excesses described by Mr. Garis and myself. [*The Nation*]

21 October 1950 As one who has considered Beecham to be one of the world's great musicians I have been disturbed by tendencies revealed in some of his performances of the last year or two—the tendency to slow up the music so that it has seemed static instead of forward-moving; the tendency to over-elaboration and exaggeration of phraseological inflection, accentuation and so on. The new Columbia LP record with his performances of Mozart's Symphonies K.551 (*Jupiter*) and 504 (*Prague*) provides further evidence of these tendencies. Thinking that possibly it was my taste that had changed, I played the recordings he made of the same works with the London Philharmonic a number of years ago, but found that what I had thought beautiful then I still thought beautiful now, and that the new performances were distressing distortions and caricatures of the old. What I mean is such things as the excessive fussing with the violins' transitional measures (43-46) leading from the end of the exposition to the beginning of the development in the second movement of K.551, or the excessive accentuation in measures 59 and 107 of the first movement, or the excessive retardation at measure 95 for the so-called second subject in the first move-

10 March 1951

ment of K.504, as compared with the treatment of the same details in the old performances. And all this apart from faults in the new performances which were also faults in the old—e.g. the adagio tempo of the second movement of K.551 as against the prescribed andante, the discarding of the mutes in the course of the movement, the perversely slow tempo of the minuet movement. [*The Nation*]

10 March 1951   One had a demonstration of Koussevitsky's continuing powers under favorable conditions, at the first Carnegie Hall concert of the Israel Philharmonic. The favorable conditions were that he was conducting two of his favorite pieces —Prokofiev's Fifth Symphony and Tchaikovsky's Fourth—which he had played with the orchestra a number of times, and that he and the orchestra were therefore operating with relaxed assurance. The result was playing which had the refinement of execution and sonority characteristic of Koussevitzky performances, and which, in the process of demonstrating his powers, also demonstrated what the orchestra was like and what it could do under a virtuoso conductor's direction: the fact that it had excellent strings which could produce tone with the silky sheen Koussevitzky aims for, that it had good woodwinds, and that even its undistinguished brass section could be got to play with discretion if not with beauty of tone.

The next night Leonard Bernstein conducted the orchestra in Mozart's *Linz* Symphony with a warmth of feeling for the music and a distinguished taste in its treatment that Koussevitzky knows nothing about; but the beauty Koussevitzky had created was gone from the string tone, and raucous sounds from the brass were heard in the coarse-toned performances of Chavez's *Sinfonia India*, which Bernstein played very well, and Schumann's Second Symphony, which he played with an excess of emotion and an insufficiency of taste. [*The Nation*]

7 April 1951 Listening to Charles Ives's Second Symphony, which Leonard Bernstein performed with the New York Philharmonic, I heard nothing that should have kept it from being played fifty years ago, but on the other hand nothing that called urgently for performance now. The great to-do about Ives's having used this or that revolutionary technique years before this or that famous European composer is about something irrelevant and unimportant: the important thing is what music he produced with whatever technique he used. It is especially irrelevant in the Second Symphony, which contains nothing horrendous that should have frightened conductors fifty years ago. And when one considers this work in and for itself as it reveals itself to the ear, one hears this bit of lovely writing here, that bit of lovely melody there, but in sum a constant shifting from one thing to another in one tempo and another in a succession that rambles on with no integration and no cumulative effect.
[*The Nation*]

21 April 1951 My recollection of Flagstad's first New York performance in *Tristan und Isolde* in February 1935 is documented by the first recording of the finale that she made at the end of that season. One of the amazing things about the voice at that first performance was its freshness after twenty years' use which had included very little singing of Wagner; and listening to the record at the time it was issued I heard the loss of this freshness after the wear and tear of a few months of Isoldes,

21 April 1951

Sieglindes and Brünnhildes, sometimes four in one week. But listening to the record now I cannot recall or imagine anything beyond the flow of vocal splendor in long phrases that it reproduces; and it confirms my recollection that what I heard at that first performance was nothing less than a phenomenon—as unique a phenomenon among soprano voices as Caruso's voice among tenors.

That is still true of what I heard at Flagstad's last *Tristan* performance at the Metropolitan recently, even with what had been lost after sixteen years. The unique splendor which used to be heard throughout the entire range of the voice was gone from the upper portion; and gone also were the breathtaking high C's of the frenzied opening passage of the second-act duet. But if *this* had been the performance in which Flagstad was singing her first New York Isolde at the age of forty-two, and if she had sung with such lustrous beauty in the lower range of her voice, with such clarity and power in the higher notes up to the B of the first-act narrative; if, moreover, she had produced those long phrases, including the final *"höchste Lust,"* on one breath; and even if she had managed only the first high C in the second-act duet and substituted A for the second—one would have thought the singing phenomenal. And as the performance of a woman of fifty-eight the phenomenon was even greater.

So with her singing in *Fidelio*—above all her sustained legato singing in *Komm Hoffnung,* her long unbroken phrases, the second rising to high B, on *"sie wird's erreichen,"* her long phrases also in the fast part of the aria, and at the end the climactic rise to G-sharp followed by the rapid scales from a low E to high B. Even with the high notes that lacked the beauty of the lower ones, even with the break for breath before the last rush to high B, it was singing which would have been extraordinary from a woman of forty, and which was even more so from a woman of Flagstad's age. It was in fact singing such as Lotte Lehmann had

1 *September 1951*

not done even at forty, by the evidence of her Parlophone recording of the aria. But Lehmann's singing on the record is suffused with the affecting personal warmth and dramatic animation which Flagstad's lacked. That brings me perilously near to the subject of what Flagstad looked and acted like in this opera —from which I retreat as fast as I can. [*The Nation*]

1 September 1951 Columbia also has made a contribution of immortal performances of the past—four LP records with forty-eight of the performances which Louis Armstrong recorded with his Hot Five (1925) and Hot Seven (1927), with Earl Hines and supporting players (1928), and with commercial bands (1929). The records document Armstrong's trumpet-playing and singing from the time when they operated in the framework and context of the integrated performances of the Hot Five and Seven that were still very close to their New Orleans origins of group improvisation, to the time when a band merely provided a plushy background for the solo entertainer who began with a sensitively ornamented trumpet statement of a current song hit, continued with an extravagantly free vocal treatment of it, and carried this to its climax in a final spectacular trumpet solo. They enable us to see, in the words of Wilder Hobson, that "Armstrong himself . . . has . . . remained substantially the same artist," but "the material he has worked with, the types of musical combinations with which he has played have widely differed." And the results too have differed—in quality. This is the first time I have ever listened to all these groups of performances together; and it has enabled me to perceive how much better the Hot Fives and Sevens are, as wholes, than the performances of the Earl Hines combination, brilliant and exciting though these are; and to perceive also how much better Armstrong's

1 September 1951

own work is in those early performances, superb and beautiful though it is in the later ones—e.g. the 1928 *Muggles* and *West End Blues*, the 1929 *I Can't Give You Anything but Love*. Within the framework and context of the integrated Hot Five and Seven performances, Armstrong's solos, no matter how impassioned, how fantastic, how breathtaking in their virtuosity, remain under control and complete their developing structure; but already in the performances with Hines we hear the spectacular getting to be formless at times, as in those series of ever higher high notes; and we hear this carried to its occasionally incoherent extreme in the concluding exhibitions of trumpet virtuosity of the 1929 performances.

Columbia gives us not only performances of the past but music: the Arthur Schwartz-Howard Dietz songs of one of the most memorable of musical revues, *The Band Wagon*, which are as delightful today as in 1931, and are sung with a little too much charm by Mary Martin; and the songs of one of the finest of the Rodgers and Hart series, *Pal Joey*, with Vivienne Segal again singing *Bewitched, Bothered and Bewildered*, and Harold Lang contributing his appropriately voiceless singing to *In Our Little Den of Iniquity*. Also the songs of Cole Porter's *Anything Goes*; but these call for an Ethel Merman rather than a Mary Martin. One hopes for more: *The Boys from Syracuse* and others of the Rodgers and Hart series; *Funny Face* and others of the pre-*Strike up the Band* Gershwin series.

Of the present is *Guys and Dolls* (Decca), with Frank Loesser's wonderful comedy songs—above all *Adelaide's Lament* (in which the stanza with the marvelous line about the naked feeling one gets from the absence of an engagement ring on one's finger is omitted) and *Take Back Your Mink* ("take back your puhyils") as sung by Vivian Blaine and the lifelike replica of a raucous-voiced night-club chorus. [*The Nation*]

8 and 15 September 1951 In his book on Mozart, Dr. Alfred Einstein, speculating on what model Mozart could have had for the first of his string quintets with two violas, which he wrote in 1773, refers to Boccherini, "the fame of whose quintets began to spread through the world in the late 1760's. Boccherini cannot have been wholly unknown to Mozart even as early as 1770, and perhaps his influence had something to do with Mozart's later, Vienna quintets." And Einstein remarks in parentheses: "It may be mentioned in passing that Boccherini himself apparently did not write quintets for any other combination of strings: he does indeed call the second viola 'alto violoncello,' but its part is notated in the viola clef throughout and is almost unplayable on the violoncello." These statements were characterized, in a letter from Charles B. Farrell, as error typical in, among other things, "the bland serenity of its assertion within the aura of a mighty reputation quietly defying correction." The blandly serene assertion and mighty reputation, Farrell might have added, command belief that Einstein is speaking with a scholar's knowledge of evidence which he considers unnecessary to supply in this book for the general reader. And there is also his statement, "I cannot boast that I know all of Boccherini's 113 quintets"—implying the knowledge of a large number that he *could* boast of. But the authoritative work of scholarship and source of information about Boccherini, said Farrell, was Picquot's book, *Notice sur la Vie et les Ouvrages de Luigi Boccherini*, in which was assembled all the available documentary material, including Boccherini's own autograph catalogue. And this book—which one would expect Einstein to know, but which he evidently did not know—gives the date of composition of Boccherini's first set of quintets as 1771, and the date of publication as 1774—which means that his quintets couldn't have been famous in the late 1760's and known to Mozart in 1770. Moreover, Picquot, who did know 112 of the 113, describes them

8 and 15 September 1951

constantly as works for two cellos, and quotes similar descriptions of them in the autograph catalogue and on the title pages of the early editions. And here we come to an interesting fact: the title pages of the edition of Janet et Cotelle describe the works as "quintets for two violins, viola and two cellos," but add that "the part of first violoncello can be replaced by an alto violoncello"; and with the five original parts the edition provides an additional alternate part for the "alto violoncello," which is merely an arrangement of the first-cello part for viola (hence the viola clef) that the publisher caused to be made so that the edition would be useful and salable to more people (and a professional cellist assured Farrell that the original first-cello part was entirely playable on the cello). Apparently Einstein encountered a copy of this particular edition with this alternate part for viola; and on this alone he based his statement that the Boccherini quintets were not for two cellos but for two violas.

Einstein's *Mozart* appeared in 1945; already in 1948 Ulrich's *Chamber Music* cited Einstein's belief "that Boccherini's 113 quintets with two cellos are actually for two violins, two violas, and one cello; the 'alto violoncello' part is written in viola clef throughout." And the error will be picked up by the next writer from Ulrich, by one writer after another from his predecessors—the result being another of the countless examples of the *fable convenue*, as Ernest Newman has called it, that becomes our knowledge of all the matters we cannot possibly learn about through our own investigation. This was the process which produced the myths about Berlioz and his work that are still current many years after they were corrected by Wotton (and note that we were in no position to determine by our own investigation the credibility of Wotton's statements).

So with the famous critic Hanslick. We have got our ideas of him not from our reading of his reviews but from our reading of what has been written about his reviews by writers whose

8 and 15 September 1951

knowledge was acquired in the same way as ours. However, we have also read about them in Ernest Newman's *Life of Richard Wagner*, whose documented text has supported his claim to be replacing *fable convenue* with the facts established by first-hand examination of source material. And we have therefore had confidence in his statements that the vogue of Hanslick's "fluent, superficial journalism" resulted from his "presenting the reader with bright reading matter that had a minimum of connection with the work of art under discussion"; that "there was hardly a contemporary work of genius or high talent in connection with which he did not demonstrate ... the limitations not merely of his intellect but of his taste—from 'Tristan' to 'Aida,' from 'Carmen' to 'Die Fledermaus' he was consistently wrong"; that as one of the Viennese critics who "distinguished themselves by the fatuity and the malice of their remarks on [Wagner's] concert" in May, 1872, "Hanslick sagely opined that if all operas were to be composed in the style of 'Tristan' their audiences would soon be in the lunatic asylum, whither they would be followed by the conductors and the orchestral players if these made a habit of the Wagnerian elasticity of tempi."

But now a volume of Hanslick's articles, *Vienna's Golden Years of Music*, gives us the opportunity to learn about them for ourselves. And we discover that they are indeed fluent, graceful, urbane and witty, but in the formulation of judgments which reveal great knowledge and understanding and thorough preparation (e. g. by study of the scores of new works) in support of excellent critical perception that is in close contact with the music. Like most critics—and most people—he is out of phase with certain minds and their manifestations in art: the composers of program music, the mature Wagner, Bruckner. But if this makes him incapable of appreciating even the lovely things in *Die Meistersinger*, a listener of today finds him accurately perceptive about the wearisome declamatory style, the absurd

8 and 15 September 1951

philosophical pretensions, the horrible verbal jargon of the other mature works; and what he says about Bruckner's symphonies describes what one has heard in them. There is nothing about *Carmen* in the book; but there are articles on Verdi's *Requiem* and *Otello* which reveal not only full recognition of Verdi's powers but accurate understanding of them and of their development. To the contention that *Otello* shows the influence of Wagner he replies that mere examination of the score had convinced him that "there is not a scene, not a measure, for which Verdi owes any obligation to the composer of 'Tristan und Isolde,'" and Boito and Ricordi confirmed this subsequently by telling him Verdi had heard nothing of Wagner's after *Lohengrin*. *Otello*, he says, represents only the further development of Verdi's own powers and style: "The sharp, challenging rhythms and melodies of his first period ('Nabucco,' 'I Lombardi,' 'Ernani') are more rounded in his second ('Rigoletto,' 'Il Trovatore,' 'La Traviata'). In 'Aida' and 'Otello' they achieve noble simplicity"; and whereas *Otello* has more fidelity to the text, *Aida* has more beautiful melodic ideas.

Moreover the volume of Hanslick's articles contains the review of Wagner's concert described by Ernest Newman; and we discover that in it "Wagner is recognized as a brilliant conductor," and "his spirited reading of the 'Eroica,' with its fine, individual nuances, was, on the whole, a real pleasure." We discover also that Hanslick finds it necessary to insist that this was not the first good performance Vienna has heard of the *Eroica*—in contradiction of Wagner's contention in his essay on conducting (presumably echoed by the fanatical Wagnerians) "that our conductors have no idea of tempo and that the Beethoven we have learned to know through public performances is a 'pure chimera.'" And so he points out that Wagner's principle of frequent modification of tempo works out successfully in the final variation movement of the *Eroica*, that "the Funeral

8 and 15 September 1951

March was beautiful, particularly the gradual dying away of the main theme," but that the "conspicuously slower" tempo of the so-called second theme in the first movement, after the very fast beginning, diverted "the 'heroic' character of the symphony toward the sentimental." And he observes in conclusion:

Wagner approaches conducting as he approaches composition. What suits his individuality and his utterly exceptional talent must be accepted as the one and only universal, true, and exclusively authorized artistic law. From his highly personal poetic-graphic-musical endowment he evolved a new theory of opera which has led him to brilliant and original accomplishments, to compositions whose imaginative sincerity is their own accreditation, and which are effective because they are Wagnerian. But not satisfied with that, he denounces all other opera styles as "colossal errors," overlooking the fact that his own, in the hands of any other composer, would be only a caricature. If all other opera composers were to write in the style of "Tristan und Isolde," we listeners should inevitably wind up in the madhouse; and if Wagner's "tempo modifications" were to gain general ascendancy in our orchestras, then conductors, fiddlers, and wind players would soon be our companions in lunacy.

If there is any "fatuity and malice" it would appear to be not in the comments of Hanslick but in their misrepresentation by Newman.

Now this is not the first instance of such malpractice by Newman; nor is the business about Boccherini's quintets the only thing of its kind in Einstein's writings. In fact, the extraordinary and important thing one discovers about these renowned scholars and their formidable products—and at this point I remember to include Barzun and his *Berlioz*—is that their elaborate and rigorous documentation at one point or in one book seems to make them feel privileged to speak elsewhere without any documentation, or without rigor in their documentation, and without regard for the facts which contradict them; and that the docu-

8 and 15 September 1951

mented portions confer their authority and authenticity on the products of pure invention or scholarly malpractice. And one reason why this is important is that most of us, as I said earlier, are in no position to detect it; and that includes most of the writers who have the task of informing the public about these books. The result, in fact, is that the general public almost never reads a genuine and adequate review of them. The performances, instead, range from Barzun's amusing single statement, in a *Harper's* book column, that he can only marvel at the scholarship and handsome format of Einstein's monograph on the madrigal, to the lengthier evasions of a Taubman filling a *Times* review of Einstein's recent *Schubert* with statement after statement about its scholarship and deep comprehension and so on, or of a Winthrop Sargeant automatically describing Einstein's *Music in the Romantic Era* as "a heavily documented, scholarly study" and getting on with the writing of his own piece on romanticism, though he is equipped to perceive at the very least what was reported to me by someone who read the book—that it is as undocumented as Einstein's other books for the general public.

And as a matter of fact there are usually some things in these books which even a person with only the critic's presumed familiarity with music should be able to perceive and report. Someone who hasn't done the digging into the material on Boccherini that Charles B. Farrell happens to have done will not be able to detect the inaccuracy of Einstein's statements about Boccherini's quintets; but anyone who knows Mozart's Quintet K.515 is in a position to see that Einstein's characteristic comment, that the minuet movement "is more of a *tempo di minuetto*, with a Trio in the subdominant, which itself grows into complete song-form," is about everything except what is important in that extraordinary movement; and anyone familiar with the last movement of Beethoven's Quartet Op. 130, and

22 September 1951

the last movement of Schubert's posthumous Sonata in B-flat, is in a position to see that Einstein's assertion of their relation is —like most of his endless twitterings about derivations of one piece of music from another—nonsense.

But since the general public never reads anything like that in the reviews of books like Einstein's, the writer who does point it out runs into trouble. Faced with a painstaking demonstration that Einstein's way of writing "informally" for the general public is to write not merely, as he says, without formal documentation, but without even informal regard for factual evidence; or that Barzun's *Berlioz* is the product not only of scholarship but of fluent invention, and that its scholarship is not above selective quotation of a supporting sentence out of its contradicting context—faced with a demonstration of such shocking things the unprepared public is shocked, but so shocked and so confused about what it is shocked by, that in the end the shocking thing is not what Einstein or Barzun has done but the demonstration that he has done it. The public doesn't wonder whether personal friendship has influenced Roger Sessions's praise of Einstein's *Mozart*, but it does wonder what personal grievance has led Haggin to cite such damning evidence in dispraise of this book or of Barzun's *Berlioz*, and would find it difficult to believe that no personal grievance was involved—that what caused Haggin to cite those damning details was their presence in the book.

[*The Nation*]

22 September 1951   Considering Virgil Thomson's latest collection of his *Herald Tribune* writing in and for itself one finds again examples of his marvelously accurate perception and formulation, such as the summation of Koussevitzky's career, or the comment on De Sabata's overplaying of a Morton Gould piece:

22 September 1951

"This composer's Spirituals for String Choir and Orchestra, overdressed as it is orchestrally and harmonically, has its own rhythmic life, supports no imposition of any merely theatrical animation. Itself all trickiness, the addition of jugglery from another school plain breaks its back."

One also finds again examples of his spinning of trains of thought about data made up in his head, such as the descriptions of Rubinstein's and Curzon's piano-playing, or the article *Tradition Today*, which is about the conductors, dominantly exemplified for Thomson by Reiner and Monteux, who operate as the preservers of "the traditions of interpretation as these have been handed down," as against men like Stokowski and Koussevitzky who operate rather with "a highly personalized ability to hold attention"; about our own conductors of this second type who "have the excuse of having passed their youth out of contact with a major musical tradition, of not having known the classics early enough to feel at home with them"; and about one of them, Leonard Bernstein, who "knows what American music is all about, but the western European repertory he is obliged to improvise. . . . That is why, I think, he goes into such chorybantic ecstasies in front of it. He needs to mime, for himself and others, a conviction that he does not have. He does no such act before American works of his own time. He takes them naturally, reads them with authority." Thomson once made a similar statement to me about Toscanini—that whereas Toscanini had learned the operatic traditions in the opera house, he had found himself at the age of fifty having to deal with the symphonic repertory with no knowledge of *its* traditions, and had solved the problem by doing a complete streamlining job on it. Actually Toscanini began to conduct the symphonic repertory soon after beginning to conduct opera, and after learning about it until then as everyone does—by hearing it performed and studying the scores, and by hearing varied performances of

22 September 1951

Beethoven, Mozart and Schubert grouped around ever-changing norms which did not represent a line of piously handed-down tradition going back to an authentic first source, because there had been no such source. These European performances were transferred to this country, and were what our own conductors, including Bernstein, learned the classical repertory from. Bernstein, as it happens, first studied conducting with Reiner—which is not, however, why he plays Mozart with evident warmth of feeling and distinguished taste; and only last spring a violinist mentioned he had just come from recording a piece by Aaron Copland in which "Lennie did his usual dance act."

And one also finds again examples of Thomson's method of demonstration by *pointilliste* pronouncement, which do not make coherent understandable sense in their own terms—e.g. *The Intellectual Audience*.

For Thomson the book is, in addition, the occasion for a retrospective glance over the ten years of his writing in the *Herald Tribune*; reviewers, therefore, have taken it as an occasion for an estimate of this writing; and I now propose to consider how it is that the man who has written such distinguished criticism has also written such irresponsible nonsense.

Thomson once stated his belief concerning the critic's function—that it was "to defend contemporary musical composition, not to attack it"; and more recently, that it was to "stick his neck out." Actually the critic is confronted not by contemporary musical composition but by individual contemporary pieces of music; and his function with them is not to defend contemporary musical composition but to look at the individual object placed before him and report faithfully what he finds in it. If he finds nothing in it of significance or value he must stick his neck out (and have his throat cut) with that finding; and I might add that when he does he is not attacking contemporary musical composition.

22 September 1951

I have used the example of contemporary music to make clear my own idea of the critic's duty: to keep his eye strictly on the object—the piece of music, the performance, the book—before him, and not let it be deflected therefrom by anything, even so admirable an aim as defending creative originality. For it is my belief that Thomson has written his distinguished criticism when he has been able to keep his eye on the object; and that when he has written nonsense it is because his eye has been deflected from the object. I would say that in some instances it has been deflected by the fact that he was putting on a performance—which is to say that his eye has been partly on the effect he was making, and by that much less on the thing he was writing about. And in some instances it has been deflected by his fondness for schematization, which has made him not only indulge in remote-from-fact schematizations of his own but fall for those of other writers—among others Max Graf's of the critic as "interpreter of the artist to the public" versus the critic as "spokesman of the public against the artist" (the critic in reality being neither of these). The result in that instance was Thomson's failure to see what contemptible trash most of the material in Graf's book on criticism was; and that failure led to Thomson's performance with the recent volume of Hanslick's criticism.

Here, instead of keeping his eye on Hanslick's writing, Thomson let it be deflected by Graf's section on Hanslick—which is to say that he made his article largely out of material in that section, principally Graf's contention that Hanslick, who opposed Liszt, Berlioz, Wagner, Bruckner, Verdi, Wolf and Richard Strauss, did not really care for Brahms but "was clever enough to raise the banner of Brahms as the banner of counter-revolution" against the others. "Dear Mr. Pleasants," wrote Thomson in reply to the protesting editor and translator of the Hanslick volume, "I did not get all my thoughts about Hanslick out of Max Graf's excellent 'Composer and Critic,' which I quoted.

29 September 1951

I have read some others about the period." "Dear Mr. Thomson," Mr. Pleasants could have answered, "you should have got your thoughts about Hanslick's book, which you were supposedly reviewing, from the book. If you had, you would have noted that with Hanslick's praise of each new Brahms symphony there is criticism, and that both are perceptive, concerned with the things we perceive in the works today—which is to say they are genuine, and provide evidence of as much genuineness in the attitude expressed in the articles as if these had been written by someone today. You might then have mentioned the accusation that the attitude was not genuine, adding that this might be established by other evidence (which you admit is not decisive) but was not supported by the articles. And if instead of copying Verdi's name from Graf you had read Hanslick's articles on the *Requiem* and *Otello*, you would not have your mistaken thought about his opposition to Verdi."

But these defects and failures of Thomson which take so much space to document are those of a man who has given us some of the finest music criticism written anywhere. And—applying Tovey's observation about Schubert again—his occasional inequalities of performance cannot make that man a critic of less than the highest rank. [*The Nation*]

29 September 1951 "Don't sleep!" Toscanini roared during a rehearsal of—as it happened—an inconsequential piece by one of the minor Italian opera composers. "Put your blood! *I* put *my* blood!" And if a Toscanini is to be written about, it should be only by someone who likewise—in whatever he does—"puts his blood."

Mr. Taubman's way of operating, in the years I have observed it, has involved no such expenditure. It is well exemplified by

29 September 1951

the passage in his review of a Stokowski book in which he described what Stokowski had to say about the physical basis of music: "When he gets around to the physical side of music Mr. Stokowski writes more illuminatingly than most musicians. For his is a bold far-ranging, searching mind. Not content merely to study and conduct symphonies, he has gone to the roots of his art. He has made himself an expert on the science of sound. More than any major conductor in this country he knows the science of acoustics and the possibilities of the new fields being opened by scientists. . . . Many other writers have set down their views. But Mr. Stokowski covers the field with a fresh, broad point of view. Etc." This, to my ear, is the writing of someone who hasn't read what he is pretending to describe—the writing, then, of a journalist, in the usual and worst sense of the term: one who doesn't need to read a book to produce the words about it which fill the space assigned to it and which as such constitute, for a newspaper, "coverage" of the subject. And a man who has made a career of producing lifeless words that betray the absence of genuine experience behind them is incapable of understanding something like the intensity of Toscanini's involvement in his work, or of describing it in words that have the ring of authenticity; certainly he doesn't achieve this authenticity by employing artificially colored language to write "how thoroughly his blood stream and very nerve ends are soaked in the stuff [music]" or how "the notes have long since left the page and come alive for him, and yet he returns again and again to the printed page to see whether the flesh and bones are in the right places and whether the blood courses warmly enough."

A Taubman writing about Toscanini the man, then, sets one's teeth on edge; nor have I ever detected in Mr. Taubman's critical writing the slightest evidence of genuine musical perception that would have made him easier to read on Toscanini the musi-

29 September 1951

cian; and the journalist without musical understanding proves to be an inaccurate reporter of some of the stories he says he has been collecting for twenty years. Thus: "He confided that he had made a recording of Mozart's Divertimento for strings and two horns for the benefit of his colleagues, the conductors. . . . In the slow movement, he had always felt something lacking and decided that what was needed was a cadenza for the first violin. After he had made this addition, Toscanini found a letter from Mozart to his wife which confirmed his hunch." Toscanini did perform the divertimento to show certain conductors how to play it. But even if I didn't know what he said about the cadenza in the slow movement I would know it couldn't possibly have been what Mr. Taubman reports: the journalist collector of stories dropped this one through the wrong slot. There have been many instances of Toscanini reaching a conclusion about something in a score which had troubled him (the conclusion, for example, that Mozart must have intended the Larghetto movement of the Concerto K.595 to be played *alla breve*) and having it confirmed later by documentary evidence. But in the case of the divertimento the entire point was the fact that the score itself calls for a cadenza in the usual way—the music coming to a halt on the anticipatory six-four chord, followed by a rest for the interpolated cadenza, and then a trill for its conclusion—which any musician should understand. And Toscanini, listening to Koussevitzky's Tanglewood performance, had been horrified at this point to hear the orchestra pause on the six-four chord, break off for the rest, and then simply play the trill and go on. "This man is no musician!" was Toscanini's verdict. "He is *ignorante!*"

There remains the purely factual biographical material; and this I expected would be the valuable material of the book. For the publishers' statement that Mr. Taubman had had "the close friendship and cooperation of several of the Maestro's immediate

26 April 1952

family," Mr. Taubman's own statement that he had "talked to his friends, colleagues, and family," the fact that he had talked with Toscanini himself during the 1950 transcontinental tour—all these led me to believe that although this was not an authorized biography it presented accurate biographical material obtained from these dependable sources. But encountering details which I knew to be incorrect (e.g. the rehearsal of a Brahms symphony with the New York Philharmonic in 1942, on p. 265), and others which seemed questionable, I inquired, and learned that except for the remarks of Toscanini and anecdotes about him that Mr. Taubman had picked up on the tour, the book was mostly a journalist's rewriting of the material in older books and articles, including their inaccuracies. I say "a journalist's rewriting" because such rewrite-jobs are standard practice in the production of articles in newspaper offices; and I will add that the paper's only requirement concerning the statements in such an article is that the writer be able to show they appeared somewhere in print, because that seems to have been the only requirement Mr. Taubman imposed on himself. Which is to say that it was enough for this journalist on the run to read somewhere about Toscanini's having been distressed to discover "that his father had gone to his father-in-law to seek a loan" (p. 70), and did not seem to him necessary to check the story with the Toscanini family, who would have informed him that Carla de Martini's father had been dead a number of years when she married Toscanini. And so with other details. [*The Nation*]

26 April 1952 The mail has brought me a sumptuous brochure from NBC about the television première of Menotti's *Amahl and the Night Visitors*, with quotations not only of Toscanini telling Menotti, "I think it is the best opera you have ever done," but of experts like Philip Hamburger writing, "Musically, 'Amahl' struck me as being Menotti's finest work," and John Crosby pronouncing Menotti "a magnificent composer" and speaking of the "rare melodic sweetness" of the music—to say nothing of some gaudier products of other professional word-slingers (e.g. Jay S. Harrison's "Once again Mr. Menotti has demonstrated that the lyric stage is his destiny. It is a destiny which becomes him as golden robes do a prince"). After all this dare I say that I listened to *Amahl*, as I have listened to Menotti's other operas, with incredulous amazement—finding it difficult to believe I was really hearing these sugary, trashy tunes, that they could even have occurred to anyone operating as a serious composer today, that he could not have been too embarrassed by the mere thought of them to let anyone else hear them, and that other people could have considered them worth publishing to the world. At one time I would have felt the same incredulous amazement as I read the critical estimates I have quoted; but now I think I can account for them: once again Menotti has used a dramatic idea whose development has so powerfully engaged the interest and emotions of his audience as to mislead even its professional members into thinking their interest and emotions were being powerfully engaged by the music. Moreover, his dramatic gifts don't stop with choice of subject, but extend to every detail of staging—which is to say that the audience's emotions have been engaged, and its musical judgment confused, by young Chet Allen. But one would expect the professional's ear to be proof against this sleight of hand.

[*The Nation*]

31 May and 7 June 1952 Roger Sessions's *The Musical Experience of Composer, Performer, Listener* includes much material that isn't relevant to his essential line of thought. It begins, for example, with material on the psycho-physiological basis of

31 May and 7 June 1952

musical communication, which is no more necessary to a discussion of the composer's, performer's and listener's operations in music than analogous material on the basis of linguistic communication is necessary to a discussion of the writer's, speaker's and listener's or reader's operations in poetry. And actually what Mr. Sessions says later about the composer's and performer's operations he does not relate to the bodily conditions he discussed at the beginning.

Moreover, after he has shown that the composer creates a course of events which the performer makes audible to the listener "in terms of its articulation, its contours, and its proportions," playing "not so much notes as motifs, phrases, periods, sections . . . and rhythmic groups," the next step should bring Mr. Sessions to the listener's experience in apprehending this course of events. Instead he first digresses on the subject of the large-scale business operation in which entrepreneurs and performers are engaged as producers for a mass consumer of what this consumer's demand makes profitable and what the various appreciation books, courses and radio programs persuade the consumer to buy. He drags this in on the pretext that to understand the listener "we must see him . . . not as an abstraction but as an existing and concrete figure in our musical society"—a pretext, since in this book we have not had to understand the composer or performer as a figure in musical society and do not, really, have to understand the listener as one. And the irrelevance of the digression is admitted in the statement Mr. Sessions uses at the end of it to get himself back to what he should have been talking about: "But it is not mainly in his role of consumer that I wish to speak of the listener. The question for us is rather his own experience of the music"—which is in fact the only question in this book.

Dealing now with the listener's activity in relation to the course of events in a piece of music, Mr. Sessions distinguishes four stages in its development: first, hearing ("following . . . the

31 May and 7 June 1952

music in its continuity"), then enjoyment, then understanding ("He needs to be aware of the progression of the bass as well as of the treble line; of a return to the principal key or to a subsidiary key; of a far-flung tonal span . . . as events which his ear witnesses and appreciates as a composition unfolds"), and finally discrimination. And with discrimination the listener becomes a critic: "The critic is, in fact, the listener who has become articulate, who has learned to put his judgments and his values into words."

This statement about the critic is correct as far as it goes, but incomplete: what must be added is the assumption underlying the critic's public articulateness—that he can give his readers the benefit of powers as a listener greater than their own. That is, he can point out to the listener the "progression of the bass line," the "far-flung tonal span," and other details in the course of events that the listener might otherwise not be aware of. And to say this is to continue the scheme of Mr. Sessions's book: the course of events which is created by the composer and is re-created by the performer and must be apprehended by the listener—this course of events is pointed out to the listener by the critic.

But Mr. Sessions does not say it, taking off instead on a discussion of the critic's "true function," which he sees as the exercise of powers of discrimination developed "to the point where he becomes conscious of values in a generalized sense" and can "contribute strongly to musical life through illumination of the real issues which are vital in any particular time and place." And in a state of hoarse moral fervor he summons the critic to his high duty. Formerly, he says, when our music was the imported product of a tradition developed elsewhere and the critic's task was to interpret that tradition to the American public, he had merely to "take due note of judgments and values that had already reached maturity elsewhere. Today, with the ever-increasing development of a rich musical life of our own, he is forced to swim in more perilous waters and to discover values of his own. It is small wonder that he often shows a certain reluctance to do this and takes refuge in writing long columns on the season's sixth performance of 'Tristan,' or indulging, to cite a ghastly example I shall never forget, in vituperation of Critic B because the latter had written an unfavorable review of a book by Critic C, of whom Critic A (the author of the review in question) approved because he (Critic C) had written disparagingly of Critic D's book on Mozart. A veritable tangle of critics, with poor Mozart, in this case representing the only actual music involved in the whole matter, four steps away!"

I was about to say that Mr. Sessions's idea of the situation fifty years ago—that the score of a European symphony was imported for the conductor together with a little box of European values for the critic—hadn't the slightest relation to reality, when I realized that there probably were critics who accepted any European work unthinkingly. But there were others who operated as a critic should—who listened for what life they could themselves discover in the symphony and made their own evaluations of it. That is what the critic does today too when he is confronted with a new symphony by an American. And today when he writes a long column on the season's sixth *Tristan* it isn't because he shrinks from the task of discovering the life in that symphony, but because a new singer is singing in *Tristan* for the first time and this too is something which calls for critical evaluation. So does a book about music; and it wasn't because I shrank from the task of dealing with Mozart's music (I had, only a couple of months earlier, dealt with the unfamiliar Piano Concerto K.503 that Schnabel had played in New York for the first time*) but because I had Einstein's book on Mozart to evaluate that I wrote the review Mr. Sessions cannot forget,** in which I (Critic A) began with the observation that reviews of books sometimes were amusing performances to watch; cited

11 October 1952

the example of Mark Schubart (Critic B) condescending to Virgil Thomson's (Critic C) *The Musical Scene* in the *Times*; explained that I wasn't condescending to Schubart's youth but thinking of the quality of his own critical writing; went on to say that the performances on the Einstein (Critic D) book had been staggering, but that Thomson, whose reviews of books were usually poor, had made the only perceptive comment I had seen on this one; quoted his comment; and then took off from it with my own comments on what Einstein had written about Mozart and his music. An entirely untangled progression of thought—the "veritable tangle of critics" being what Mr. Sessions contrives to make of it in a lecture a few years later at the Juilliard School where Schubart is now Dean.

Which brings me to my last point. Taking the critic's primary task to be the illumination not of issues but of the object—the piece of music, the book, the review of a book—that he has before him, I would say that this task imposes on him a duty: the duty of describing this object accurately, which means the duty of looking at it with an eye unaffected either by friendship or by animosity, by gratitude for a beneficial act, or by anything else of this sort. Criticism, in other words, is one of the forms of human behavior, in which the critic has the duty, simply, of behaving honorably, and which does, then, involve moral issues. Not the issues Mr. Sessions is concerned with, but others which he seems to be unaware of. [*The Nation*]

---

11 October 1952   By virtue of a book about Berlioz noteworthy, among other reasons, for its author's inability to say any-

* See the article in the *Nation* of 13 January 1945, reprinted in *Music in the Nation*.
** In the *Nation* of 19 May 1945 and on pages 232-5 of *Music in the Nation*.

20 December 1952

thing illuminating about Berlioz's music, Jacques Barzun has become the man to review performances and recordings of Berlioz's works in the *Saturday Review* and to compile *Pleasures of Music: A Reader's Choice of Great Writing About Music and Musicians*. In the customary editor's introduction, entitled *Music and Words*, he envelopes the subject of writing words about music in a haze of diffuse bright chatter, and more relevantly offers explanations of the preponderant number of items in the collection that are not writing about music but merely involve music indirectly in some way—e.g., excerpts from novels, Barnum's account of the Jenny Lind tour, Prokofiev's confession of error after the Zhdanov denunciation. Mr. Barzun also states his criteria of selection: "the representative worth of the sample, the greatness of the mind that conceived it, and the felicity of the prose"; but a large number of the selections are not to be accounted for by these values or any others; nor has he chosen the best work of even the great writers. What he has done in this collection is to demonstrate again, as in his book on Berlioz, the enormous amount and range of his reading, and his astounding lack of discrimination. And one begins to see the process which produced both books: a lifetime of indiscriminate collecting of bits of material into files, then an equally indiscriminate emptying of the files into books. [*The Nation*]

20 December 1952 Tuning in for the broadcast of a performance of *La Forza del Destino*, I heard Mr. Bing, in his little speech of welcome to the radio audience, say that no better singers could be heard anywhere in the world today than those who were to sing the leading roles that afternoon. My first thought was that Mr. Bing undoubtedly knew better than he

17 January 1953

spoke—knew, for example, of Renata Tebaldi and knew that she was a better singer than Milanov today—until I remembered his engagement of the tenor Del Monaco. My further thought was of the danger of telling the public Milanov's tremulous shrillness was the best singing it could hear anywhere: the public might, in Shaw's words, say reverently, "This is classical music. This is above our heads, this is," and decide not to listen to it anymore —until I remembered that the public applauds bad singing as loudly as good, Del Monaco as much as Bjoerling, Milanov as much as Steber. And my final thought was that an enlightened director presenting opera to such an unenlightened public will not take advantage of its lack of discrimination but will rather try to develop in it the discrimination it lacks—will try, that is, by letting the public hear only what is good, to give it the ability to perceive that something is bad (which requires, of course, that he himself be aware of the difference between Del Monaco's hard-voiced yelling and Bjoerling's lustrous-voiced lyricism).

[*The Nation*]

17 January 1953 Musicians' lives have always been news, which it used to be the publicity man's job to get into the papers. What we have today—and what the present-day publicity operator's job is to get into the news magazine that originated it and is its chief publication medium—is the news story with built-in critical estimate. An outstanding example is the story of the Monteux career as that of one of the giants to whom recognition has come belatedly, with its built-in estimate of Monteux as one of the giants. This one has been kept rolling for several years by one writer after another incapable of hearing Monteux's repeatedly demonstrated musical mediocrity, until it

7 February 1953

is now part of the body of accepted belief in terms of which most writing about music and musicians is done.

Only recently launched is the story about the soprano Milanov as someone who, having at last achieved the control she didn't have of her beautiful voice years ago, now occupies "the long-vacant throne of Rosa Ponselle" and, with the retirement of Flagstad, has "the grandest operatic feminine voice at the Metropolitan"; and one wonders whether this one will stand up very long in the face of the painfully audible fact that what Milanov has learned to control is a voice that has lost all its former beauty. As for the grandest feminine voice at the Metropolitan, rereading my report of Milanov's phenomenal singing in a performance of *Norma* in 1944, only a few days after her tremolo-ridden stridency in *Un Ballo in Maschera*, I came to a similar report of Steber's singing in *Figaro*.* Previously, I wrote, "she had begun every performance with a strong tremolo which sometimes had cleared up and sometimes had not. This time, however, the very first tones of *Porgi amor* were clear and lovely; and her technical security continued to produce such tones, which her musical taste molded into long, continuous and exquisite phrases." Since then I have reported other occasions when the slow vibrato in Steber's singing has become a clouding tremulousness, but also occasions—notably a performance of *Così Fan Tutte* last year—when her lustrous voice has been clear and she has done what I consider the grandest singing one can hear at the Metropolitan today. [*The Nation*]

7 February 1953 RCA Victor continues to make available again in its Treasury of Immortal Performances series of LP records items not deserving of immortality, such as the Menuhin-Landowska and Menuhin-Enesco performances of Bach's Sonata

* See pages 47-8.

7 February 1953

in E and Concerto in D minor, but also things like the Casals performances of Bach's Suites Nos. 2 and 3, of which I will say again what I said when they were first issued: "The life which these works have . . . is the life created by the coloring, the movement, the tensions of Casals's phrasing. . . . This is something you would almost not believe you had heard in a performance, after it was over; but you can put the needle back at the beginning of the Sarabande of No. 2 and find that it did happen; and there it is on the record for all time." Which now—thanks to Victor—is true again.

And if Victor hasn't yet got around to reissuing the Kreisler-Rachmaninov performances of Beethoven and Schubert sonatas, the Elisabeth Schumann performances of Mozart arias and Schubert songs, the earlier performances of Frieda Hempel, it has on the other hand placed the public enormously in its debt by making available for the first time the Schnabel performances of Beethoven sonatas in Volumes 1 and 2 of the Beethoven Sonata Society, which HMV issued in 1935 only in small limited editions. The two LP's not only make it possible for many people to hear again those unique performances of Op. 111 and Op. 109, and for many more to hear them for the first time; they also make it possible to study in the performances the distinctive way of dealing with the music that so extraordinarily enlarged its meaning.

Toscanini once spoke of the difficulty of playing Mozart as one of knowing what to do between the mere *p* here and *f* eight bars later; but actually there is the same difficulty with Beethoven whose directions are much more numerous and closer together: there still remains what must be done between and around them. This is something one appreciates when one plays first the Solomon performance of Op. 111 that was issued last year and his performances of Opp. 109, 53 (*Waldstein*) and 54 on a new Victor LP, and then the Schnabel performances of the first two on the new LP's and the one of Op. 53 on the old

7 February 1953

HMV 78's. The difference—most striking in the slow movements—is between Solomon's mere obedience to every p and f in the score, and what Schnabel does in addition: the expansion, the distention in time, the intensification by dynamic force, which place the sounds in significant, powerful relations in sharply contoured successions with cohesive tensions that are built up to the salient points and then released. And this produces the further difference that the slow movement of Op. 53, for example, as Schnabel plays it has a spaciously, profoundly meditative and powerfully dramatic expressive effect that it doesn't have in Solomon's performance.

That meditative character of Schnabel's playing led some people to characterize it as a product of intellect without emotion; whereas actually, though the involvement of a powerful intellect is evident, so is the operation of powerful emotion. It was excess of emotion, not of intellect, that produced the flaws in the performances—the occasional distention of phrase to the point of distortion, the occasional tempo too fast for clarity, the occasional fortissimo beyond the limit of agreeable sound; though it was mere limitations of technique that produced the inaccuracy and confusion that is to be heard in some of the difficult passage-work in the first movement of Op. 111. If one can't endure these flaws one can have smoothly rounded perfection from Solomon; if one *can* endure them one gets in addition what Solomon doesn't offer: the dramatic power that Schnabel imparts to the first movement of Op. 111; the sustained continuity and intensity of the progression from the spaciously reflective opening of the second movement to the superearthly illumination of the end; the similar sustained continuity in the conclusion of Op. 109—the crescendo of intensity in the extraordinary final variation to the trills that subside into the affecting restatement of the theme. [*The Nation*]

4 April 1953 Though almost everyone involved in *The Rake's Progress* at the Metropolitan contributed to making it the distinguished and stimulating occasion it was, the principal contribution was of course Stravinsky's. In fact the other contributions could have been regarded as an *hommage* to the composer of a score which was like a summation of his artistic experience and activity. A score, that is, in which a way of thinking and operating developed in the succession of previous works now produced a great deal that was familiar—ranging from the well-known ostinato figures to the gravely dissonant writing that one recalled from *Orpheus* and that now provided the opera's most affecting music in its last two scenes. But for the situations of the earlier scenes Stravinsky had produced a wide variety of invention that was astonishingly and delightfully new: fanfares, processional music, arias in sustained melodic style, even an aria (Baba's *Wretched me*) in an amusingly extravagant florid style. True enough, even in what was new Stravinsky had followed his old practice of working with materials taken from his musical experiences—the themes and styles of other composers and other periods—and of producing, in effect, personal commentaries on those experiences. That is, considering it appropriate that a play laid in the eighteenth century be set in the operatic style of that period, he had produced arias in a lovely melodic style, but with the tensions they acquired in the process of being geared with orchestral parts whose acrid dissonance and rhythmic intricacy kept one constantly aware of, and stimulated by, the presence and activity of the Stravinsky mind.

[*The Nation*]

16 May 1953 The year has given us the Metropolitan's production of Musorgsky's own *Boris Godunov* and HMV's record-

16 May 1953

ing of the Rimsky-Korsakov version. It has been possible, then, to hear what Rimsky considered to be "the fragmentary character of the musical phrases, the harshness of the harmonies and modulations, the faulty counterpoint, the poverty of the instrumentation, and the general weakness of the work from the technical point of view" that called for his corrective revision; and to discover that nothing in Musorgsky's writing called for correction, that everything sounded right, true, powerfully effective, achieved with assurance and mastery, and that Rimsky's changes to make the music conform to his taste were a falsification of Musorgsky's work. This was true even of the orchestration: Musorgsky's "sonorous image" (to borrow Aaron Copland's term) had been right, but his instrumental realization of it hadn't carried effectively in the opera house; and what this had called for was a more effective realization, such as Karol Rathaus had attempted for the Metropolitan production, not a substitution of the sonorous image of *Le Coq d'Or*.

It may seem extraordinary that at this late date, when the Metropolitan at last produced Musorgsky's *Boris*, HMV recorded Rimsky's. But in this episode it isn't only what has happened to Musorgsky's work that is extraordinary, but the way people's minds have operated, and continue to operate, in relation to it. Thus, for years it has been the accepted belief that whatever might be said of Rimsky's changes they had enabled a work that had failed in its original form to be performed with success. That belief goes back to Rimsky's statements in justification of his revision; and it has continued, amazingly, in the face of his own testimony to the contrary: the passage in *My Musical Life* in which he says Musorgsky's *Boris* was produced in 1874 "with great success" and continued to be performed "with uninterrupted success" until 1882, and in which, discussing possible reasons for the cessation of the performances, he speaks of "rumors that the opera had displeased the imperial family . . . gossip that its subject was unpleasant to the censors," but says

16 May 1953

nothing about defects or difficulties of the work itself. With that contradicting passage plain to read in the 1942 edition of *My Musical Life*, Carl Van Vechten wrote nevertheless in his introduction that Rimsky "made it possible for Musorgsky's music drama to be performed"; and even the compilers of the documentary material in *The Musorgsky Reader* quoted and accepted the statement in *My Musical Life* that the revision satisfied the "need of an edition for performances, for practical artistic purposes," but did not quote the passage which revealed there had been no need of such revision for that purpose. As a result those who listened to Musorgsky's own *Boris* this year did so with the idea that they were hearing a work whose inept crudities had caused it to fail when it was first produced; and some must have been unable to hear the work whose remarkable qualities brought it success from the start.

More important: poems, novels, paintings have been criticized, but I don't recall anyone ever having gone so far as to rewrite or repaint what he considered to be faulty in someone else's work. Moreover, if it had ever been discovered that this had been done, there would have been no debate about whether the work was more effective with the changes or without them, and whether they should be retained or not: it would have been taken as a matter of course that they had no validity and that the original work must be restored (though certainly if some academician had "corrected" what for him were the faults and crudities of a Van Gogh it would have been recognized that the result was not an improvement but a falsification). But in the case of *Boris* we find the celebrated Ernest Newman writing after a production of Musorgsky's first version that the problem of which *Boris* to produce is one of choosing not merely between Musorgsky's own two versions, each complete and with merits of its own, but from these two and Rimsky's, since "rail as the specialists may at Rimsky-Korsakov . . . he has given the theater a good practical proposition"; and that the ideal solution is to

16 May 1953 (1964)

give all three. Even more perceptive critics like Desmond Shawe-Taylor and Edward Sackville-West also decide, "after frequent hearings and examinations of both versions, that the case against Rimsky has been overstated," and that the differences in the *Farewell and Death of Boris* "are comparatively small."

And even the most accurately perceptive and clearest-minded of present-day English writers, Gerald Abraham, who recognizes in the booklet of the HMV recording that by applying to *Boris* an art whose "essence . . . is brightly tinted transparency, clear-cut harmonies and part-writing realized in primary orchestral colors" Rimsky "imprinted his own personality over the entire work"—even Mr. Abraham goes on to conclude that "the result is—like Mozart's rescoring of 'Messiah' . . .—a fascinating posthumous collaboration of two very different but very fine musical minds, and we must accept it (as we do Mozart's 'Messiah') for a masterpiece in its own right, without clouding our pleasure by overmuch reference to the quite different values of the original version." Which is to say that he fails to perceive the difference between Mozart's rescoring of Handel's *Messiah* and Rimsky's recomposition of Musorgsky's *Boris*, and the incompatibility and disparity of the mind that produced *Boris* and the mind that produced *Le Coq d'Or*.

After all this the simple good sense of Mr. Bing's reasoning—that if one is going to give Musorgsky's *Boris* one should give the *Boris* Musorgsky wrote—becomes something of a miracle.

[*The Nation*]

Postscript 1964 It turned out some years later that the good sense had been not Mr. Bing's but that of Max Rudolf and Fritz Stiedry, his musical advisers at that time. In 1960, with Erich Leinsdorf as his adviser, Mr. Bing replaced Musorgsky's *Boris* with Shostakovitch's reorchestration and partial rewriting of the work, which gave it an impress of his vulgar mind that falsified it no less than the impress of Rimsky's mind had

19 September 1953

done. And this provided an explanation of the puzzling inconsistencies in Mr. Bing's operation: his seemingly exhibiting intelligence, judgment and taste by producing Musorgsky's own version of *Boris*, but then producing rubbish like Giordano's *Andrea Chénier* or a feeble piece of *ersatz* operatic glamor ("old wine in old bottles," in the words of a friend) like Samuel Barber's *Vanessa*; his lavishing new scenery and costumes on *Chénier* and *Vanessa*, but putting on *Boris* with various bits of old scenery from the storehouse; his securing Eugene Berman's amazingly beautiful scenery for *Rigoletto*, but then offering in *Don Giovanni* a permanent set of Charles Elson's, which had the singers spending most of their time and energy clambering over the ramp that filled much of the stage, and which had the first-act ball and second-act dinner taking place, apparently, in the street (an error corrected a few years later with Berman's scenery and costumes for *Don Giovanni*, which surpassed even his previous achievements in visual beauty and effectiveness in relation to the proceedings on the stage.)

19 September 1953 About once a year I get a letter questioning my practice of discussing other critics' opinions. One interesting thing about this is that there would be no such question if I discussed a book by one of these critics—even a book that was a collection of his newspaper reviews; what is objected to is my discussing the reviews when they appear in the newspaper; and this distinction is obviously absurd. But no more absurd, surely, than the idea that the critic is to evaluate what the artist does, but nobody is to evaluate what the critic writes about the artist. And if it is conceded that his writing is subject to evaluation, who is to evaluate it if not another specialist in the field? Is the rule for music critics to be different from the rule for historians, anthropologists and philosophers, who are considered to be the right ones to evaluate each other's writings? Or different

19 September 1953

from the rule for literary critics, who constantly discuss each other's ideas?

All this aside from the fact that as someone intensely interested in music I am bound to be interested in what is written about it—to get pleasure from an illuminating statement, pain from a misleadingly unperceptive one. And the ideas about music published in books, magazine articles, newspaper concert reviews, record blurbs are a part of the musical scene that it is the critic's function to comment on—an especially important part since it affects people's understanding and thus influences the rest of the scene. If it is the critic's duty to object to a performance that gives people a false idea of a piece of music, it is equally his duty to object to a statement which gives them a false idea of it.

But, my questioners point out, since critics deal with what is not objectively measurable, and their judgments are mere personal opinions, can one of them contend that his opinion is right and another's wrong? To my questioners the answer is very clear that he cannot; and they would approve of what Virgil Thomson said when I asked him once what the *Herald Tribune* music staff had done in its course in music criticism at New York University: "On the democratic assumption that any opinion is legitimate that can be expressed in clear prose, we taught them how to write." But I would say the democratic assumption he referred to holds only for the opinions of private belief and conversation, not for those of published criticism; and that the assumption underlying the publication of an opinion is that it is worth publishing because it embodies the special critical perception that most people lack. Thomson might say he was speaking only of opinions of this sort; and my questioners undoubtedly would point out that their question is concerned with differences in opinions of this sort.

10 October 1953

I would say then first that if one concedes the possibility of the critic having greater perception than his lay readers, one has to concede the possibility of one critic having greater perception than another. And my second answer is to say how I think criticism operates. The piece of music is a communication; as such it may impress different minds differently; and the critic reports to his readers the effect it has on *his* mind. But in this he acts only as a sort of guide-post, saying in effect: "At this point I hear this detail, this quality, this meaning, this value"—after which his reader listens and may say: "Yes, I hear all that too." But his reader also may say: "No, I don't hear that, I hear *this*." What the critic says about a piece of music is true for his reader only if it is confirmed by the reader's ears; and each critic writes for the group of people who have found his perceptions and evaluations confirmed sufficiently by their own experience. The critic, in other words, writes not what is true, but what is true for him, and what becomes true for other people who find it to be so when they listen. And this is so not only when he writes about a piece of music or a performance, but when he writes about another critic's statement.

One thing that is true for me is that there are a lot of people writing about music on nothing but Thomson's democratic assumption. To practice medicine or law or engineering a man has to prove himself qualified; but all he has to do is persuade somebody to publish what he has written, and he is a music critic, about whom I will be asked how I know I am right and he is wrong. [*The Nation*]

10 October 1953   Irving Kolodin's *The Story of the Metropolitan Opera* begins with a chapter, *Patrons and Purposes*,

10 October 1953

which tells how the social ambitions of the new millionaires of the eighties, who were denied boxes in the Academy of Music by the old millionaires, led them to build the Metropolitan Opera House and arrange to have opera produced in it, and describes the part these men and their successors played in the subsequent history of the building and the producing companies. The next chapter, *House and Home*, discusses the characteristics and defects of the building as a theater, and gives its history as a meeting-place of New York's aristocracy of wealth. Then comes the major portion of the book, *Opera and Artists*, with a season-by-season listing, description and evaluation of operas, performing artists and productions from the opening in 1883 through the season of 1951–52.

An unavoidable weakness of the book is that it must derive its evaluations of the early seasons from contemporary newspaper reviews by critics, in some instances, no more worth reading now than they were then, and even the best of whom, W. J. Henderson, shakes one's confidence with his opinion that Verdi's *Don Carlo* was "both tuneless and unvocal" and "machine-made from beginning to end." Kolodin does his own evaluating of recent seasons; but I have described in this column some of the experiences with his critical writing that have made it not writing I would read for dependable information about a work or performance.

A major defect of his earlier book on the Metropolitan was its endless descriptions of casts and changes of casts, which he justified by the fact that the book was intended as a factual record for reference purposes. The new book seems to me to have less of this material, possibly because the complete record is now available in the Seltsam book which simply gives all the casts in block style. But there is still too much, some of it concerned with appearances by obscure singers that are of no importance whatever. And whereas Seltsam's listings in block style are interesting

10 October 1953

to glance through, Kolodin's prose listings are made worse than boring by the quality of the prose.

Which brings us to a major defect of the book: the writing, and not just about casts. A man who perpetrates "The absence of Wagner during the war years blemished no opening," or "The complications of critical coverage of New York's music events prevented close attention to several new ventures that may be isolated in time, if not by quality," is plainly someone unable to use the English language; though things like "The unspirited if conscientious work [in *Louise*] of Fourestier, Parisian though he was, left as much dissatisfaction as the cool, collected singing of Kirsten, American though she was," or "Peace had [in 1945] indeed come to all theaters of war by fall, but not to all theaters of opera. The easy acceptance of incompetence [in the war years] now imposed a period of extrication to balance the one of implication," plainly reveal the writer's belief that he is turning out specimens of very fine writing and impressive thinking indeed. The pretentious gestures are like a woman's coquetries that presume the attractiveness she lacks; and they produce writing and thinking—especially in the passages of summation—that are sometimes difficult to make coherent sense of.

For me what is valuable in the book is the factual material of the opening chapters. From the time I began to frequent the Metropolitan, in 1914, the public was given to understand that it was the princely generosity of the millionaire members of the Metropolitan Opera Company (the producing company, as distinguished from the Metropolitan Opera and Real Estate Company, the owner of the building), and above all of Otto Kahn, that made possible the continuation of opera there. But the fact is that opera at the Metropolitan earned a profit uninterruptedly from 1910 to 1930, and when the deficits began the millionaires of the Opera Company called on the public to make them up, retaining control but escaping financial responsibility through

23 January 1954

the transformation of the Company into the Metropolitan Opera Association. As for the $4,500 a boxholder paid each year, this was an assessment for maintenance of the building which the boxholders owned as members of the Real Estate Company; and since they received the use of the boxes instead of rent from the Opera Company, the $4,500 was in effect their payment for six box seats for every subscription performance of the season—which is to say it was not philanthropy but payment for value received.

All this is interesting in connection with Toscanini's leaving the Metropolitan in 1915. It is, characteristically, not clear whether Kolodin merely speculates that the reduced profit for the season of 1914–15 *would* have "argued for retrenchment on rehearsals, to which Toscanini would not accede," or that he means that such a difficulty about rehearsals *did* occur; but he considers it certain that an unsatisfactory performance of *Carmen* "was the spark that ignited the explosion." My authoritative information is that the spark was Kahn's insistence that instead of five extra musicians being hired to play on stage in *The Masked Ball*, five men be taken from the orchestra in the pit. Presumably this was not the first instance of the kind; and, as we have seen, it was not as though the money would have had to come out of Kahn's pocket. [*The Nation*]

23 January 1954 Recently I spoke of those whose ears go along with the accepted view of Bach's *B-Minor Mass* as a towering masterpiece from first note to last, instead of hearing the uninspired music in parts of the work. This is of course only one instance of many in which people hear not the actual music or performance but what this is transformed into by their own loy-

23 January 1954

alties or generally accepted ideas. Thus, recordings exist of the superbly phrased and shaped performances Beecham used to give of certain works of Mozart—recordings that enable us to perceive that his present performances are distortions of them; but there are people who hear the distortions of the present performances as the superb phrasing of those of years ago. In this instance they are influenced by loyalty; in others they are influenced by current ideas—the idea, for example, that since Monteux conducted the first performance of *Le Sacre du Printemps* his performance must be the definitive one, instead of the hard fact of Stravinsky's own recorded performance, which should enable anyone to hear that the work in Monteux's performance hasn't the power it should have.

Now one can see the possibility of argument over a conductor's phrasing; but one would think nobody could fail to hear the unpleasant sound or the tremolo of a singer. Actually, however, Beecham and Weingartner command nothing comparable with the passionate loyalties to singers. When I reported Traubel's tremulously acidulous singing in a performance of *Tristan und Isolde* a few years ago I received letters of protest that sounded as though they had been written in tears; and it was evident that the tremulously acidulous sounds had reached the writers' ears as the opulence of earlier years. And a year ago, discussing the news magazines' news story with built-in critical estimate, and the way such a story, once started, was kept going by one writer after another and got to be part of the body of accepted belief, I cited as an example the then current news story of Milanov's having at last achieved the control of her voice that now made it "the grandest operatic feminine voice at the Metropolitan"—a story accepted by writers and listeners who should have been able to hear the actual threadbare and tremulous voice, the scooping, the sagging pitch.

6 March 1954

A couple of years ago there was the story of how Mr. Bing's ear had detected the soprano voice hidden by the contralto of Margaret Harshaw, and how as Brünnhilde in *Die Götterdämmerung* she had revealed herself as Flagstad's successor. This line of thought was continued in subsequent writing (as recently as the January 4 issue of *Newsweek*); and it is the reason for the enormous applause after Harshaw's successive exhibitions of tremulous stridency in the recent Metropolitan performance of *Don Giovanni* I attended—to say nothing of her inability to cope with the florid passages of *Non mi dir*.

In the title role was Nicola Rossi-Lemeni, largely as a result of the news story, in the fall of 1952, of the sensational debut in San Francisco of a bass of Chaliapin-like stature. And this must have been the reason also for the ovations after singing which was rough-textured in full voice, more agreeable—but also more mannered—in half-voice. Or perhaps some of the applause was for a curious dramatic performance which gave the impression of his playing with the part rather than in it. [*The Nation*]

6 March 1954 The few hundred people who made the trip to Circle in the Square on the rainy afternoon of February 21 for one of Alexander Schneider's chamber music concerts were rewarded with one of the great concerts of the season—great by virtue of the music it presented, Schubert's Trios Opp. 99 and 100, and the compelling ensemble performances by the trio comprising Schneider himself, the cellist Frank Miller, and the pianist Horszowski. The performances would have been compelling anywhere; but in this small place one was close enough to the players to be affected by the intensity with which they operated—and to discover incidentally that it was on his most delicate inflections of phrase that Miller expended his greatest,

20 March and 1 May 1954

most audible effort. At this close range one also heard with Miller's impassioned cello tone the sounds of bow on strings that aren't heard in the distances of the concert hall; but no such sounds accompanied Schneider's lyrical violin tone. As for Horszowski, he could produce nothing better than the glassy tone of the piano that had been provided for the concert.

From Circle in the Square Miller presumably rushed up to Carnegie Hall for Cantelli's final broadcast with the NBC Symphony, while I rushed home to listen to it. There was this time a performance of Beethoven's Fifth which—like earlier performances of Haydn's No. 88, Schubert's No. 9 and Tchaikovsky's No. 4—was something completely and beautifully achieved and finished, accomplished with complete control and yet with relaxed ease, and with the youthful lyricism and purity of intention that are so touching in Cantelli's work. I was especially grateful for the repetition of his performance of Tchaikovsky's No. 4—the first in my forty years' experience that gave me an accurate realization in sound of what Tchaikovsky set down in his score, and one that showed him to have been a better composer of his music than Stokowski, Koussevitzky, Mengelberg and all the others who have insisted on recomposing it for him.

[*The Nation*]

20 March and 1 May 1954   Virgil Thomson's objections to Cyril Ritchard's direction of the Metropolitan's new *Barber of Seville* as "a rowdy English farce rather than as commedia dell' arte" sounded convincing when I read them, but turned out not to apply to the performance I attended. For one thing Thomson had found that only Fernando Corena, as Dr. Bartolo, "clowns in the grand Italian manner," whereas "the others flounce about naturalistically," and Cesare Siepi in particular, "as the music teacher, climbs over furniture"; and he had thought it less effective to have "Dr. Bartolo and Don Basilio . . . played for an identical buffo effect instead of for contrast . . . of the one as an ebullient comic and the other as a sad, even sinister comic." But I found that the two *were* contrasted in this way by costumes, make-ups, and movements—in particular Siepi's sinisterly sinuous movements of his hands, which in the crescendo of *La Calumnia* extended themselves into sinuous movements of his body, including, at the climax, a gigantic movement over his chair. And in general the action contrived by Mr. Ritchard didn't seem to me to be excessive and out of character in this comedy, in the way the clowning had been that Alfred Lunt introduced during some of the most tender and poignant music of *Così Fan Tutte*, with Thomson's enthusiastic approval.

Not that there weren't things wrong in the *Barber* performance, and that Thomson didn't describe them accurately: "Merrill is never still. Miss Peters is saucy like a night-club soubrette." But these excesses, it seemed to me, were not imposed on Merrill and Miss Peters by Mr. Ritchard's direction; they were rather imposed on his direction by Merrill's and Miss Peters's one objective in the performance—of putting themselves over to the audience with a bang. For this they used not only their acting but their singing: Merrill hurled at the audience big sounds that were made unpleasant by the hoarseness his voice has exhibited this year; and Miss Peters, who has acquired a secure technique that enables her, as Thomson put it, to "rip out scales like a keyed instrument," used this ability in a relentless socking of the audience between the eyes.

But there were more things that were right, and a couple that were wonderful. In addition to the acting and singing of Siepi as Don Basilio and Corena as Dr. Bartolo there was Cesare Valletti's singing as Count Almaviva, with a beauty of tone and phrasing that made one think of Schipa. And the sensitive, finished playing of the orchestra under Erede—though I would have liked to

20 March and 1 May 1954

hear more sharpness of accent and contour, and less patient waiting for Miss Peters to complete her exhibitionistic interpolations. But the glory of the performance was Eugene Berman's scenery and costumes—above all the first-act house-front which, as the curtain rose, took one's breath away with the beauty of its design and color, the audacious fantasy of its ornaments of luminous fans matching the fans on the false proscenium. With a good Rosina and Figaro this would be one of the Metropolitan's most distinguished productions (as a later performance with de los Angeles and Capecchi demonstrated).

As I watched Corena and Siepi and thought of what Virgil Thomson had written about them, I wondered how irrelevant newspaper criticism could get to be. As irrelevant, one might answer, as a recent statement, ostensibly about Cantelli, but really intended to convey the fullness of long-accumulated experience and understanding out of which Irving Kolodin could pronounce: "That degree of musical culture and experience which can settle, almost instinctively, on proper tempi and sonorous values for such works as the ... Mozart [Divertimento] are not yet his"; and the further statement about a performance that had flowed with relaxed ease and grace and a beautiful and moving lyricism: "... almost all the movements were too fast and nervous, over-accentuated, lacking lilt and songfulness." It appears that what Mr. Kolodin writes about a Cantelli performance he heard has as much connection with reality as what he writes about a Beecham performance that never happened.*

Readers continue to question my commenting on what other

* (1964) In the first edition of his *Guide to Recorded Music* Kolodin wrote concerning Beecham's recording of Mozart's Symphony K.201: "It has been my reaction, after hearing Beecham's more recent performances of this work, that the interpretation he recorded was a transitional one, tending toward the conception he holds today." An accidental meeting with Beecham enabled me to confirm my impression that there had been no "more recent performances" of the work either in the concert hall or on records.

27 March 1954

critics write about music; and I continue to wonder at their doing so, which to me indicates their failure to understand what critical writing is. Apparently they think of it as entirely an exercise of judgment, and don't realize that the critic's exercise of judgment on the artist's public performance is itself a public performance, and as such properly subject to evaluation. What Berlioz expresses with literary brilliance, gaiety and wit in his critical writing is musical perception that deals rigorously with its material; and with this integrity there is an intensity, a passion, a nobility in the operation that brings tears to my eyes whenever I read him. As against Berlioz's way, and Shaw's, and Turner's, there is the way of Kolodin and his brethren, which arouses altogether different emotions. [*The Nation*]

27 March 1954 It was interesting, on a Sunday afternoon, to hear Cantelli conduct the New York Philharmonic in the Mozart Divertimento K.287 that Toscanini recorded a few years ago—interesting, that is, to hear how different Cantelli's performance was, and how beautiful in its different way. Some of the fast movements were slower-paced and more easy-going, making possible the outlining of smaller details within the flow of the larger phrases—a flow that had a beautiful and moving lyricism and grace, as against the powerful impulse operating in Toscanini's treatment. This was the difference also in their performances of the slow movement—a beautifully shaped and eloquent vocal aria as Cantelli played it; one to which Toscanini's power imparts a largeness of span and expressive effect, a tension, a grandeur that become overwhelming.

That power, creating a continuous tension in the flow of tone, and doing this in the quietest music no less than in the most forceful, is one of the distinctive characteristics of Toscanini's work. And it was impressively evident later the same day in his

24 April 1954

NBC Symphony broadcast—in the lovely slow movement of Vivaldi's D-minor Concerto Grosso no less than in Verdi's wonderfully beautiful *Te Deum* and the Prologue to Boito's *Mefistofele*. [*The Nation*]

24 April 1954 The continuing tension and power in a Toscanini performance was a manifestation of the power that was actually being exercised—exercised to hold the hundred men of the orchestra in precisely balanced relation to one another; to maintain the strands of continuing sound in the similar precise balance that produced the unique clarity of texture; to keep everything in the progression in coherent relation of sonority and pace to what preceded and followed. That power was exercised in the performances of the Vivaldi concerto, Verdi *Te Deum* and Boito *Mefistofele* Prologue one Sunday; the next Sunday one heard that it was not being exercised in the performance of Tchaikovsky's *Pathétique*, in which there was no continuity of impetus and tension, and one thing was not in coherent relation to the next. The power was exercised again at the dress rehearsal for the final broadcast, in magnificent performances of the Prelude to *Lohengrin*, the *Forest Murmurs* from *Siegfried*, and the *Dawn and Rhine Journey* from *Die Götterdämmerung* up to the point where Toscanini stopped to correct a mistake he had corrected the day before,* and then, angered by its recurrence, walked out and did not return. But it was not exercised at the broadcast the next day; and the last performances were a cruelly tragic conclusion to the unequaled achievements of this great and dedicated musician.

As I listened to Aaron Copland's score for *The Tender Land*, the new opera produced by the New York City Opera, I was

* It turned out that the mistake both days was Toscanini's.

1 May 1954

struck first by the loveliness that was being achieved with the assured mastery one is always aware of in Copland's operation; then, as the work continued, by the variety and unfailing adequacy for the dramatic purposes, the power when this was called for; and in the end by the rich profusion of the invention and elaboration. This seems to me to be Copland's largest and most richly filled-out canvas, so to speak; and the one in which that mastery is most impressive. As for the drama it serves so well, the subject of Horace Everett's libretto is an incident in the life of a simple rural family, of which it makes something high-flown that I for one cannot believe in. One should perhaps listen to the last scene of *The Tender Land* in the way one listens to *Il Trovatore*; but there is the difficulty that what is unbelievable in *The Tender Land* can't, because of its immediacy in time and place and its English words, be put out of mind as easily as what is unbelievable in *Il Trovatore*. [*The Nation*]

1 May 1954   The New York City Opera's announcement a year ago of its intention to produce *Show Boat* in order to realize the musical values of the work that hadn't been realized on Broadway led me to comment that the music of *Show Boat* was some of the loveliest of its kind but I knew of no values in this kind beyond the ones realized in the Broadway productions of such works—which was to say, none of the kind an opera company was concerned with. And concerning the actual production I must report that it not only fails to offer additional musical values unrealized on Broadway but fails to offer some essential theatrical values the Broadway productions did realize. The music is sung beautifully by Robert Rounseville, Laurel Hurley and Helena Bliss; but the top-notch musical-show performers and sumptuous scenery and costumes with which the Broadway pro-

26 September 1953 and 12 June 1954

ductions put over the painfully corny play are missing. Not only do works like *Show Boat* have no place in the activities of an opera company, but they shouldn't be attempted by a company that hasn't the money for the Broadway-style production they call for. [*The Nation*]

26 September 1953 and 12 June 1954 The "searching insight" of Horowitz's performances of Schumann's *Kinderszenen*, a Scarlatti sonata, a Brahms Intermezzo convinces Roland Gelatt, in *Music-Makers*, that Horowitz is fully capable of playing the "non-acrobatic" music he doesn't play, as is assumed in Horowitz's explanation of why he doesn't play it. Early in his career, he says, when he played in small halls, he did play Bach and Mozart; but this music intended for the intimacy of a small room would bore the thousands of people he plays to in large halls today. So with Schubert's B-flat Sonata: "It is too long, too introspective. You cannot keep the attention of five thousand people through four long movements of Schubert." As for Beethoven, in general the piano works are inferior to the orchestral works ("It's not that Beethoven's piano writing doesn't sound the way *I* want it to; it's because his writing doesn't sound the way *he* wanted it to"); and the last sonatas are for him like Cézanne's last paintings—gropings toward a new style, incomplete, and "not of sufficient listening-value . . . for recitals in large auditoriums."

But the assumption that Horowitz can play the music he doesn't play is incorrect; and the alternation of brio and affetuoso teasing that is the sum total of his playing would make Mozart, Beethoven and Schubert intolerable even to a few hundred of the thousands who, long before the Horowitz era, used to listen in Carnegie Hall to Josef Hofmann play one of the last Bee-

26 September 1953 and 12 June 1954

thoven sonatas, and in recent years filled Hunter College Auditorium to hear Schnabel play these works and sonatas of Mozart and Schubert. And on the other hand Schnabel's performances of these works would bore even a few hundred of the thousands who attend Horowitz's recitals to be alternately excited by his supercharged virtuosity and titillated by his affetuoso teasing. The true Horowitz situation is that of a pianist and an audience on the same level of musical understanding—the level indicated by Horowitz's ideas about Beethoven.

And also his ideas about Musorgsky. The *Musorgsky Reader* is filled with contemporary statements about Musorgsky's powers as a pianist, especially in dramatically and pictorially imaginative invention; and I remember my amazement when, after years of the Ravel orchestration, I heard the original piano version of *Pictures at an Exhibition* and heard how completely achieved an imaginative creation it was. But Horowitz, says Gelatt, made his arrangement "on the principle (hardly to be controverted) that Musorgsky did not understand the piano's full potentialities"—Horowitz's and Gelatt's way of saying that Musorgsky, like Beethoven, was guilty of the inadequacy of not thinking in terms of the Horowitz fireworks. Horowitz changes only the piano "scoring," says Gelatt, whose own musical understanding doesn't extend to realizing that details like the reiterated off-beat F-sharp inserted in the bass in the last ten bars of *Con mortuis*, with rhythmic and pedal effects unintended by Musorgsky, are substance, not "scoring." And the result—as monstrous as Stokowski's completion of Bach's Chaconne—Gelatt considers "Horowitz's interpretative masterpiece."

As for Schubert's B-flat Sonata, Gelatt is in a flutter about the performance which—at the time he was writing his book—Horowitz had allowed only his friends to hear. Gelatt feels it is something the public should not be deprived of; and Horowitz did play the sonata at a recent recital which RCA Victor re-

26 September 1953 and 12 June 1954

corded, making it possible for me to satisfy my interest in the performance of the sonata and comment on it here.

The comment is that from the very first phrase one hears Horowitz operating in what apparently is the only way he can operate. That way is the excessively mannered affetuoso melodic style that incorporates the infinite gradations and varieties of tone he produces from the piano. The mannered style and the fussing with tone are facts; in addition I will mention an impression I get from those facts. When Schnabel played a phrase of melody I had the impression that his fingers were producing the sounds that realized his idea of the phrase; when Horowitz plays the phrase I have the impression that his fingers are using it to produce their gradations of tone, and that these gradations of tone are responsible for the affetuoso style rather than the other way around. This, I repeat, is only an impression; and to accept it is to take the worst view of Horowitz's playing; but even if one limits oneself strictly to fact and believes that the affetuoso style is the way Horowitz thinks of melody, and the fussing with tone is dictated by this way of thinking, then one is taking the best view of the playing, but it is hardly a good view.

For Horowitz's way of playing a phrase of melody—any phrase of melody—the first phrase of Schubert's sonata—the phrases that follow—isn't a good way. It isn't a good way even for Chopin and some of the other composers Horowitz customarily plays; and it isn't a good way for the tranquilly sustained opening of Schubert's sonata; nor does it suit any better the expressive character of the sections that follow. The series of jaunty staccato B-naturals that Horowitz, concerned with varieties of tone, produces in place of the *portato* series indicated by the slur over the dots, at the bottom of page 4 (266) of the Lea original-text edition, and the sprightly legato he produces immediately afterward, are startlingly incongruous in the impassioned context; and they are only two of the many examples of the consequences of

17 July 1954

Horowitz's absorption in his fussing with tone and phrase-contour with no regard for the character and requirements of the music. [*The Nation*]

17 July 1954 In his letter of resignation to David Sarnoff, Toscanini recalled the invitation in 1937 "to become the musical director of an orchestra to be created especially for me for the purpose of broadcasting symphonic music throughout the United States," and wrote that "the sad time has come when I must reluctantly lay aside my baton and say good-bye to my orchestra." For NBC, apparently, certain consequences followed from his statements: that the orchestra created especially for him, allegedly as a contribution to good music in this country, should be discontinued now that he laid down his baton, and the money it cost need be spent no longer. For me these consequences don't follow at all.

In the first place the group of players assembled for Toscanini in 1937 is today one of the world's finest orchestral instruments, with a claim to continued existence even without him. Anyone who cares about music would no more destroy this instrument than he would a Stradivarius violin (to disregard for the moment the human aspect of the matter). And a broadcasting company which created the orchestra as a contribution to good music in 1937 would continue it today—with Cantelli, with other gifted younger conductors like Solti and van Otterloo, with some of the older men. This of course would cost money—more money than the fee for broadcasting the Boston Symphony next year; and so I come to the second point.

Actually NBC did not in 1937 create an additional new orchestra especially for Toscanini or give him any orchestra for his exclusive use. NBC's Red and Blue Networks already had a staff

17 July 1954

orchestra of 115 that was used in various "services"; from this the required ninety-odd players were drawn whose weekly services now included the rehearsals and performance for Toscanini's broadcast; and he complained bitterly and legitimately about having to work with players spoiled each week by what they did under less competent conductors in their other services, and who sometimes came to his rehearsal tired after a long rehearsal of a program of dance music, or who on occasion had to leave his rehearsal surreptitiously for another service.* What *was* done for Toscanini was to replace about sixty men in the staff orchestra with higher-caliber players who were—in the first years—paid higher salaries. And when NBC had to give up one network it had to engage extra players to bring the basic group of about forty-five from the staff orchestra of sixty-five up to symphony size for the Toscanini broadcasts.

Certainly this cost money; certainly Toscanini and the other conductors cost additional money. But the suitable comment on that was made by NBC itself repeatedly in the fall of 1946, when it kept informing listeners to the NBC Symphony broadcasts that their cost that year was being borne by the network itself out of revenue from sponsored programs, and that they were thus part of "a balanced service of the world's finest programs" which, "sponsored directly or not," were "all dependent on the sound American plan of financing radio by advertising revenue." Which

* (1964) NBC Symphony men have told me about the most notable such occasion—the late-afternoon rehearsal on the day before the 1940 performance of Beethoven's *Missa Solemnis*. After a number of men, including the first viola, had crept out without being noticed by Toscanini, his eye was caught by a bassoon moving like a periscope as it was held by the player creeping toward the door. Stopping in astonishment, Toscanini became aware of the empty chairs of the men who he was told had had to leave for a Cities Service broadcast; and in a fury of outrage and disgust over what he denounced as NBC commercialism he left the stage swearing never to return. And though he was induced to conduct the performance the next day, and finished the season, the men of the orchestra were not surprised to find his name missing from the list of conductors for 1941–42.

17 July 1954

is to say that in 1946 NBC rightly considered its expenditure on the symphony broadcasts a fulfillment of its part of the bargain of the American system of broadcasting—the bargain that in return for the use of part of the public domain to make money the broadcaster undertakes to spend part of the money for programs of public service. That was NBC's position also in the early years of the NBC Symphony broadcasts, when, if I remember correctly, it considered them unsuitable for commercial sponsorship. And that should be its position today, when it discontinues the orchestra because it cannot get a sponsor without Toscanini.

Actually, moreover, the cost of the NBC Symphony broadcasts was not money spent on a public service program; it was money spent to acquire for NBC and RCA the prestige of Toscanini's name, which NBC profited by in its sale of time and programs to advertisers (as CBS profited by the prestige of the New York Philharmonic), and which RCA profited by in its sale of radios, phonographs and records, including those Toscanini made with the NBC Symphony. It was, in other words, an investment which right from the start brought a financial return even with the broadcasts unsponsored, and which brought an additional return in the later years when they were sponsored. And lest anyone think I point this out in disapproval, let me say explicitly that I strongly approve of a broadcasting company, under the American commercial system, investing in a symphony orchestra and getting a return on its investment. But I contend further that even when there is no financial return on the investment, the company under the American system has the obligation NBC acknowledged in 1946.

Concerning those statements in 1946 about the "world's finest programs . . . dependent on the sound American plan of financing radio by advertising revenue" one could say then that the British plan of financing radio by license fees from owners of sets had proved equally sound and had given the British public even

18 September 1954

finer musical programs: the BBC, solely out of regard for music, had set up its BBC Symphony ten years before NBC, with one eye on the commercial value of Toscanini's name, set up the NBC Symphony (to say nothing of the difference between the American networks' broadcasting chiefly of the big-name orchestras and soloists and the Metropolitan Opera, and the BBC's systematic presentation of the entire musical literature). Today one can point out that the orchestra which the BBC created solely out of regard for music and paid for with license revenue still exists, whereas the orchestra which NBC created largely out of regard for the commercial value of Toscanini's name and paid for out of the advertising revenue his name helped to bring in has, with his departure, been discontinued.*

This, said one of the members of the orchestra, was something they had seen coming and were prepared for. What they had not foreseen and were shocked by was that nobody—from Mr. Sarnoff in his letter to Toscanini, all the way down to the executive who dictated the formal notice of discontinuance on the bulletin board—thought of saying, in public or in private, one word of appreciation of the orchestra's distinguished achievements.

[*The Nation*]

18 *September 1954* In her second or third season in this country Flagstad, at a Town Hall concert, sang an aria from *Aida* in such electrifying fashion as to raise the question, why not at

* (1964) Even the one hour or less of the Boston Symphony's Saturday night concert—enough for only the third and fourth movements of Beethoven's Ninth, only the *Kyrie* and *Gloria* of Bach's *B-Minor Mass*, only a Walton cello concerto and the first two movements of Beethoven's Fourth—that NBC in 1954 felt compelled to offer the public as a replacement for the NBC Symphony broadcasts, was dropped after two or three years, leaving the few televised performances of opera each season as NBC's total contribution to music on the air.

18 September 1954

the Metropolitan. When I put the question to her she answered that "they did not ask me"; and similarly when I inquired why she allowed herself to be dangerously overworked (four Wagner performances in one week, and on one occasion three on three consecutive days) her answer was that "they asked me." For the explanation of these answers I had to wait until *The Flagstad Manuscript*, the story of her life as she told it to Louis Biancolli. And at this point I will add that in our brief talk I got the impression of a wonderfully decent person. I mention this because it makes her a credible witness for me in this book; and also because such decency is the only thing she claims for herself.

A key to everything that has happened in her life is her statement "I am not an artist except when I am dealing with art, and when I am not dealing with art I am the most commonplace person in the world." The typical celebrated performing musician is someone who early in life made his art and career paramount, and who accepted the distortion of his personal life by their conditions and exactions. But Flagstad from the start wanted what the commonplace person would want—"a simple and tranquil home life, and a husband to love and respect me"; her talent, at first, was a means of achieving this personal happiness; her art, much later, was something carried on by the artist, whose interference with that personal happiness the commonplace person had to endure.

As the child of two hard-working professional musicians—her father a violinist and conductor, her mother a pianist—she got involved with music as the child of two cooks would have got involved with cooking; and the piano-playing and singing that began as something to do for pleasure became something to do well, and eventually something with which to earn a living in whatever musical jobs came her way. Whether it was, at fifteen, to play dance music at a ball, or to accompany a lady's recitations of poetry, or, at seventeen, to sing her first role in opera, she

18 September 1954

thought of herself as a professional musician doing the job she had been given to do; and this continued to be her attitude in all the years that followed. In those years, also, she continued to regard this professional activity as one to be carried on, as any other trade or profession would be, within the frame of a normal personal life.

And so when in 1930 she married her second husband, a wealthy business man, although the commonplace person felt able to give up the hard work of professional singing for a quiet married life and an occasional concert, the professional musician felt impelled to take on now this, now that challenging new role, to accept the opportunity to sing at Bayreuth, then at the Metropolitan. So too, although in a position to limit her work, the professional who did whatever job she was given to do accepted the heavy load of Wagner performances at the Metropolitan and concerts on tour that soon damaged the voice whose unflawed beauty all the way to high C, at her first Metropolitan appearances, was the result of its never having been taxed in this way until then. "At that time I took the high C's regularly," she says of her first Metropolitan rehearsal in 1935: when she said this to Biancolli in 1941 she was no longer taking those squarely attacked and full high C's that were one of the sensations of her first *Tristan* performance. And so, on the other hand, in the spring of 1940, "exhausted to the verge of hysteria," she decided she had done enough and planned not to return here the following season, but to do only a little more singing in Europe and then retire.

The German invasion of Norway kept her here an additional year; and we now have her statements about the incidents in which she was accused of impropriety. She shared the grief of other Norwegians here (she gave a concert for Norwegian Relief in Chicago, and canceled the one in New York only because of difficulties created by the man in charge of it); she went back to

18 September 1954

Norway because she wanted to see her family; and she didn't know of her government's opposition to her going. The arrangements about passage and visas were made entirely by her management, and in entirely normal fashion with the airplane office and consulates—which is to say no favors were asked of the German chargé d'affaires in Washington and he was not given his box at her Washington concert: presumably he bought it at the box-office. Nor was it any different in Norway. She stayed because she felt she should be with her family and her people; and her life was private, unpolitical and unprofessional: her only public singing was done in Switzerland, where she went twice for a couple of months, and in Sweden, where she gave two concerts. For these trips the Germans granted exit permits and visas; for a third trip to Switzerland they refused them. As for her husband, he had originally joined the National Socialist Party because he had considered it a defense against radicalism; when she got to Norway she found he did not approve of its war-time role and was waiting for an opportunity to resign, which he did in July 1941; and she tells us he did nothing thereafter that justified his arrest after the war. The arrest tied up their property; and the prosecutor, a personal enemy, kept her from leaving Norway to resume her singing on the pretext that she was needed in the investigation of her husband's financial affairs. At one hearing the old charge about the Washington concert was brought up; and her denial led to an admission by the Norwegian Embassy that there was no evidence of her having invited the German chargé d'affaires to the concert. And eventually she was allowed to leave. She was, she insists, not cleared—because she was never accused by her government of anything that she had to be cleared of.

That I was politically inactive when others were sacrificing their lives I am prepared, along with millions of others, to admit. That I was neutral in my feelings toward the horrible tragedy that overtook my country is the grossest falsehood, and for a woman who loves

25 December 1954

Norway as I do, the cruelest unkindness of all. Nor do I think it fair of anyone to hold it against me that to the very end I believed in the goodness and decency of the man I had married.

Flagstad, as she tells it, was not a Furtwängler or a Gieseking.
[*The Nation*]

4 December 1954   In recent years Virgil Thomson has combined journalism with an increasing amount of concert activity; and one learned to anticipate, in the Sunday article about a university chorus and orchestra in some remote place, the inevitable "In a performance of this writer's cantata. . . ." His appearance as conductor at a recent concert of the Concert Society of New York signalized his complete substitution of concert activity for journalism for the purposes of earning a living and furthering his career as a composer. And since an enlightened public is as important in music as in politics, Thomson's departure from the *Herald Tribune* is a disaster. He could be irresponsible, he could be nonsensical, in recent years he was increasingly bored and wrote more than ever about what he imagined rather than what he heard; but he had the equipment of critical perception that is the one essential in criticism; and when it was allowed to operate on what was before him it produced the only newspaper criticism of music worth reading. For he was the only one with this equipment; and now there is no one. Or rather there is worse than no one: there is his successor on the *Herald Tribune*, Professor Paul Henry Lang. [*The Nation*]

25 December 1954   The Quartetto Italiano couldn't fill Town Hall for the Concert Society; but Elisabeth Schwarzkopf did. And the additional people appeared to be those who used to

26 February 1955

pack Town Hall for Lotte Lehmann's recitals, and who now come to Schwarzkopf's because *she* now puts on the sort of performances for them that Lehmann used to. Let it be understood that Schwarzkopf is, like Lehmann, a very gifted woman. She is, for one thing, a very gifted singer, with a beautiful voice and the capacity for exquisite musical phrasing; and at her recitals, as at Lehmann's, one is every now and then held spellbound by a piece of flawless sustained singing. She is also, like Lehmann, a singer with a gift of dramatic projection; and one is, as one was at Lehmann's recitals, often moved or charmed by that. But unfortunately these gifts, like Lehmann's, serve an inclination to ham; and Schwarzkopf's hamming—her exaggerated pouting and pertness and archness, her gasps and whispers—delights her audience as Lehmann's used to. Exaggeration means lack of a controlling sense of measure, fitness—what is summed up in the word taste; and Schwarzkopf is capable of lapses of taste even worse than Lehmann's—for example, her singing and miming of *In dem Schatten meiner Locken*, at this recent Hugo Wolf recital, in the style of Marlene Dietrich for the patrons of *Der blaue Engel*, which especially delighted the people who filled Town Hall. [*The Nation*]

26 February 1955 The collective brainstorms of the New York reviewers every now and then are like nothing so much as the sudden commotions in barnyards that flare up and die out for no discoverable reason. There was the one about Maryla Jonas several years ago; and last year there was the one about Backhaus. It was set off by his recital in Carnegie Hall on 30 March 1954, after an absence of twenty-eight years, which elicited from Mr. Downes the opinion that it "must be ranked as one of the great-

26 February 1955

est evenings of the interpretation of Beethoven's piano music heard here in as long a period," and from one of the others the statement that Backhaus had "played Beethoven as he hasn't been played here in twenty-eight years." I hadn't attended the recital; but I found the statements difficult to believe—not only because of my recollections of performances of Beethoven by Schnabel in those twenty-eight years, but because of what I remembered of Backhaus's playing before 1926, and what I had heard more recently on his records. In the twenties he had been a pianist of prodigious technical powers who had produced the figurations of Chopin's Etudes and the Paganini-Brahms Variations with incandescent ease and grace; but a pianist also of completely phlegmatic temperament whose playing of music of high expressive content was at best dull, and even worse when he tried for expressiveness. And recent records had revealed an inevitable loss of the dazzling speed and smoothness in Chopin's Etudes, with no gain in ability to give expressive effect to a Beethoven sonata.

As it happened the recital was recorded and has now been issued by London; and the performances justify my skepticism. Listening to Op. 31 No. 2 I was shocked first by the crude accentuation in the opening section of the first movement—crude in its treatment not only of the music but of the instrument—then by the sentimentalizing expansion of tempo in certain melodic phrases. The slow movement and finale were played simply and agreeably to the ear, but the simplicity amounted to ineffectiveness: notes merely succeeded each other, now soft, now loud, but with no cohesive tension from one note to the next, no giving of continuous outline to the phrase, of coherent shape to the movement. This is the ineffective way he plays Op. 81a; and it is the disastrous way he plays Op. 111. It is hard to believe that anyone—and least of all a pianist of Backhaus's age and experi-

26 February 1955

ence—could play the introduction to the first movement of Op. 111 without awareness of what is happening in it—awareness, for example, of the increasing dramatic suspense in measures 6 to 9 as the increasingly hushed chords of the two hands draw closer together in the middle of the piano, and the dramatic effect produced after this by the left hand's low octave; but Backhaus's perfunctory playing of this passage, and indeed of the entire introduction, is on the record for all time to demonstrate the actuality of the unbelievable. And so with the passage that momentarily interrupts the course of the slow movement—the continuing trills up above creating tension and suspense in which the left hand strikes in powerfully down below: it is hard to believe anyone could play this with the unawareness that Backhaus demonstrates with his perfunctory playing of it.

I should add that comparable insensitiveness was exhibited in Mr. Downes's review of Backhaus's performance of this movement, when he referred to "the often inept and ill-considered spacings of the writing of the deaf master." Mr. Downes appears to have listened to his friend Horowitz instead of listening to Beethoven. It is depressing to think of a pianist with Horowitz's technical competence not having the musical understanding that would enable him to perceive the expressive effect achieved with absolute precision and rightness by those trills continuing up above while the left hand strikes in down below, and not having the humility that would keep him from calling his lack of understanding a miscalculation by Beethoven. But it is appalling to think of a reviewer in Mr. Downes's position and with his influence on the public not having the musical understanding that would enable him to perform his function—which is to rebuke Horowitz's ignorance and arrogance, not to be taken in by them.

[*The Nation*]

16 April 1955 Flagstad, here on a personal visit, broke her retirement for two appearances with the Symphony of the Air and Edwin McArthur. If I were to speak only of what was to be heard at the second concert I would report that once again there was the shock, when she began to sing, of the loss in vocal beauty since the last time; then the amazement as the voice gained in luster of lower notes and power of higher ones, as it went with complete assurance wherever the phrase required it to go, and as it operated with complete flexibility in the inflections the phrasing required it to make. With all this, certainly, there was a loss since the last time: one noted that when the voice rose to a soft high note it produced that note carefully as a head tone; that climactic high notes, though astoundingly clear and powerful, were less powerful this time. Nevertheless it was true this time as last that even with what it had lost, the singing—the lustrous lower notes, the clear and powerful high ones, in the sustained phrases so exquisitely and touchingly inflected by musical feeling and taste—would have been considered remarkable if it had been done by a woman of thirty; and one heard it being done by a woman of sixty.

That brings me to what there was to see. It was five years since the concert in which I had last seen Flagstad without stage costume, make-up and wig; and there was an additional shock from the changes in her appearance: the graying blond hair now totally gray, the head and shoulders slightly hunched together, the face shadowed and impassive. All this as she stood waiting and listening; then, when the moment came for her to sing, one saw her face amazingly become animated, transfigured by what produced the beautiful phrases one heard. And this made the occasion moving in the way Toscanini's concerts had been in recent years, when one had seen the manifestations of increasing age and then heard the manifestations of continuing great musical powers.

17 September and 1 and 22 October 1955

Nor was this the only way the occasion recalled Toscanini. I wrote once how everything he did in working with an orchestra was equal to each momentary situation but never more than equal to it, and how this economy in the operation of those extraordinary powers was a form of honesty in relation to the situation that made the performance, in addition to everything else, a moral experience which I found intensely moving. There was a similar honesty in the singing which employed the beautiful voice in the simplest, most direct way to produce a beautiful statement of the musical phrase—an honesty especially impressive to someone with Tebaldi's self-indulgent vocal manipulation still fresh in his memory. And it added a similar affecting moral beauty to the musical beauty of the unforgettable performances.

[*The Nation*]

17 September and 1 and 22 October 1955 Reviewing Kolodin's *Guide to Recorded Music* years ago, Jacques Barzun took the line that the whole idea was absurd—that things had reached the point where "a man is an ass who thinks of going into a shop and using his own ears, long or short, in selecting a disc." I don't know what to call a man who exhibits so little regard for the realities that cause people to read and be guided by record reviews, and so little awareness that they are much the same as those which cause people to read and be guided by reviews of books and plays, which Barzun presumably would not think absurd. To determine for oneself—by reading or seeing it—whether a book or a play is worth reading or seeing is to risk discovering that one has wasted time and money; and so most people make use of the judgment of someone else—someone with the special powers of perception and evaluation of the professional reader of books or observer of plays—the critic. Not that they passively

17 September and 1 and 22 October 1955

accept what he says: they test it with their own experience of the book or play he has recommended; and their willingness to accept the recommendation this time is based on previous tests in which their experience confirmed his judgments. Similarly the record-buyer who makes use of the record critic's judgment doesn't give up his own: he reads and accepts the recommendations of the critic whose judgments have been confirmed by his own in the past; and he continues to subject each new recommendation to the same test. And I must point out that a record-buyer who did want to depend on his own ears would face the fact that even in shops in big cities he is rarely able to try records on a phonograph good enough for him to form dependable opinions about what is on the records, and in little towns the shop may not even have the records to try; so that he has to depend on the critic to tell him whether the performance is reproduced with agreeable or disagreeable sound, and to give him similar information about other objectively perceptible matters like tone and phrasing in the performance.

Unfortunately, just as much of the criticism of books and plays is worthless, so much of the criticism of records isn't dependable even for the objectively perceptible matters I have mentioned. The thing for a reviewer of a record guide to do, therefore, is not to deride the man who depends on someone else's ears, but to recognize what he has to depend on them for, and to report whether the guide supplies it. And concerning the three volumes of *The Guide to Long-Playing Records* I must report that the reader who accepts their guidance will acquire a number of poor records and miss a number of good ones.

In the volume on vocal records, for example, Philip L. Miller doesn't inform him of the shockingly bad condition of Hopf's voice in the Bayreuth *Meistersinger* or of Mödl's tremulous shrillness in the Bayreuth *Parsifal*, of the poorly balanced reproduction of the *Parsifal* or of the unclear and unclean sound of

17 September and 1 and 22 October 1955

the *Meistersinger*. The statement about De Sabata's "clean musicianship" in a performance of Verdi's *Requiem*—in which "Verdi's indications as to expression and dynamics are respected, though the singers are allowed to spread themselves within the bounds of good taste"—doesn't inform the reader of De Sabata's excessively slow tempos in the face of Verdi's metronome markings, of his fussing with dynamics and phrasing, of his allowing Schwarzkopf *her* fussing, pouting, whispering and gasping and Di Stefano his sobbing. And "a nicely paced production typical of the better-grade present-day Italian opera stage" doesn't adequately describe the *Traviata* in which the conductor meekly follows wherever the singers' self-indulgence leads. Nor, on the other hand, does the statement about "the much-heralded Toscanini recording" of *La Traviata*—that the singers "have little chance, led through their arias at such a pace. In the good old Italian tradition they want to spread themselves in their big moments, but the conductor keeps them strictly in line"—give the reader correct ideas about the nature of that "good old Italian tradition" and the superb Toscanini pacing and phrasing that don't follow it. And "hers is not the gift of simplicity" is only one of the references to Steber that describe incorrectly her beautifully phrased singing.

In the volume on orchestral records Irving Kolodin does the writing he has always done: a churning of words and thoughts concerned less with the supposed purpose of informing the reader about the subject than with the evident purpose of impressing him with the writer—the results being what can be expected when the critic's eye is on the effect he is making instead of being on the object he is describing. With Cantelli, for example, Kolodin has been the mature listener who perceives what immature talent cannot know: "That degree of musical culture and experience which can settle, almost instinctively, on proper tempi and sonorous values for such works . . . are not yet his";

17 September and 1 and 22 October 1955

with the result that he has failed to perceive in the performance the manifestations of Cantelli's unfailing instinct for just such "proper tempi and sonorous values." And the result in the present book is not only that Kolodin, in the high-flown preface, includes Cantelli with mediocrities like Jorda and Dorati among the conductors who have shown "hopeful promises of things to come," but that he doesn't list even one of Cantelli's distinguished performances. The reader is to be impressed by the unawed Kolodin ear that can hear in a Casals performance of Schumann's Cello Concerto "offenses against musical taste in phrasing, dynamics, phrase-endings" which in fact are not there to be heard; but a real thing on a record that is important for the reader to know—Patzak's painful struggle with an old voice in a performance of *Das Lied von der Erde*—he isn't told. Though Beecham has been, for Kolodin, a name to stimulate the flow of sonorous praise with no relation to anything in the performance, good or bad, a momentary attention to what actually came off the record of Mozart's *Jupiter* Symphony causes him to report correctly for once "the flow of the melodic line . . . retarded by arbitrary pauses, the rhythmic impulse not . . . steady"; but the reader who is told of the "flow of keenly controlled spirit" in the performance of Mozart's *Paris* Symphony and the "refinement and elegance" of the one of Haydn's No. 93 will not know they are two more of the ponderously fussy and distorted Beecham performances of recent years. If he is led by Kolodin's unqualified praise to acquire Scherchen's performances of Haydn's Nos. 98, 100, 103 and 104, he will only then learn of Scherchen's eccentricities of tempo in them. And on the other hand if he is steered away from the performance of No. 102 by Kolodin's statement that it is "a tribute to the consistency of Scherchen rather than to his best capacities as a conductor of Haydn," he will miss the one performance without those eccentricities, and an excellent statement of the work.

17 September and 1 and 22 October 1955

As for Harold C. Schonberg's volume on records of solo instruments and chamber groups, one would think the beauty of Pierlot's oboe tone and Rampal's flute tone in some Vivaldi pieces is an objective fact no ear could fail to perceive; but to Schonberg's ear "none of the soloists is an outstanding workman." Someone who had heard the Juilliard Quartet only in Schönberg and Bartók might not expect the grace and exquisite inflection of its playing in Mozart's K.499, but—one would think—could not fail to hear what is so plainly to be heard in this performance; however, Schonberg hears that "Mozart is not the Juilliard's dish of tea. The phrasing is stiff, and there are some strange tempos." Nobody, one would suppose, could fail to hear the difference between the Budapest and Schneider Quartet performances of Haydn's Op. 76—the refinement and smoothness of the Budapest's playing as against the Schneider's more energetically detailed inflection and sharper rhythm; but Schonberg writes that "the Budapest's playing is a little fuller in tone and stronger in concept" and "the Schneider . . . is frequently more gracious and intimate-sounding." Nothing could be more striking than the contrast between Wührer's simple, straightforward, dull playing in Schubert's posthumous Sonata in B-flat and Kempff's fussing with phrase and tempo; but to Schonberg "Kempff and Wührer are pianists very much in the same style. Both exhibit the Teutonic style of playing; both work in broad, massive strokes." And in Schumann's Fantasy "Yves Nat . . . has interesting ideas, but the veteran pianist is no longer up to the technical demands"; but Schonberg doesn't say what the "interesting ideas" are, and actually there is nothing out-of-the-way in Nat's fine performance, for which he has all the necessary technique.

These volumes do not offer a record-buyer the dependable information and guidance he needs. [*The Nation*]

3 December 1955

3 December 1955 Since the members of the Symphony of the Air (the former NBC Symphony) have to accept jobs that sometimes conflict with the Carnegie Hall concerts, there were a number of temporary changes of personnel at its opening concert. For one thing the Bervs were absent from the horns, and additional brass were present for the Mahler symphony; as a result there was not the fabulous sound like that of one instrument, which the orchestra's own brass section used to achieve. And though, with the other changes, there was the playing of a great orchestra, I did not hear the refined beauty of sonority, the precision and finish, that I used to hear. The reason may have been not only the changes in personnel but lack of sufficient rehearsal, or Bernstein's conducting, or even the fact that I sat too close to the stage.

It was close enough to perceive the real contact between Bernstein and the orchestra, and close enough to be distracted and embarrassed by some of the movements Bernstein used to get the orchestra to do what he wanted. They were the movements of the warm-hearted extrovert who at the end embraced the concertmaster and blew kisses to the audience, who himself writes huge sprawling symphonies concerned with matters like the age of anxiety, who therefore feels drawn to a work like Mahler's Second, and who, with all the impressive effect he gives the work at times, damages it at other times. What is damaging in Bernstein's performance is the same lack of a controlling sense of measure that one hears in the Mahler symphony. In the lovely Andante moderato second movement, for example, the lilting opening melody returns with a countermelody of the cellos which engages all of Bernstein's attention and on which he lavishes all his emotion, oblivious to the fact that his lingering over it is slowing down the lilting melody to the point where its lilt is destroyed. This is only one of many instances; and whereas skillful performance like Bruno Walter's conceals the work's discon-

28 January 1956

tinuities with a contrived coherence that makes its length less noticeable, Bernstein's preoccupation with the effect of the moment—with one effect after another, each carried to its extreme—emphasizes the discontinuities and the already excessive length that it increases by an additional quarter-hour. [*The Nation*]

28 January 1956   The interest at the concerts of the Symphony of the Air under Leonard Bernstein is not only in the music and performances but in what is happening to the orchestra and to Bernstein. What is happening to the orchestra is the inevitable: changes in players, and therefore changes in the playing. A year ago the Symphony of the Air *was* still the NBC Symphony in personnel, and *played* still like the NBC Symphony—with the discipline, the unity, and consequently the precision, finish and tonal beauty, that had been achieved by the years of rehearsing and playing under Toscanini. This year, with a number of new players and with no Toscanini to drill them and fuse them into the ensemble, the Symphony of the Air no longer *is* the NBC Symphony, and therefore no longer sounds like *it*. That is to say, the orchestra which Bernstein conducted at the recent Mozart concert was an aggregation of players of virtuoso caliber, responsive and fine-sounding; but it was not the one he conducted a year ago, and did not produce the fabulous refinement of execution and sonority one heard then.

As for Bernstein himself, during much of the evening he operated within the limits he seems to accept when he conducts Mozart. And the results were admirable: a tremendously powerful performance of the slow introduction of the Overture to *Don Giovanni*, followed by a brilliant performance of the Allegro; a graceful, warm and exquisitely modeled performance of the lovely Symphony K.201; and sensitively adjusted orchestral

28 January 1956

contexts for the singing of Jennie Tourel in three arias. In these Bernstein revealed the specific gift for conducting opera, most impressively in his dealing with the preliminary recitative of the aria *Ch'io mi scordi di te* K.505. And in this aria he also played the obbligato piano part very effectively, giving the elaborately ornamented melodic writing superb rhythmic continuity and dramatic force.

This brings me to the concluding work of the concert, the Piano Concerto K.453, in which Bernstein played the solo part, conducting the orchestra from the piano. The concerto, as I observed a couple of weeks ago, is one of the greatest in the series; and its first movement, a supreme example of Mozartian instrumental high comedy, calls for playing that points up its sharp-witted animation. It got such playing from the orchestra that prepared the listener for the entrance of the solo piano; but from Bernstein, when the piano entered, it got a lingering and melting over the melodies, a softening of their sharp contours, a finicky inflection, that sentimentalized them and reduced them to miniature. In the Andante, one of Mozart's most extraordinarily organized and affecting slow movements, a poignant opening statement recurs several times, played now by the orchestra, now by the piano, and pausing each time before an extended sequence of thought takes off from it; and this opening statement not only was lingered over excessively by the orchestra but was sentimentalized beyond endurance by Bernstein on the piano. And in the finale the suddenly hushed and ominous variation in minor, with syncopations that create powerful tensions, was played by Bernstein in the finicky miniature style of the first movement. The fussy playing, moreover, was done with much rolling of the wrists and much hunching over them by an intensely swaying body; and it all adds up to the fact that in the concerto the seemingly irrepressible exhibitionist in Bernstein had himself a time after all.

18 February 1956

As for Tourel's singing, it was small in volume and projective force, but flawless in tone and phrasing. [*The Nation*]

18 February 1956 Television offers possibilities of scenic illusion—including quick and illusive changes of scene—which the stage cannot equal; and these can increase the effectiveness of an opera like *The Magic Flute*. But scenes of large spectacle in such an opera lose by their reduced scale in the small televised image. This image is suited only to close-ups of action involving two or three persons; but the close-range relation of performers and spectators that television creates in place of the long-range relation of the opera house is not entirely advantageous for opera.

There are some who argue that opera is drama which must be understood from word to word as one listens to the music, and that it must therefore be performed in English. They include Samuel Chotzinoff, producer of NBC-TV Opera Theater, who in an interview a couple of years ago contended that opera, when it is given in a large theater where the listener is too far from the performer for dramatic meaning to come through to him, can be only a recital in costume; and that television, by bringing the performer close to the listener, "can make [opera] dramatic all over again." For this purpose, said Mr. Chotzinoff, Opera Theater gives opera in English; and he mentioned other things it had done to make opera dramatic. For example he described how, in cutting Britten's *Billy Budd* to make it fit into the allotted hour and a half, Peter Herman Adler, Opera Theater's musical director, had found it necessary to omit Claggart's big aria; how Chotzinoff had objected that this aria was needed to provide the motivation for the villain's actions; and how "it was discovered . . . that we could compensate for the aria by showing Claggart in some evil visual action . . . that did in one minute what it would have taken ten minutes of music to do.

18 February 1956

The aria was never missed."

I might begin my comment on these statements by mentioning that Chaliapin's Boris was only one of many dramatic performances that came through to me in the top gallery of the Metropolitan. Certainly I would have got even more from his performance if I had been closer; but the next thing to say is that *Boris Godunov* can stand such intimacy, but that to be brought close to most operatic dramas, as one is by television and English translation, is to discover the advantage of being kept at a distance from them, as one is in the opera house and by the foreign languages. Who would spend an evening in the theater for a performance of an English translation of the text of *I Puritani, Il Trovatore, Aida, Die Walküre, Tristan und Isolde?* And who would want to understand every word of these texts as he listens to the music—rather than have a mere general idea of the developing dramatic situation which the music is concerned with?

The fact is that opera is not drama but drama realized through music; that for the sake of the music we accept in the opera house dramatic nonsense that we wouldn't waste time on in the theater; and that the less nonsense we are aware of as we listen, the better for our experience of the music. Opera, I repeat, is not drama but drama realized through music; it is not just Claggart's villainous thoughts but these villainous thoughts communicated through the aria Chotzinoff omitted—which means that if one performs the opera one includes the aria, and if one substitutes for the aria an equivalent visual action one is not performing the opera. Similarly, if one performs *Pelléas et Mélisande* one retains the orchestral entr'actes that Chotzinoff decided could be omitted from his televised production because they weren't needed to provide time for changes of scene—the reasons for keeping them being that they perform the important musico-dramatic function of taking the listener's mind from one scene and preparing it for the next, and that, as it happens, they do

18 February 1956

this with some of the most impressive music in the Debussy score.

As it happened, NBC-TV Opera Theater's recent production of *The Magic Flute* was one of its best achievements. The cuts made to fit the work into the allotted two hours included music as important as the second-act trio of Pamina, Tamino and Sarastro and a large part of the scene of Tamino and the Two Armored Men; and the overture, instead of preparing the listener for the opera to come, served as a background for the credits at the end. But these were few and small defects in an outstandingly beautiful performance of the music, in which one heard not only the Queen of the Night's florid arias sung brilliantly by Laurel Hurley, but the music of Pamina, Tamino and Papageno sung for once with the suitably youthful voices of Leontyne Price, William Lewis and John Reardon.

The dramatic performance gained too from the youthful handsomeness of Lewis and the amusing face and comic gift of Reardon; it also benefited by the quick and illusive changes of scene, but lost by the close view of rocks that appeared to be made of Christmas wrapping paper. Moreover the scenes of spectacle, as I mentioned earlier, were made ineffective by the small televised image; and this amounts to saying that much of the potential profit from having Balanchine as stage director was lost. But the potential profit from having W. H. Auden and Chester Kallman produce the English text was largely realized. A great deal that is obscure in the opera house—the large philosophical ideas, the enmity of the Queen and Sarastro—remained obscure in this performance, in which even the English words at the close range of television often couldn't be understood in the arias and ensembles. But what was clear in the spoken dialogue—the love of Pamina and Tamino, his submitting himself to the trials, the less high-minded preoccupations of Papageno—was made distinguished and at times delightful by Auden's and Kallman's words.

[*The Nation*]

10 March and 14 April 1956

10 March and 14 April 1956 After a recent Metropolitan performance of Musorgsky's *Boris Godunov* it seems to me that one must say of this work—and indeed of his entire output—what Tovey said of Schubert. Tovey warned against regarding Schubert's weaknesses and inequalities as evidence of his being an artist of less than the highest rank: "Even if the artist produces no single work without flaws, yet the highest qualities attained in important parts of a great work are as indestructible by weaknesses elsewhere as if the weaknesses were the accidents of physical ruin." And I contend that it doesn't matter, in *Boris*, that much of the scene in Pimen's cell is boring, or that much of the scene in Marina's garden is tawdry: they don't alter the quality of what is heard in the two scenes of the Prologue, the scene in Boris's apartment, and above all the three scenes of the last act. Here one is moved not only by the moment-to-moment invention as such, but by its demonstration of extraordinary powers operating with an incandescent adequacy for every dramatic point they are called on to deal with. They are the powers which, for example, transform the brutal four-note ostinato figure accompanying the bailiff's entrance in the first scene into the lamenting ostinato figure of the introduction to the St. Basil's scene, and which then gives us the Simpleton's song and the chorus's plea for alms. And I believe that if we had only this scene to judge by, or only the scene of Boris's death, or only the final scene in the forest of Kromy, we would have to say the man who produced it was a great master.

I speak of these scenes as written by Musorgsky himself, which one now hears at the Metropolitan in place of the ubiquitous Rimsky-Korsakov revisions. And if one thinks of the history of this work in the world's opera houses one must conclude that in nothing else he has done has Mr. Bing exhibited more intelligence * and courage than in his production of the Musorgsky

* See the postscript on pages 134-5.

31 March 1956 and 18 October 1952

original ("Musorgsky's so-called original," as Winthrop Sargeant put it in his loaded prose). Certainly he has exhibited less intelligence and courage in his further decision to piece together the production out of whatever odds and ends he could find in the storehouse. I haven't seen everything at the Metropolitan, but there cannot be anything more shabby, clumsy and confused than this *Boris*. Yet such is the power of Musorgsky's music that the audience stays to the end and cheers after the final Kromy scene. [*The Nation*]

31 March 1956 and 18 October 1952 The filmed *Don Giovanni* provides an interesting close-range view of Furtwängler's conducting, and specifically of his fuzzy beat, which makes it a mystery how the men of the Vienna Philharmonic manage to begin and stay together. Evidently Furtwängler had whatever else it takes to control and manipulate an orchestra—the specific powers for conducting like Heifetz's for the violin and Horowitz's for the piano. Heifetz and Horowitz have taught us that the gift for playing an instrument is not inevitably associated with taste in the playing of music; Stokowski has demonstrated that this is true also of conducting; and Furtwängler provided another such demonstration. It has been argued that he was effective only in the nineteenth-century German music with which he was, as a German, able to identify himself; that he exhibited inadequacies in Verdi, in French music, even in Mozart's music with its Italian and French influences, but understood German "music of philosophical conception"—Beethoven, Schubert, Brahms—as few other interpreters ever have, played it "more eloquently, more movingly, more compellingly" than anyone else, and exhibited in his performances of it "a supreme sense of form." But I found it impossible to accept what Beethoven was made to mean by the self-indulgent moment-to-moment vagaries and excesses which destroyed all coherence in the works. Only in the amorphous music of Wagner did Furtwängler operate with a sense for continuity, and therefore with impressive effect; and the complete *Tristan und Isolde* issued by Victor a couple of years ago is for me the monument to his capacities as conductor and musician.

I have held onto a paragraph in Kingsley Martin's column in the *New Statesman and Nation* on the occasion of Furtwängler's reappearance in London: "H. M. Brailsford sends me a note of the facts proved before the DeNazification Tribunal which acquitted him. Never a party member . . . in 1933, when few realized what Nazi rule would mean, he accepted the vice-presidency of the Chamber of Music. The title of Staatsrat was then conferred on him. After some experience of the regime, Furtwängler in 1934 wrote a formal letter of protest and resigned his title, his vice-presidency, his official post as director of the State Opera, and his conductorship of the Berlin Philharmonic. . . . Fearing its ruin, the orchestra besought Furtwängler to return. So he met Goebbels and consented to come back on conditions; he should rank as a private musician only, should never be called on to conduct at official functions, would not 'Heil Hitler' at his concerts, etc."

This was written after the publication of Berta Geissmar's *Two Worlds of Music* (*Dictator and Jackboot* in England), in which Furtwängler's devoted secretary writes bitterly of Goebbels's ingratitude for the success as political-cultural propaganda of a tour by the Berlin Philharmonic in Italy in April 1934 that she arranged on condition that Furtwängler be received in audience by Mussolini who gave him an Italian decoration. She writes also about Furtwängler's first appearance after his submission (for it was that), in April 1935, which was at an official function, the *Winterhilfe* concert attended by Hitler and the

7 April 1956

entire government, and at which occurred the famous cordial handshake of Hitler and Furtwängler that Dr. Geissmar rightly calls a "symbolic gesture." And I might add that only a couple of months ago a friend told me of having turned on the radio for a Furtwängler performance of Beethoven's Ninth from Paris in 1937, and having turned it off when Furtwängler, after playing *Deutschland über alles*, began to play the *Horst Wessel Song*. By 1937 everyone knew what Nazi rule meant; but even in 1933 it was evident that it meant the silencing of Schnabel, Bruno Walter, Klemperer and other Jewish musicians; and this was as evident to Furtwängler as to Fritz Busch, who made a gesture of protest and solidarity with his fellow artists by leaving Germany. Principle would have caused Furtwängler to leave too; opportunism caused him to stay, to associate himself with the regime that persecuted his fellow artists, to lend himself to its purposes. His offense, in the words of the *Times* correspondent who covered his trial, was that of "so overlooking moral values and fixed principles that he was . . . willing to make maximum use of a regime which he alleged was obnoxious to him." [*The Nation*]

7 April 1956 "What she wants other people to know," Edmund Wilson wrote once about a novelist, "she imparts to them by creating an object, the self-developing organism of a work of prose." The statement occurred to me as I listened to the Stravinsky program in which Leonard Bernstein conducted the Symphony of the Air; for I was hearing Stravinsky, in each piece, creating an object, this one the self-developing organism of a work of musical sound, and was observing with what assured mastery he did so.

The creative mastery was evident at every point in the early *Firebird* Suite, though most impressively so, perhaps, in the two-

30 June 1956

plane construction of the marvelous transition from the *Berceuse* to the finale. It was evident also in the moment-to-moment operation of the perversely rhythmed Capriccio for piano and orchestra, in the employment of the grim ostinatos and monumental vocal styles of *Oedipus Rex,* and in the fashioning of details like the simple but overwhelming phrase of Oedipus to the words "All now is made plain."

Actually, of course, the composer creates his object only in his mind, and notes down in a score the directions for the performance that creates it in living sound. And even with inadequate soloists, but with the excellent orchestra and a fine-sounding male chorus trained by Hugh Ross, Bernstein produced a powerful, eloquent and touching performance of *Oedipus Rex* which I think Stravinsky would have accepted as the object he intended. But in the Capriccio exhibitionism took over, with Sanroma punching out each statement of the piano's theme in the first movement with ostentatious jangling violence, and with both conductor and soloist whipping themselves into a visible frenzy that got cheers from the audience but would not, I suspect, have got them from the composer. And judging by Stravinsky's own way of playing the *Firebird* Suite I think he would have reacted violently to what Bernstein's dramatized lingering and melting and fussing made it. [*The Nation*]

30 June 1956   Listening to Oistrakh's performances of Mozart's Concerto K.218 and the Mendelssohn E-minor with the Philadelphia Orchestra under Ormandy on a Columbia record, I recalled a statement by Paul Henry Lang last fall about the visiting Russians—that their playing exhibited inadequacies which were the consequence of their having been cut off from the musical life of the Western world. And while I was thinking

30 June 1956

about this a letter arrived in which a perceptive young reader remarked on Professor Lang's tendency "to criticize . . . in what he considers his brilliant manner, however different the performance may turn out from his preconception." Even the preconception in this instance, though plausible, disregarded the fact that Moscow and Leningrad had themselves been important centers in the Western musical world for a century or more; that Soviet Russian musicians had remained in contact with those of the West through radio and in some degree through phonograph records; that some of them had had direct contact at international competitions in which they had exhibited enough expertness in Western practice to win over their Western competitors. And Professor Lang made his statement in the face of the actual performances by Oistrakh and Gilels which exhibited full command of Western practice, and which were good or bad, as are the performances of Western musicians, by virtue of the personal musical taste that operated in the practice.

What delighted one in Oistrakh's Russian recording of Mozart's Concerto K.219 a few years ago was the excellent taste evident in the pure tone and simple sustained phrasing—a taste manifested in much the same way by Isaac Stern in his first years; what shocked one in Oistrakh's performance of the work with the New York Philharmonic last fall was the deterioration in taste evident in the excessive vibrato that made the tone overrich, the swells and portamentos that made the phrasing over-expressive—the sort of thing one has heard also in Stern's recent playing. And what one hears now in Oistrakh's recorded performance of Mozart's K.218 is not his unfamiliarity with the ways of Western violinists, but an all too great familiarity with them: it is the fat-toned, high-powered performance, without delicacy and grace, that one might get from a Western violinist throwing his virtuosic weight around. The same kind of playing is heard in Mendelssohn's Concerto, instead of the impassioned elegance which the work calls for. For both works I recommend Grumiaux's performances on Epic records.

[*The Nation*]

11 August 1956 The Columbia record *Golden Jubilee Concert* offers dubbings of imperfect but listenable recordings of a number of Josef Hofmann's performances at the concert in November 1937 at which he celebrated the fiftieth anniversary of his American debut, and provides the only available documentation on records of this famous pianist's playing. For some it documents unequaled pianistic and musical mastery. "Hofmann was not only the world's greatest pianist; he was also the pianist's pianist," says Abram Chasins, a pupil of Hofmann, in the accompanying booklet. "His greatest colleagues (even Rachmaninov ...) placed Hofmann on the highest peak, the absolute monarch of the pianistic realm." And in an article in the *Saturday Review* Chasins welcomes the record's documentation of piano-playing in the "grand manner" of an earlier day, no longer to be heard today, which he says gave the Romantic repertory— and specifically the music of Chopin—the correct and effective style it doesn't have in performances of today. Chasins describes what Chopin himself demanded for correct performance of his music: "a controlled spontaneity, a direct cantilena, a variety of coloring, pedaling and rhythmic accentuation, an elegance of ornamentation which have all but vanished from the concert platform." And of Hofmann's performances of the Chopin pieces on the record Chasins says the art "is Chopin's own art . . . Chopin's Chopin was precise and classical. So is Hofmann's Chopin."

Not, however, to my ears. What I hear on the record is evidence, rather, that the piano-playing of Chasins's "exponents

11 August 1956

of the grand manner" was similar to the singing of their contemporaries of the "golden age," who treated music as something to use to show what they could do with their voices. The record, in fact, provides documentation of my observations on Hofmann in this column a couple of years after that golden-jubilee concert. The virtuoso pianist, I said, presented himself to his audience for the same purpose as the acrobat—to exhibit all the things he could do with his instrument and the music; and he regarded the instrument and music in the way the acrobat regarded his trapeze—as things to use for his purpose. He learned his pianistic and musical tricks in a certain number of works in his youth; and he continued to elaborate and add to those tricks in the same works thereafter. Thus Hofmann, in the twenty-five years in which I had observed him, had repeated a limited repertory—mostly a lot of Chopin, some Schumann, a few major sonatas of Beethoven—which didn't include Beethoven's *Diabelli Variations* or last Bagatelles, or a single sonata of Mozart or Schubert, but did include a large quantity of trashy salon and display pieces. And in his performances one had heard things like the left-hand octaves or chords crashed out suddenly for no musical purpose but only to surprise and impress the audience; the series of notes extracted from within accompaniment chords to astonish the audience with a counter-melody unknown to the composer; the exposition of a sonata movement played one way the first time and a different way the second time, to amaze the audience with the ability to do that. ("He would," writes Chasins, "enunciate a theory and then sit down at the piano to illustrate it . . . and just as one had concluded that this was the way, the *only* way, he would turn the theory upside down and prove it equally valid.")

The Columbia record has a couple of trashy pieces by Moszkowski and Rachmaninov that Hofmann used to play. And in the performance of Mendelssohn's *Spinning Song* there are the

11 August 1956

unexpectedly accented left-hand note, the sudden eruption of hammered-out accompaniment chords, the succession of perverse accents in the accompaniment, which have no relation to the ends of the piece itself, but are contrived for their own effect of shock and excitement by their unexpectedness, their exhibition of daring wilfulness and perversity. So with the octaves banged out by the left hand at one point in the Chopin G-flat Etude, and the perverse decrescendo that follows in place of the crescendo the music calls for. So with the succession of loudly accented A-flats in the left hand near the end of Chopin's *Berceuse*, in which, moreover, the excessively fast tempo makes the execution of the delicate ornamental passage-work breathtaking but the piece not a lullaby. And so with the succession of such ostentatious perversities of tempo, phrasing and accentuation in Chopin's G-minor Ballade, the accompaniment chords at one point that are made louder than the delicate passage-work they accompany, the concluding three forceful chords that are played loud—unexpectedly soft—loud. Pianistic mastery certainly is exhibited in these performances, but not what I regard as musical mastery. And not Chopin's own direct cantilena, his own classical art.

These are the performances which, year after year, thousands came to hear—among them the many students, teachers and pianists with the professional's interest in the mere doing of things on the piano and with the music, who came to Carnegie Hall to marvel at the things this "pianist's pianist" did. Chasins and I, when we began to hear Hofmann in our teens, were piano students with that interest; and the explanation of the difference in our present evaluations of the performances on the record is, I think, that he has retained that interest to this day, whereas I lost it, and by the time of Hofmann's jubilee concert I had stopped going to hear him use music to show what he could do

1 December 1956 and 19 March 1955

on the piano, and had begun instead to go to hear Schnabel use the piano to illuminate music. [*The Nation*]

Postscript 1964 Some who are impressed by Hofmann speak of Schnabel as a pianist with noble musical conceptions which he couldn't realize for lack of the necessary technical equipment. Actually even the melodic legato of Schnabel's large-spanned enunciation of the cantilena of the great Andante of Mozart's Concerto K.467—the legato that creates note-to-note continuity of tension and outline in sounds which begin to die out as soon as they are produced—is something done by a highly accomplished musician who is also a highly accomplished pianist. And actually Schnabel was not only a great musician but a superb pianist, with a technical equipment which in all but a few instances—such as the especially awkward passage-work in Beethoven's *Hammerklavier* Sonata, his Sonata Op. 111, the Brahms concertos—completely and effectively satisfied every demand. Moreover the greatness of his playing in most of the first movement of Beethoven's Op. 111 wasn't lessened by his imperfect execution of some of the passage-work; nor did this flaw the perfection of his unique performance of the concluding movement.

1 December 1956 and 19 March 1955 The much-written-about Maria Callas has made her first appearances at the Metropolitan, exhibiting a voice that has lost most of what caused so much to be written about her. The recordings of the last couple of years have documented the deterioration in that remarkable voice; and by now its original bloom and loveliness are gone, it has a bad wobble, and as often as not it produces a climactic high note off pitch. That is what one heard during much of the

1 December 1956 and 19 March 1955

Metropolitan's third performance of *Norma*; but in an occasional quiet phrase employing its lower range the voice approximated its former beauty. And all the singing, whether agreeable or not in quality of sound, still exhibited Callas's unfailing sense and concern for continuity and shape of the musical phrase, which at times was very exciting.

In the Metropolitan her singing did not project the compelling power that it does at microphone-range on records. Nor did she, on the stage, radiate any of the force of personal presence or dramatic projection that her carefully studied poses and movements were evidently meant to convey. They were meant also to make the performance a prima-donna-assoluta-grand-style operation; and in this too they failed. All this was bad enough; but what was appalling was the audience's response to it: the same storms of applause, the same cheers and yells, as for the successful operation of a Lehmann or a Flagstad.

Nor did this happen only with Callas. In the *Norma* performance one heard also the frayed, rough, coarse bass of Siepi, the unpleasantly rasping tenor of Del Monaco, the contralto of Barbieri, beautiful in quality, but shattered a good deal of the time by tremolo; and each elicited the storm of applause, the cheers and yells. We have, then, not only a deterioration in performance, but a deterioration in public taste that is to some extent responsible for it: not only does the Metropolitan offer performances with singers some of whom would not have appeared on its stage fifty years ago, but it does so because, for one thing, the public goes into frenzies over a Del Monaco or a Harshaw today as it did over Caruso and Destinn fifty years ago. Nor does the public behave in this way because it isn't acquainted with beautiful voices and great singing: it hears Steber, Bjoerling, de los Angeles, Valletti.

One doesn't expect musical taste of the public, and wouldn't be surprised by its enthusiasm for a new Gigli; but one is amazed

8 and 29 December 1956

by its loss of its former ability to perceive the objective fact of a pleasant or unpleasant vocal sound, and by the frenzies for a Del Monaco or a Harshaw. And not only the public: I don't see all the reviews, but I have yet to encounter one—even by one of the voice- and opera-cultists—that has discussed the voice of Del Monaco or Harshaw that I have heard. [*The Nation*]

Postscript 1964 Callas's vocal powers, peculiarities and deficiencies—not only her range, agility and power, and the strangely beautiful timbre of her lower voice, but even her unpleasantly shrill high notes—promised an effective Lady Macbeth in the Metropolitan production of Verdi's *Macbeth* two seasons later; but it was lost through Mr. Bing's loudly proclaimed dismissal of her, allegedly for reasons which did not justify his action. Her decision not to sing *La Traviata* in alternation with *Macbeth* was not only understandable but the sort of thing that happens in opera companies all the time, and the sort of thing that is always handled and settled by private persuasion and mutual accommodation, not by the public martinet-like assertion of power that Mr. Bing seems to like to indulge in when he can (when he can't—when he has to yield to demands by a singer he needs—he doesn't proclaim it in the newspapers).

8 and 29 December 1956 Subjects like the difficulties of the New York Philharmonic or the New York City Opera are invitations to fancy or pretentious idea-spinning that usually has no relation to fact. Thus, in explanation of the Philharmonic's poor performances last season Winthrop Sargeant argued that it resulted from the orchestra's having to play under a group of conductors—Mitropoulos, Walter, Monteux, Szell and Cantelli—"far too numerous and disparate in its methods of conducting."

8 and 29 December 1956

Very impressive—until one remembered the beautiful performances last season of the London Philharmonia, whose manager has made it a point to have the orchestra work under a large number and variety of conductors. Concerning Cantelli in particular Sargeant remarked that his "claims to distinction as a symphonic maestro have always seemed to me rather dim"; but the claims that were dim to him were impressively clear to the not easily impressed Toscanini and musicians of the NBC Symphony; and the true reason for the Philharmonic's poor work under Cantelli was talked about among informed orchestra men: "The orchestra has stopped playing for him." This is something which the Philharmonic could not possibly admit, and which the public may find it difficult to believe; but I believe it and write it because I got it from sources I consider reliable, and because it has happened before in the orchestra's history. In the thirties one heard the Philharmonic one week play like a great orchestra under Toscanini, and one saw it the next week sit back and take things easy under another conductor and produce playing in which one couldn't recognize the orchestra that had played under Toscanini. I was reliably informed that this was the reason for Stokowski's withdrawal a few years ago; and last April someone who had seen Cantelli almost every day during his few weeks with the Philharmonic told me what Cantelli had reported to him immediately after the first rehearsal. It had been a rehearsal of a Beethoven concerto with Backhaus; and Cantelli said he had spent the morning knocking himself out against the wall of the orchestra's indifference—an indifference which it hadn't been ashamed to exhibit in Backhaus's presence. This misbehavior had continued in the weeks that followed; and as a result, said my informant, Cantelli was attempting to get the Philharmonic management to release him from this year's contract.

The young conductor to whom the Philharmonic misbehaved

22 December 1956

was of an order of distinction that made his first appearance here in 1949 a memorable event. With Toscanini approaching the end of his activity, it was exciting to hear in Cantelli's first performances with the NBC Symphony something similar to Toscanini's operation in attitude, method and results. There were differences too: as against the power creating a continuous tension in the flow of a Toscanini performance, one heard in Cantelli's performances a youthful lyricism and grace. These qualities of youth the performances exhibited, but not the immaturity about which some critics pontificated to show their discernment (e.g. Irving Kolodin's "That degree of musical culture and experience which can settle, almost instinctively, on proper tempi and sonorous values for such works as the Mozart are not yet his"): the performances certainly would change in time, but each as it was produced then emerged as a completely, satisfyingly achieved entity, "as fresh and glistening as creation itself." And Cantelli's extraordinary technical and musical equipment, his fanatical personal dedication, won the respect and response not only of the conscientious musicians but of the hard-boiled specimens of the genus New York orchestral player in the NBC Symphony.

The destruction of this distinguished talent is a heartbreaking loss; and one's grief is the greater for the knowledge that Cantelli was killed on the journey to an engagement which he regarded as a waste of his energies and from which he had tried to escape. [*The Nation*]

22 December 1956 Berlioz, who was one of the great musical creators, was also a great critic; and I use the word 'great' to indicate not only the magnitude of his critical perception and literary gift but the personal qualities which shine through the writing. The perception that formulates itself with literary brilliance and delightful gaiety and wit is at the same time one that deals rigorously with the work of art before it; and in addition to this integrity there are intensity, passion and nobility which, expressing themselves in a rhetorically heightened style, are very moving.

Berlioz did the daily musical journalism he hated, in order to earn the living he could not earn by writing the music he loved; and since the French public that was indifferent to his music enjoyed his criticism, he published collections of his prose writings to earn additional money. Of these collections one, *Les Soirées de l'Orchestre,* has an unusual and amusing framework: the author spends a number of evenings in the orchestra pit of an opera house; and when a worthless opera is performed the members of the orchestra read, tell stories or talk about music, providing the opportunities for Berlioz to introduce his articles. Though the volume includes pieces of serious criticism, like the long study of Spontini or the report on music in London, its contents are mostly the lighter, sometimes extravagantly fantastic or satirical, but always accurately perceptive writings, like the pieces on the art of the claque, the life cycle of the opera tenor, the miseries of being a critic. *Les Soirées* is the only one of the collections that has been published in this country: a translation by Charles E. Roche appeared in 1929; and now we have *Evenings with the Orchestra,* translated by Jacques Barzun, the title page informs us, "at the request of the Berlioz Society."

When it announced the project to its members the Society said its first idea had been a reissue of the Roche version, but it had decided, "after consultation with Jacques Barzun and other authorities, to . . . work for a completely new translation." Presumably it was influenced by Mr. Barzun's opinion, stated in his book on Berlioz, that Roche had translated *Les Soirées* "so clumsily and with so many blunders . . . that it ought to be done

22 December 1956

over." And though Mr. Barzun, in a note on his translation, now concedes that the Roche version "had occasional merit, and wherever it contained a happy turn of phrase this has been preserved," he still contends that "as a whole the rendering was inaccurate and unidiomatic." Actually, Mr. Barzun's version is only a little less old-fashioned in its English than Roche's and is less accurate. For it is not the "completely new translation" which the Berlioz Society commissioned; instead it is largely the Roche translation with an occasional word or phrase by Mr. Barzun which as often as not replaces a happy or correct turn of phrase with something less good or less correct.

There is space for only a few typical examples. Where Roche has "He took unto himself a wife" instead of "He married" for Berlioz's *"Il se maria,"* Mr. Barzun only makes it "He took a wife." On the other hand, where Roche translates *"ton jeune courage"* simply as "your young courage" it is Mr. Barzun who makes this "your fledgling valor." When Berlioz asks the tenor dizzy with success not to condescend to the composer: *"Quand, du haut de votre élégant cabriolet, vous apercevrez dans la rue, à pied, Meyerbeer, Spontini . . . ,"* Roche keeps Berlioz's image in "When, from the height of your elegant carriage, you see in the street Meyerbeer, Spontini . . . afoot . . . ," but Mr. Barzun changes it with "When, from the depths of your elegant carriage . . ." And when Berlioz has Cellini exclaim: *"Il est donc vrai! tu composes pour le grand-duc! Il s'agit même, dit-on, d'une oeuvre plus vaste et plus hardie . . ."*—"So it is true! You are composing for the Grand Duke! Even, they say, a grander and bolder work . . ."—Roche weakens this a little with "It is, then, true that you are composing music for the Grand Duke! Even, as they say, a work . . ."; but Mr. Barzun waters the impassioned outburst down to "If what I hear is true, you are composing for the Grand Duke; composing a work . . ." This illustrates an

22 December 1956

important fact about Mr. Barzun's renderings: that they tend toward a prissy urbanity which is not Berlioz's.

This brings us again to Mr. Barzun's note on his translation, which is his answer to the criticism of his volume of Berlioz letters two years ago. His way of translating, he says, is a "recomposition" to achieve what "would express precisely this thought in English today"; as such, he foresees, it will disappoint those who like to be aware of a foreign author's foreignness, and will annoy those "who in a text can see only words," not "atmosphere and continuity of thought, rhythm and emphasis, allusion and local intent," and who consequently will "make an outcry when they compare the original 'meaning' revealed to their college French with equivalents of the kind I have tried to give."

I cannot speak for the possessors of college French; but I can speak for myself. I happen to have learned French as a boy of eleven in Vienna, with the result that today, although I cannot speak it with any ease, it is for me, when I read it, a living language, a medium of communication of "atmosphere and continuity of thought, rhythm and emphasis." Not, of course, to the degree that English is, but enough for me to be able to perceive that Mr. Barzun's "If what I hear is true, you are composing for the Grand Duke . . ." does not achieve in English the rhythm and emphasis and atmosphere of Berlioz's *"Il est donc vrai! tu composes pour le grand-duc! . . ."* I admit that when I read a French writer I think I should be aware that he is French; certainly when I read Berlioz I want to receive a communication of the mind and personality of Berlioz. Mr. Barzun contends this is achieved in English by his recomposition—which amounts to saying that if Berlioz wrote in English today he would write the prose of Mr. Barzun. And this seems to me rather unlikely.

[*The Nation*]

23 March 1957

16 February 1957 Thanks to NBC-TV Opera Theater we have at last heard Prokofiev's *War and Peace,* which turns out to be a work of little value. In the scenes of personal drama concerned with Natasha and Prince Andrei one hears only the operation of a resourceful craftsmanship capable of turning out music in any quantity for any descriptive or expressive purpose; in the historical scenes this craftsmanship operates at times for the purpose of wartime patriotic exhortation: in this work written during the Nazi invasion of Russia, an aria of Kutuzov begins with pretty music about the beloved Moscow he is sacrificing, changes to sinister music at the words "the treacherous foe invades our land," and rises to grandiloquent affirmation at the end.

Life, for Toscanini, meant a score to study, an orchestra with which to translate that score into living sound; for him, therefore, life in a real sense must have ended when he stopped conducting three years ago; and mere physical death must have been of no consequence. And so with the rest of us: we suffered our real loss when he retired; and his death now merely reminds us of it and tells us it is beyond recovery. [*The Nation*]

23 March 1957 With his superb performances of Mahler's Second Symphony (*Resurrection*) with the New York Philharmonic Bruno Walter concluded what he has announced is the last of such periods of guest-conducting with this orchestra or any other. He was eighty years old this year; and though he will continue to conduct he is reducing his commitments. Thus the career of another of the major figures in the musical life of the past fifty years is nearing its end.

The observances of Walter's eightieth birthday in the press

23 March 1957

and elsewhere have been concerned not only with the musician but with the person; and Columbia's have included not only the new recordings of the Mozart *Requiem* and Symphonies K.543 and 551 but a record for free distribution, *Bruno Walter in Conversation with Arnold Michaelis,* on which Walter "speaks to us from the serene plateau of mature understanding about music, musicians and life." And on the envelope of a popular-priced promotion record, *Bruno Walter: The Sound of Genius,* a collection of bits of Mozart, Beethoven, Schubert, Brahms, Johann Strauss and Mahler, Columbia printed an appreciation of Walter by the English critic Neville Cardus, who writes among other things that Walter "has maintained a balance between mind and imagination, reason and feeling," and that "there has always been courtesy in Bruno Walter's conducting, as in the man himself. He does not tryrannize music or musicians; he draws the best out of both by love and good manners. He is less happily described as the Maestro than as the Chevalier or Grand Seigneur."

I remember Walter's first appearance with the New York Symphony in 1923, and his performance of an unfamiliar Mozart symphony with a lightness, grace and sparkle that were a revelation in Mozart style; and I remember that his performance of Strauss's *Don Quixote* made me laugh more than any I have heard since. I also remember a delightful performance of *Così Fan Tutte* which he conducted in Salzburg in 1928; but in Vienna a few months later I heard *Così* conducted by Strauss in a sharper-contoured, keener-witted manner that made Walter's performance seem soft and amorphous; and thus I was made aware for the first time of the defect that Toscanini described in an observation reported to me in Salzburg in 1937: "When Walter comes to something beautiful he melts." The melting over Mozart, Beethoven and Schubert has continued in the years since then, and has produced performances which have been

23 March 1957

increasingly nerveless, soft and flabby. But the amorphously sprawling musical structures of Mahler, paradoxically, Walter tightens and makes coherent; and the performances of Mahler's Second with which he ended his engagement with the New York Philharmonic were impressive demonstrations of his capacities operating at their best.

As for Walter the Chevalier and Grand Seigneur, the picture is marred for me by an incident I witnessed some years ago. The occasion was a Saturday morning Philharmonic rehearsal for the evening concert at which Mozart's Piano Concerto K.595 was to be played. If the pianist had been Schnabel the entire rehearsal would have been devoted to achieving homogeneity of phrasing and precision of execution in the joint performance of orchestra and soloist. But the pianist was a young American; and while this appearance with the Philharmonic was of enormous consequence to him it was of no importance to Walter. So the young American sat waiting while Walter continued to rehearse the Suite from Korngold's *Much Ado About Nothing* and time grew shorter, until there was barely a half-hour left. At this point an official of the orchestra intervened and insisted on Walter's taking up the concerto. There was time only for one hurried and uninterrupted run-through; and the result was an ineffective performance at the concert. The Walter of this incident was no Chevalier and Grand Seigneur, but instead a man of no artistic conscience and of ruthless inhumanity.

[*The Nation*]

23 *March* 1957 * The volume *Olin Downes on Music* is a collection of what are offered as some of the best of Downes's

* (1964) This is the entire column of which the *Nation's* literary editor refused to publish anything but the first paragraph. I should add that in August 1955 the magazine's editor refused to publish two of my weekly

23 March 1957

writings between 1906 and 1955 and are considered worthy of permanence as a historical record of the period, as examples of excellence in critical writing, and thus as evidence of a task well done. And it is my duty to report my opinion that the collection is made valueless and unreadable as a record by the quality of the taste, mind and prose style of the man who for thirty-one of those years spoke for the *Times* on music. Thus, a statement in a 1944 review—"The Menuhin who played the Mendelssohn Concerto is now the matured artist, no longer the student of genius emerging from a certain master's superintendance. Poise and elasticity, stability and lyricism, an authority that never deserted him, an ease which comes only with authority, throughout characterized his playing"—is followed characteristically by qualifications: "It is true that the concerto has, on some other occasions we can mention, burned with a more incandescent flame, and that the slow movement, while it was in no sense breathless or without serenity, was played as fast as its nature would reasonably permit, and with some loss of *Innigkeit*"; but these qualifications give the impression of dealing with small and unimportant matters, and do not give even a hint of what was so saddening in Menuhin's change from student to matured performer—that the tone which had been compact and sweet was now coarse and blowzy, that the phrases which had been long-breathed, sustained and serene were now finicky and chopped up

---

columns in which I discussed what Downes had written about the policies of New York's City Center; and a month later he killed a column which included an obituary paragraph on Downes (I pointed out to him that when the *World* had done this with columns of Heywood Broun the *Nation* had called it censorship and suppression of opinion; but he disagreed that it was censorship and suppression of opinion when the *Nation* dropped a column of mine). In January 1956 the magazine's literary editor and publisher rejected a column in which I reviewed *High Fidelity Record Annual 1955*, because they didn't think it was the business of a critic to review the writing of other critics. Moreover, in all the columns of mine that the *Nation* did publish that last year and a half I had to accept some of the literary editor's changes in the writing; and I wouldn't want anyone to think this was something only I had to complain of.

23 March 1957

by accents and swells, that much of the playing was now mere high-powered fiddling, rhythmically unsteady and stylistically undistinguished. Downes's review is, then, made inaccurate as historical record by a failure either in critical perception and taste or in candor. (His views on *Fidelio* are a failure in perception and taste; his report on Paderewski's final broadcast a failure in candor.) As for the unprecise mind and its expression in the unprecise writing, here is one of the briefer examples, concerned with the freedom of American criticism from the provincialism of European criticism: "If there is one advantage that we have over other countries of the world where musical traditions are in the ascendant, it is in our degree of orientation toward any fixed tradition, and freedom, in our big musical centers, from the domination of the petty provincial influences."

However, if one is to evaluate Downes's performance as a critic accurately one must consider relevant and important material which the collection doesn't include. Thus, in an article on the right of the critic to "get mad when he hears a piece of music to which he feels acute objection," Downes says it is occasioned by letters protesting against his comments on a Mahler symphony; but he doesn't quote any of his statements that caused the protests. Certainly a critic has the right to say he doesn't like something; he has the right to speak with anger; he has the right even to express his dislike in the terms that an outraged reader quoted to me from a Downes review of a Mahler symphony:

It has been remarked that in the breast of every Frenchman there slumbers Massenet. We doubt not that in the breast of many, if not most middle-Europeans, there slumbers a Mahler, with his shoutings and posings, attitudes and exaltations, his fiery sincerity on this page, his windy mouthings and false naïveté on another. These Faustian protestations strongly affect the quite young and the impressionable old. Here is romanticism of a bad sort, which strikes a certain wistful echo. There are even those who pride themselves upon being sophisticates, intellectuals, abhorrent of sentimental protestation, who find in Mahler's luxuriant self-pity a sympathetic

23 March 1957

recognition. Secretly they see themselves as old souls, hapless victims of *Weltschmerz*. And do they fall for it! With all the sausage and the bunkum involved. The tears fall into the beer-mug, which is very, very deep.

But a critic who exercises the right to speak in such terms has to accept the consequences of so doing—the contempt merited by the arrogantly unembarrassed vulgarity of mind which those terms exemplify.

Because the collection is limited to Downes's writings on music itself, it omits another important part of his operation—his comments on the related matters that a music critic is called on to deal with. The book doesn't contain any of his denunciations of the attempts by composers or orchestral players to "exact all that the traffic will bear" (the composers' fees, it turned out on one occasion, averaged $50, with many works offered at $25 for a single performance or $35 for a pair, and this to be divided between composer and publisher). It doesn't contain his objections to the attempt to unionize the Boston Symphony, which he said was paid more than union orchestras (it was paid less). It doesn't contain the two articles which clouded with indirection and evasion the issues in Rodzinski's dispute in 1947 with Arthur Judson and the New York Philharmonic (whether Judson, a manager of concert artists, should be manager of an orchestra which engaged such artists, and whether he should have anything to say about the orchestra's artistic operations). Downes's writing on these subjects merited as little respect as his writing on music itself.

In one of those 1947 articles on the Philharmonic Downes described as "still a mystery" the Philharmonic's earlier retention of Barbirolli "for seasons after he had conclusively demonstrated his insufficiency," so that reviewers had become "embarrassed to record the level of mediocrity, or worse, in the performances." But the Philharmonic had retained Barbirolli partly because of reviews such as the one in the *Times* of 11 October 1940 (not

Summer 1957

included in the published collection) of a Barbirolli performance of Sibelius's Second ("a paean to the unconquerable spirit that is man"), in which Downes wrote that it "was read, for the greater part, in bardic vein. There was breadth and sweep of line in places where interpreters have fussed with detail," but then "there was sensitive treatment of details of delicate and haunting instrumental effects," and "a thoughtful reading was distinguished prevailingly by fine proportions and a real sense of form," but then "this feeling was lost . . . in places where tempo was too suddenly whipped up or slowed down," but then "the impression was of a too calculated performance, with many fine attributes, one which, had all previous calculations been forgotten, and the music given its head, would have been a complete instead of a conditioned success." This was no embarrassed recording of mediocrity; and the blowing hot and cold contrasted with the forthrightness of Virgil Thomson's statement—in his very first *Herald Tribune* review—that the music was "vulgar, self-indulgent and provincial" and the playing "dull and brutal." [*The Nation*]

Summer 1957 The critic's operation as I understand it and value it is the one described by E. M. Forster at the Harvard Symposium on Music Criticism ten years ago: the critic, according to Forster, considers the work of art before him as an object, an entity with an internal life, and tells us what he can about this life. Most writing on music exhibits the writers' inability even to describe the object accurately; and so when a reader, several years ago, sent me a few articles by Joseph Kerman in the *Hudson Review* to see whether I agreed with his high estimate of them, it was a pleasure to find accurate perception and knowledge about Mozart, Stravinsky and Tovey formulated in clear and forceful prose.

Summer 1957

But I also found ostentation in the writing—a show, a performance of being very learned, very intellectual, very severe. It may be asked what difference this made; and the answer is that when a critic's eye is partly on the effect he is making instead of wholly on the object before him, he is likely not to see the object accurately and may as a result deal with it not as it is or as it deserves; and this happened occasionally in Mr. Kerman's writing. Thus, in an article on Bach's choral music there was a reference to what I had written about Bach: that operating as a busily engaged musical craftsman—which meant operating with invention now momentarily inspired and incandescent and expressively moving, and now only mechanically expert—Bach produced some pieces that were great and affecting works of art and others that were no more than accomplished exercises of his craftsmanship. Or rather, there was a reference to "the rather sour remarks of Mr. B. H. Haggin, who evidently believes that Bach tossed off most of his cantatas with unconcern and high speed, simply to satisfy his employers"; and on this matter Mr. Kerman wrote that

Bach and his contemporaries were too busy writing music to worry much about its greatness. They wrote rapidly and unerringly for occasions that followed one another too regularly to admit much pondering or polishing of scores. . . . They were craftsmen more than artists, professional musicians with a job to do and no nonsense, but their art is no less great for the absence of pomposity in their attitude towards it. You can reject this whole aesthetic if you like. . . . But it will not do to ignore it in Bach's best works and blame it for all the others. Of course much of Bach is less remarkable than his greatest pieces; it is a slim appreciation that values an art for its masterpieces alone.

All of which constituted an impressive-sounding piece of rhetoric of severity that worked itself into an all but total lack of contact with the realities of the subject and my statements. Letting the most obvious irrelevances speak for themselves, I will point out that I wrote about greatness and the absence of it in Bach's

Summer 1957

works, not about thoughts of greatness and the absence of them in Bach's mind; and while it may have been true that operating as a busily engaged craftsman Bach had no thoughts of writing greatly, it was not true that when I said some poor works resulted from his operating as a busily engaged craftsman this was equivalent to saying they resulted from his operating without thoughts of writing greatly. (Actually, Bach did think of writing well, and of writing in every instance as well as he could.) Nor was it true that because Bach operated in the same way in all his works, the manner of operation and the art it produced had to be accepted in toto: it did "do" to evaluate not the totality but the particular works of Bach's art, and to distinguish in it the poorer works that resulted from his manner of operation and the great works in which this manner was transcended by momentary inspiration and incandescence.

Both the critical perception and the ostentatious intellectualism and severity appear in Mr. Kerman's first book, *Opera as Drama*, which demonstrates that music in an opera, like poetry in a verse play, "can reveal the quality of action, and thus determine dramatic form." The critical perception is evident in much of the detail of the musical articulation of dramatic continuity that he points out in works of Monteverdi, Gluck, Mozart, Beethoven, Verdi, Wagner, Debussy, Berg and Stravinsky, which he considers outstanding examples of *dramma per musica*, and on the other hand in what he points out in works of Puccini, Strauss and Menotti, which he considers contemptible. The perception is evident, that is, in the musico-dramatic life which he describes in such objects as the trio at the beginning of Act 2 of *Don Giovanni* or the third act of *Tristan und Isolde*, and on the other hand in what he describes in *Tosca* or *The Saint of Bleecker Street*. This, the bulk of the book, is excellent in itself and valuable for its effect on the understanding and taste of its readers.

Summer 1957

The ostentatious intellectualism appears even in this writing, which at times it makes obscure and difficult to follow. It appears also in what Mr. Kerman thinks of as the additional importance and value of his book—namely, the practical effect of a reaffirmation of the true nature of opera on the situation he describes: "In our opera houses, art and *Kitsch* alternate night after night, with the same performers and the same audience, to the same applause, and with the same critical sanction. Confusion about the worth of opera is bound to exist when no distinction is drawn publicly between works like *Orfeo* and *The Magic Flute* on the one hand, and like *Salome* and *Turandot* on the other.... This may be understandable in our first flush of enthusiasm of discovery, but it is hard to think that all our operatic activity can proceed much longer without standards." This is another piece of sonorous rhetoric out of contact with realities. There have been critical voices which have drawn distinctions publicly between Gluck and Mozart on the one hand and Strauss and Puccini on the other; and just as they haven't prevented the continuing alternation of art and *Kitsch* for the same audience and to the same applause in the past, so Mr. Kerman's reaffirmation of the distinction won't prevent it in the future—which is to say that the lack of standards is no more likely to cause our operatic activity to break down in the future than in the past.

And the excessive severity appears in Mr. Kerman's standards, which it makes questionable. Because Debussy's *Pelléas et Mélisande* meets Mr. Kerman's requirements as *dramma per musica* he accepts it, although its vocal writing, after the first minutes, becomes increasingly boring; because they do not meet those requirements he ignores even the best works of Rossini, Bellini and Donizetti—even the Rossini *William Tell* that elicited the warm appreciation of Berlioz. It appears that the standards of Mr. Kerman that are to enlighten the public will also impoverish it. And the preoccupation with *dramma per musica* produces the

29 July 1957

comment that "*Rigoletto*, in spite of lapses, has an old-fashioned consistency and fire about it, thanks largely to the splendidly operatic play by Victor Hugo. . . . Yet its success did not stop Verdi from glorifying the bad old style two years later in *Il Trovatore*, a magnificent demonstration of unprincipled melodrama"—which appears to make *Il Trovatore* inferior to *Rigoletto;* whereas in fact not only is *Rigoletto* as unprincipled and absurd melodrama as *Il Trovatore*, but *Caro nome* and *La donna è mobile* are examples of a melodic writing that is far less distinguished than the writing in *Il Trovatore* which gives us *Tacea la notte* and other superb melodic structures. [*Kenyon Review*]

29 July 1957 From the Columbia recordings of the young Rumanian pianist Dinu Lipatti—of Bach's Partita No. 1, Mozart's Sonata K.310, Chopin's Sonata Op. 58, Waltzes and a few smaller pieces, Schumann's Piano Concerto—we have known that an outstanding and distinguished talent was destroyed by his death in 1950. But it is only now, in the performances on two Angel records, that we hear what this talent was capable of when operating at maximum effectiveness, and that we can realize the magnitude of our loss. For the Columbia records give us the performances of the Bach partita, Mozart sonata and Chopin waltzes that Lipatti recorded in the summer of 1950 in the recording studio, where he was completely at ease and in control of himself, and where he played with sensitiveness and lyricism, with engaging grace, elegance and verve, with unfailing taste and feeling for continuity in phrase and larger structure, with unfailing precision in the execution of dazzling passage-work and fine gradations of beautiful tone. But the Angel records give us his performances of the same Bach, Mozart and Chopin pieces at his last public recital, in September 1950, at the Besançon Festival, where he was so ill and weak that he could barely climb the stairs to the auditorium, but where by an almost unimaginable effort of will he managed to play not merely with his lyricism, elegance, verve and precision but—under the stimulation of the occasion—with these raised to sheer incandescence. The will that sustained him all through the concert failed before the final Chopin waltz, which he had to leave unplayed; but the program included two Schubert Impromptus, Op. 90 Nos. 2 and 3, which he had not recorded previously. The performances on these two records are, then, not only an exciting artistic experience but a moving personal one. [*New Republic*]

Spring 1958 Stravinsky's successive works have given us the results of the play of his mind on whatever musical material—whatever style of this or that composer or period—he happens to have been interested in at the moment; and parts of *Agon* sound like the result of his recent interest in Berg, Schönberg and Webern. My hearings of the piece thus far have made me aware of the operation of impressive powers in the making of it, but have given me little pleasure from the result. But pleasure has come, as in some previous instances, from the dance movement that Balanchine has devised for the music in the ballet presented by the New York City Ballet—dance movement which exhibits once again the powers in relation not only to his own medium but to music and the stage that make Balanchine one of the two or three greatest creative artists of our time. "The fact is," observed an actor and director I know after a Balanchine ballet, in the City Center a few years ago, "the important things that are happening in the theater today are happening right here."

A writer who had been gathering material for an article on Balanchine reported to me that some people in the dance world

Spring 1958

considered the weakness of his choreography to be that it was derived from and dependent on music. I answered that it would make as much sense to say that the weakness of Hugo Wolf's songs was their derivation from and dependence on the poems; and that a Balanchine ballet was in fact an extension of the music in very much the same way as a Wolf song was an extension of the words. The music in the Wolf song takes shape around the words as it points up their meaning; the movement in the Balanchine ballet fits among, around and across the notes of the music like an additional counterpoint that completes the texture and in so doing gives it an additional significance—the significance imparted, for example, to a crabbed-sounding motif or phrase in the music of *Agon* by visually exciting changes in an anything-but-crabbed-looking configuration of a girl's body or a larger configuration of several such bodies.

Much of this imparted significance in *Agon*—produced by the tight fitting of dance movement to the tightly-fitted-together sounds, in sequences of movement that are sharply angular and accented—is humorous. The movements in the two *Pas de Trois* are—in ways that are difficult to convey, since they are often matters of no more than the movements' angularity, energy, brevity, abrupt cessation, or their canonic imitation, or their exaggeration of charming or noble attitudes—very amusing to see; they make the music amusing to hear; and Balanchine says he had this implicit humorous character of the music in mind when he created the movements; nevertheless the music is not enjoyable by itself, and what delights one is what Balanchine adds to it. So with the climactic *Pas de Deux* to which all this fun leads: the "expressive" phrases of the music are in an idiom which is not a medium of expressive communication for me; and their expressiveness is therefore, for me, mere manner without reality; but they provide a sound-track for the successive involvements of the two dancers that hold one spellbound. It has always seemed to me that Balanchine's imagination operated at its highest potential in his invention for ballerina and supporting male dancer—the seduction in *The Prodigal Son,* the ominous *Hand of Fate* episode in *Cotillon,* the tender and playful *pas de deux* of the boy and his bride, the violent one in which the fairy possesses the boy in *Le Baiser de la Fée,* the poet's encounter with the somnambulist in *The Night Shadow,* the dance of Apollo and Terpsichore in *Apollo,* the slow movement of *Concerto Barocco,* the third theme in *The Four Temperaments.* If one saw only one of these and nothing else of Balanchine's one would know him to be a great master; and after each, one has felt certain that his imagination could go no further; but then it has gone still further in the next. So now with the *Pas de Deux* in *Agon,* which takes its place with the great examples I have mentioned: it involves the bodies of the two dancers in astounding new intricacies which appear to be the utmost imaginable by the mind that no doubt will imagine still others.

Agon got the most attention because it was a new work and a setting of a new Stravinsky score. But equally important was the revival of *Apollo,* a setting of Stravinsky's *Apollon Musagète* which Balanchine produced for Diaghilev in 1928. A ballet begins to be forgotten the moment it is no longer performed; and a number of great works that Balanchine has created in the last thirty years—notably *Le Bal, Cotillon, Mozartiana, Le Baiser de la Fée, Danses Concertantes*—have been lost in this way and probably will never be seen again. But in 1950 Balanchine managed to reconstruct *The Prodigal Son,* which he created for Diaghilev in 1929; and periodically he has revived *Apollo,* for which he appears to have an affection that is understandable, since it is his first classical ballet, in which he established the personal classical vocabulary and style, within the traditional classical idiom, that he has elaborated and extended in the works since then. This alone would make it a remarkable achievement

Summer 1958

for a man in his twenties; but in addition he produced a ballet which is not, as John Martin insisted for years, "a very young and dated effort" important only as "a historical milestone," * but a wonderfully beautiful and great work of art, of the same stature and power as the great works that followed it. *Agon* amazes one with what Balanchine's imagination continues to produce after so many years; *Apollo* amazes one with what it produced at the beginning—the visually exciting and touching dance and pantomime metaphors that express Apollo's growing consciousness of his powers and describe his involvement with the three muses: the soaring leaps around them that express his wonder and delight; the leaps that frighten them in the coda; the turns with which, fascinated, he follows Terpsichore's playful little hops; the exquisite episode in which he and Terpsichore sink to their knees facing each other, he holds out his open hands, she places her elbows on them and opens her hands, and he lays his cheek on them. [*Hudson Review*]

Summer 1958   Coming to the final sequence in the excellent *Omnibus* talk in which he described what the music in an opera does with the drama, Leonard Bernstein found the real meaning of the 'grand' in grand opera to be the way the music magnifies

* (1964) As such, Mr. Martin wrote in 1951 as a wise counselor to Balanchine, *Apollo* deserved only an occasional revival; moreover *The Four Temperaments*, though it had "some of the most stunning choreographic invention Balanchine has ever given us," regrettably had to be consigned to oblivion for lack of suitable music, and *Le Baiser de la Fée*, "another beautiful Balanchine work," needed to be returned to the storehouse until its technical problems could be solved. And though conceding the beauty of Balanchine's version of *Swan Lake*, Mr. Martin admonished him not to concern himself again with such old chestnuts—which was like admonishing a theater company not to concern itself with Shakespeare. "As a friend, and for your own good," said Mr. Martin to Balanchine in effect, "I urge you to cut your throat."

and crystallizes emotion—to the point, he added, of making words almost unnecessary. Opera reaches its highest state, he said, when the music is so communicative that the merest general knowledge of the dramatic action provides us with the key to rich apprehension. Citing as an example the end of *Tristan und Isolde*, he pointed out that we don't have to understand every word Isolde sings to feel her exaltation—don't have to know that she is saying

> *Soll ich schlürfen, untertauchen,*
> *Süss in Düften mich verhauchen . . .*

We have to know, said Bernstein, that—Tristan having died in her arms—Isolde stands over his body, ecstatic, mystically united with him, transfigured through love. And that is all we have to know for Wagner's music to do what every great work of art does—namely to create a special world of its own, into which we enter, and from which we emerge enriched and ennobled.

It was good to have this stated, and stated so well to so many people; and it would have been good for Bernstein to develop its implications. For one thing, if we don't need to understand every word in an opera, then we don't need to have it sung in English. And if it is the music in an opera that causes the drama to take place in the enriching and ennobling special world of the work of art, then it is the music that makes an opera valuable, worth performing and worth listening to, or makes it none of these. Good music translates even dramatic absurdity into a *Trovatore*, a *Rigoletto*, an *Aida*; poor music cannot make anything of a good drama but a poor opera.

I stress the primacy of the music because the tendency—of the American composer, the American public and most American critics—has been to make the drama primary, so that an interesting dramatic idea has won acceptance for music of little or no intrinsic value or dramatic force. The most spectacular successes

Summer 1958

in recent years have been won by the works that Menotti has insisted are not operas but musical dramas—much of whose music is of a trashily melodious kind that pleases the unsophisticated ear, but whose dramatic claptrap, in addition, so powerfully engages the audience's interest and emotions as to mislead it into wrongly ascribing the powerful effect to the music. *The Medium* had this success again when it was revived with *The Old Maid and the Thief* in the New York City Opera's spring exhibition (with the help of $105,000 from the Ford Foundation) of what has been achieved in opera in this country. For my part, observing the two works again after a number of years, I found that I either had forgotten, or now appreciated more keenly than before, how bad they were—*The Old Maid* with its comic cutenesses, *The Medium* with the rubbishy business of the mute boy and the games of make believe that he and the girl play when they are alone, the mellifluous third-rate tunefulness of the music of these scenes and of Mrs. Gobineau's aria, the standardized "dramatic" writing in Madame Flora's "big scenes."

In addition to the Menotti operas the works which the New York City Company's *Panorama of Opera, U.S.A.* offered as "living theater . . . created for today's audiences by today's writers" included two that actually had been written for, and produced in, the Broadway theater—Marc Blitzstein's *Regina*, with book adapted by him from Lillian Hellman's play *The Little Foxes*, and Kurt Weill's *Lost in the Stars*, with book by Maxwell Anderson derived from Alan Paton's novel *Cry, the Beloved Country*. These two I will comment on later; first I wish to speak of the others—the operas: Carlisle Floyd's *Susannah*; Douglas Moore's *The Ballad of Baby Doe*, with book by John Latouche; Vittorio Giannini's *The Taming of the Shrew*, with book by Mr. Giannini and Dorothy Fee; Marc Bucci's *Tale for a Deaf Ear*; Leonard Bernstein's *Trouble in Tahiti*; and Robert Kurka's *The Good Soldier Schweik*, with book by Lewis Allan.

Summer 1958

Of these the first had been performed by the company in 1956 and had won the New York Music Critics' Circle Award; the last was being performed for the first time anywhere; and the others, first produced elsewhere, were now given their first New York performances. In their various ways all of them captured and held attention with what happened on the stage, and carried this with music which in no instance had the impress of an original creative mind, but instead was an employment of existing resources for the needs of the text, done with more expertness or less, and in two instances with humorous cleverness. The folksong idiom of much of *Baby Doe* was not expressively adequate to the requirements of a text which at times exhibited subtle psychological insight and literary distinction; and it was used by Moore with singular feebleness. Bucci handled more sophisticated idioms with expertness; Giannini carried his expertness in producing a facsimile of the operatic-comedy style of Verdi's *Falstaff* to the point where it first made one laugh, then became irritating; Kurka devised an appropriate crude banality for the misadventures of the simple-minded Schweik. As for Bernstein, the major talent of the group, he again compensated for his lack of originality by the impressive resourcefulness in ideas and technique that made his serious music for the play about a disenchanted suburban couple highly accomplished. But he also demonstrated again that his gifts operate most successfully for comedy: the gift for mimicry and parody that he had applied with such brilliant results to the styles of Italian opera in the song *Glitter and Be Gay* in *Candide*, operated now in *Trouble in Tahiti* in the service of a sense for effective theater, which placed on the omnipresent television screen of today a dance-band trio of a girl and two boys who periodically crooned into the mike in three-part harmony their background comment on the mornin' sun that kissed the windows, kissed the walls, of the liddle white house, the liddle white house in Scarsdale, kissed the driveway, kissed the lawn,

Summer 1958

kissed the newspaper at the front door, of the liddle white house in Highland Park . . . the liddle white house in Shaker Heights . . .

Turning now to *Regina* and *Lost in the Stars*—it was in connection with the original production of *Regina* that Bernstein first stated the idea he developed in his *Omnibus* talk on musical comedy a year or two ago: that with its increasing use of the technical devices of opera—the use, for example, of the device of double soliloquy in *South Pacific*—the American musical comedy was becoming the American opera. This left out of account what seems to me the decisive factor in the matter—namely, the expressive connotation of the musical substance to which the technical devices are applied: if the musical setting of the text employs the language of serious music, the resulting expressive communication is that of opera; if it employs the language of musical comedy, the resulting expressive communication is that of musical comedy. And this is true no matter how many technical devices of opera are introduced: when the device of double soliloquy is used with substance in the language of serious music in the second-act duet of Sophie and Octavian right after the presentation of the rose in *Der Rosenkavalier*, the result is opera; when this device is used with substance in the language of musical comedy in *South Pacific*, the result is musical comedy. Nor does the musical comedy become opera when its language is used in the setting of a serious play, as in *Lost in the Stars*: the result is, rather, musical falsification of the play. *Lost in the Stars*, said the review in *Newsweek*, "offered further evidence that the boundary lines which were formerly drawn between musical comedy, musical theater and opera seem to be fast disappearing." They may be disappearing for the *Newsweek* reviewer and the director of the New York City Opera; but nothing could be more striking than the repeated change from the expressive level of the spoken portions of *Lost in the Stars* to that of the musical-comedy idiom—melodic, rhythmic, orchestral—of most of the occasional songs, the most blatant instance being provided in the final scene by the digging song of the little Negro boy, a cute little-Negro-boy specialty number straight out of Broadway, immediately after the harrowing courtroom scene that is the climax of a serious play about Negroes in South Africa.

This sort of thing happens in *Regina* too; but the first thing to speak of is the play which Blitzstein fashioned out of *The Little Foxes,* and which a friend told me represented a coarsening of the original. I suspect I would have found even the Hellman play implausible; but the speeches and actions in Blitzstein's melodramatic caricature that were intended to freeze my blood made me laugh. And dramatic plausibility was lessened further by much of the music. Not having seen the original play I can only surmise that in the final scene Regina's financial demands backed by threats of exposure caused her brother to waggle a finger at her with mock reproachfulness and call her a greedy girl; and if my surmise is correct this moment of grim humor left the continuity and tension of the scene unbroken. But in the opera his reply is *Greedy Girl,* a song with the amusingly rhymed lyric and the musical style, the expressive connotations and tone, of a humorous musical-comedy song, which breaks the dramatic continuity and tension and establishes a musical-comedy atmosphere in which the melodrama becomes unreal and absurd. And if in the original play the guests at the party whispered bitter and nasty remarks about Regina and her brothers, the dramatic situation had a sense and tone very different from what it has in the opera, where the guests sing a cleverly rhymed musical-comedy-style chorus that makes fun of—and out of—the situation. Even a serious piece like Alexandra's *What Will It Be for Me* has the style, and therefore the expressive connotations and tone, of a musical-comedy song, whose underlying assumption is that it is something not to take seriously. Actually, then, much of

Summer 1958

Regina is an American musical; and there is nothing wrong in writing an American musical, but there is something wrong, it seems to me, in writing it as a setting of the melodrama Blitzstein made of *The Little Foxes*. And if these musical-comedy portions of *Regina* testify to his gift for the genre, the other portions demonstrate that his gift is almost exclusively for that genre. He is able to work up the musical frenzy for Regina's *If You Want*, the feverish, distorted waltz for her *Do You Wish We Had Wed Years Ago* (which has some of the worst verbiage ever set to music); but the inadequacy of his musical imagination and invention for the expressive requirements of other characters and situations is evident in Birdie's short aria in Act 1 and her long one in Act 3. The inadequacy reaches its extreme in the frequent abandonment of singing and resort to speech; but it is evident in the fact that the words usually gain nothing when they are sung in Blitzstein's recitative or arioso. In *Regina*, then, Blitzstein uses his gift for musical comedy to cover his lack of the gifts required for a musical setting of *The Little Foxes*.*

What I have written amounts to saying that the New York City Opera's director exercised poor judgment in his selection of what to include in the *Panorama of Opera, U.S.A.* But the judgment was even worse than has appeared thus far. In the dozen or more years of its operation the company had itself produced one American work, Aaron Copland's *The Tender Land*, whose music gave it distinction; and in the many years of American opera elsewhere than in the City Center two other works had had music at once distinguished and dramatically effective—Virgil Thom-

---

* (1964) In his *Juno*, the following year, it was the situations of comedy and pathos of a great play—O'Casey's *Juno and the Paycock*—that Blitzstein falsified outrageously with his musical comedy lyrics and melodies, to which he added the startlingly incongruous conclusion of Juno's anguished *Where?* (more powerful as spoken in the play than with the mellifluous Blitzstein phrase for "Take away our hearts of stone . . .") and the swelling chorus of affirmation which the newer and higher musicals—the ones that have Voltaire and O'Casey as their co-authors—end with.

18 August 1958

son's *Four Saints in Three Acts* and *The Mother Of Us All*. But these the New York City Opera did not include in its exhibition of American achievement in opera. [*Hudson Review*]

18 August 1958 The Columbia recording of Ira and George Gershwin's *Oh, Kay!* gives us one of the famous classics of American musicals, and thus enables us to hear a few other engaging songs besides the best-known *Someone To Watch over Me* and *Do, Do, Do*. It also gives us an example of what might be called the classical form of the American musical—in which the book was nonsense devised to provide the principals with occasions for their songs and dances. That form has continued, giving us today *Jamaica*, in which nothing happens except the excuses for the brilliant lyrics of E. Y. Harburg and the songs of Howard Arlen that make these lyrics work so effectively.

But there have been other musicals with changes. Some of the changes have merely made the musical a better musical, by having the lyrics and songs take off from situations in a book that makes sense, as in *Pal Joey, The Boys from Syracuse, My Fair Lady*. But others have had the purpose of making the musical something else, more worthy and important—of helping it become the American opera. This has given us *The Most Happy Fella*, with its quasi-operatic setting of the entire text of its book derived from a serious play; and it now gives us Leonard Bernstein's score for *West Side Story*, with its mixture of serious and popular idioms, its application to them of the elaborate technical and specifically operatic devices that Bernstein contends are changing the musical to opera.

There comes to mind someone's observation once that art is not superfluous—that it comes into existence to communicate something which cannot be communicated in any other way.

18 August 1958

The observation is true, not only of art in general, but of each of the various arts, and also of each of the various genres of one particular art: a Peter Arno cartoon is different from a Picasso study for *Guernica*; each has its own style and form, with which it exercises its own effect, communicates its own meaning, achieves its own value and importance; and one genre cannot be derived from the other. So, it seems to me, with Gershwin's *The Man I Love* and Mozart's *Porgi amor*—which is to say, the musical and the opera. If the musical setting of the text employs the language of serious music, the resulting expressive communication is that of opera; if it employs the language of Tin Pan Alley, the resulting expressive communication is that of the musical, no matter how many technical devices of serious music and opera are introduced. And no matter if the book is adapted from a serious play: the musical language of *The Most Happy Fella* is not an expressive medium for certain serious situations of the play *They Knew What They Wanted*.

Most of the music of *West Side Story* I don't find interesting to listen to for itself (though I might find it to be good soundtrack for what happens on the stage). But Stephen Sondheim's lyric and Bernstein's intricate music make *America* a brilliant song. [*Playbill*]

18 August 1958 Paul Henry Lang's admonitions to Van Cliburn—in the *Herald Tribune* after Cliburn's concert—to forswear the path of flashy virtuosity seemed to make sense about the pianist about whom one knew only that he had wowed the Moscow public with Tchaikovsky and Rachmaninov concertos. But one discovers that they make no sense about the pianist who plays the Tchaikovsky Concerto on the Victor record and whom Lang heard play it in Carnegie Hall. For it turns out that Cliburn is, certainly, playing an inferior work of Tchaikovsky that

18 August 1958

has become a virtuoso display piece, but that the operation is—like Toscanini's performance of the *Dance of the Hours*—strictly that of a musician playing a piece of music and employing for the purpose not only a remarkable technical equipment but an equally remarkable and distinguished musical perception and taste. And one might add that the performance is that of the pianist who—it also turns out in an interview—recalls as the most wonderful moment in his Moscow experiences his having to get up four times to acknowledge the applause after his performance of a Mozart sonata; who—it turns out further—competed for the Leventritt award a few years ago with performances of two Beethoven sonatas, and earlier for the Chopin prize with a Bach partita; and who, it would seem from all this, needs no admonitions to forswear the path of flashy virtuosity.

No less wide of the mark was Winthrop Sargeant's report in the *New Yorker*, in which he described Cliburn as "a living representative of the great 19th and early 20th Century school of virtuosity, which included such formidable artists as Sergei Rachmaninoff, Josef Lhevinne and Josef Hofmann," declared it "heartening to find the traditions of this school flourishing again in one so young," and cited his "tasteful and assured use of rubato in the style of the distinguished virtuosos of the past." Lang thought he heard in Cliburn's continent playing the flamboyant style of the virtuosos of the past; Sargeant thought he had heard in their playing the continence of Cliburn's. As one who grew up on the playing of Hofmann and Lhevinne *I* am heartened by the fact that Cliburn's playing is not like theirs; and the difference is precisely in his tasteful use of the rubato which they used tastelessly. The nineteenth and early twentieth centuries were a period in which the instrumental virtuoso distorted music for the same exhibitionistic purpose, and as tastelessly, as the virtuoso singer. The practice has continued, and can still be heard in the performances of some singers, instrumentalists and conductors today; but today it is condemned by

Summer 1959

the standards of the taste exemplified in the modern practice of other performers—Toscanini, Rethberg, Flagstad, Bjoerling, Szigeti, Schnabel. And that modern taste is what one hears in Cliburn's playing: even in the Tchaikovsky Concerto his rubato is controlled by the feeling for plastic proportion and coherence in shape of phrase that Toscanini exhibits in the *Dance of the Hours*.

To listen to Cliburn is to be delighted, excited and even awed by talent so rich and so sure in one so young; it is not, however, to be electrified as one is by the very first phrase of Glenn Gould's statement of the theme of Bach's *Goldberg Variations*—by, that is, the more sharply incisive shaping and greater tension, in which one hears a more forceful mind and a more highly developed technical mastery capable of finer differentiation of tone by gradations of volume. One is electrified again by the very first phrase of Bach's Partita No. 5 that Gould plays on the Columbia record—by the power, the authority, the sustained tension that compel one's continued fascinated attention for the rest of this dull piece. And both his intellectual power and his technical mastery are evident in the amazing way in which he maintains this sustained life not just in one but in all the interweaving strands of the contrapuntal textures in the Partita No. 6 and the Fugues in E major and F-sharp major from Book 2 of *The Well-Tempered Clavier*. I can't recall another pianist achieving anything like this playing of counterpoint, or achieving everything else in these performances that makes them so extraordinary.

[*New Republic*]

Summer 1959 Reporting on the works presented in the New York City Opera's first season of American opera a year ago, I said that all, in their various ways, had captured and held attention with the dramatic happenings on the stage, not with the music, which had in no instance exhibited the operation of an original creative mind, but had instead been only a more or a less expert employment of a variety of existing idioms and styles in support of the texts. But for Winthrop Sargeant, among other reviewers, the season was a milestone in the history of American music in that it revealed—most impressively in Douglas Moore's *The Ballad of Baby Doe,* Vittorio Giannini's *The Taming of the Shrew* and Carlisle Floyd's *Susannah*—a rich sprouting of genuine American opera whose further growth required more of the financial support that the Ford Foundation had provided for the season. And the Foundation, thus assured of the excitingly beneficial effect of its first grant, came through with a second this year that enabled the New York City Company to put on another American season in which Sargeant heard further evidence of the burgeoning of the new development in American music that will no doubt persuade the Foundation to make a grant for a third season next year and so on.

Believe, if you will, Sargeant's contention that the New York City Company this year presented additions to a corpus of distinguished achievement in American opera; or believe me when I say that Menotti's *Maria Golovin* offered the usual Menotti pastiche of musical trash in the service of the usual Menotti dramatic claptrap; that Floyd's "modern" writing in this year's *Wuthering Heights* was no better in quality and no more adequate for its dramatic purpose than his traditional writing in *Susannah;* that Robert Ward merely operated with more expertness in his manipulation of unoriginal materials in *He Who Gets Slapped;* that Hugo Weisgall's "modern"-style writing in *Six Characters in Search of an Author* was unpleasant-sounding as well as expressively and otherwise worthless; and that the expressive connotations of Kurt Weill's musical-show-style writing

Winter 1960

were inconsistent with the serious dramatic action in *Street Scene* this year as in *Lost in the Stars* last year.

Glenn Gould's Carnegie Hall recital confirmed the impression I had got from his records—that this young Canadian stands out above all other pianists young and old. The playing style, with its powerful note-to-note continuity of shape and tension, is like no other. So is what it produces—the object in sound completely formed and completely achieved to the exact sonority of the last note. And so are the powers it reveals—the intellectual power with which the forming of the object begins, the technical mastery with which the extraordinarily fine and exact graduations of tone are achieved. The piece may be a dull one, or the object he makes of a great one may be unconvincing and unacceptable as a realization of the work; but the intellect and the mastery exhibited in the operation command interest and respect: one's mind is seized by the very first sounds, with their electrifying authority and force, and is held fascinated by the continuing coming into existence of the remainder of the musical object.

[*Hudson Review*]

Winter 1960 The directors of the New York Philharmonic may evaluate Leonard Bernstein by the crowds he attracts to Carnegie Hall; the players of the orchestra may evaluate him by the large amounts of money he makes it possible for them to earn; but a critic must evaluate him by the way the Philharmonic, under his direction, carries out the task that is the orchestra's reason for existence—the task of enabling the public to hear the orchestral literature effectively performed. And that was what I was interested in, after reading last year in the *Times*, *Harper's* and lesser publications about the innovations Bernstein had made in the programs, the improvement he had achieved in the orchestra's playing, the growth in "depth and maturity" of his musicianship and conducting.

The first week's program this year, as announced originally, comprised Beethoven's *Egmont* Overture, Triple Concerto and *Eroica* Symphony; as revised, it had Shostakovitch's Fifth in place of the *Eroica*; and so it ended by offering one impressive short piece and a boring long one by Beethoven and a long trashy one by Shostakovitch. And the second week's program listed Barber's *Second Essay*, one of his fluently unoriginal pieces of what Bernard Shaw called "second-hand music"; then Ives's *The Unanswered Question*, a piece with a big idea and little music (strings in the back playing quiet chords which represent the conventional life that goes on and on, while a trumpet on one side repeats a phrase which asks whether this is what life is good for, and increasingly agitated exclamations of flutes on the other side are futile attempts at an answer); then one of Stravinsky's least attractive neo-classical works, his Piano Concerto; and only then something first-class—three movements from Berlioz's *Romeo and Juliet*. A good program offers both old and new music; but it must also offer a preponderance of good, significant or at least interesting music; and this makes the Bernstein programs I have just described—only two of many of the same kind—bad.

I skipped Beethoven's Triple Concerto and the Shostakovitch Fifth, and attended the Sunday afternoon performance of the second week's program, at which the performances testified to Bernstein's competence as a conductor—i.e. for the business of getting an orchestra to play accurately and beautifully. As for his operation as a musician, the touchstone for me was the performance of the *Love Scene* from Berlioz's *Romeo*. Writing once about Berlioz's use of the four extra brass bands and sixteen kettledrums in the *Requiem*, W. J. Turner remarked that "all these things in the hands of anyone but Berlioz would have resulted in incredible vulgarity; but Berlioz could not be vulgar." And one can make a similar comment about the *Love Scene*. Its expressive content is unmistakable: the *premiers transports, premiers aveux, premiers serments* described in the Prologue; and these—which could be an occasion for vulgarity—are instead conveyed in musical terms of the most exquisite delicacy, which not only characterize the emotions of the young lovers but convey the delicacy of feeling of Berlioz himself. This delicacy is embodied not only in the melodic and harmonic substance and orchestral coloring but in the precise outlines Berlioz prescribes for the shape of the substance with his markings of tempos and dynamics. And what Bernstein did was to italicize Berlioz's delicate strokes—to linger *molto meno vivo* over what Berlioz marks *un poco meno vivo*, to slow down what Berlioz marks *senza rallentare*, to rush a tranquil melody in a section that Berlioz marks *Adagio* with a metronome marking to make sure, to linger with heavy emphasis over a wistful melody that Berlioz marks *a tempo* and *pp* for the strings and *ppp* for the winds—and in this way to vulgarize the exquisite piece.

What Bernstein did that Sunday afternoon he has been doing the past fifteen years and probably will go on doing in the years to come. He has tended to deal straightforwardly with modern and contemporary works—though I must add that recent recordings offered a frenetically whipped up performance of Stravinsky's *Sacre* and one of the *Firebird* Suite in which there was a lingering and melting over details, a fussing with exaggerated nuances of sonority and tempo, that I doubt Stravinsky would find acceptable. Also, in symphonies of Mozart he has accepted the limits set by their style, and, operating with restraint and taste, has produced fine performances—though here too I must add that in his own playing of the piano parts of Mozart concertos there has again been tasteless lingering and melting over fussily inflected phrases. But most of the standard repertory he has treated

Spring 1960

in the way he treated the three pieces from Berlioz's *Romeo*—with no restraint on what has impelled him to distort the shapes of the works and their expressive effect. That is what he has done until now; and I can think of no reason for expecting him to do anything different in the years ahead. It will not be from him that the public will get its valid performances of Beethoven, Schubert, Brahms, Tchaikovsky, Strauss, Mahler and the rest.

[*Hudson Review*]

Spring 1960 If the Moscow State Symphony's visit was intended to demonstrate Russian achievement in orchestral performance, what it demonstrated was not very impressive to ears familiar with our virtuoso orchestras. And if the further intention was to demonstrate an authentic style of performing Tchaikovsky, the performances conducted by Kondrashin demonstrated that Tchaikovsky is butchered in Russia in the same style as everywhere else. The very first measures of the small-scale Serenade Op. 48 were attacked with a vehemence which in the *Pathétique* reached such a degree of brutality and distortion that I couldn't listen beyond the second movement. Only in the two opera excerpts did Kondrashin operate with continence; and in the first of these, the *Letter Scene* from *Eugene Onegin*, Galina Vishnevskaya exhibited the usual thin and tremulous Russian-soprano voice; but in the later aria from *The Queen of Spades* the voice was steady and voluminous, though not lustrous and warm. However, with the unremarkable voice she exhibited the powers of a remarkable singing actress: a slim, attractive young woman in a low-cut black evening gown standing before an orchestra in Carnegie Hall, she created in the *Letter Scene*—with only slight movements of head and arms and slight changes of

Summer 1960

facial expression—an image of Tatiana's personality and situation that was as touching as the reality would have been.

At a later concert Kondrashin began with a vehement distortion of another small-scale Tchaikovsky piece, the engaging Suite No. 3, of which only the concluding *Tema con variazioni* is familiar from its use in Balanchine's ballet *Theme and Variations*. Then he produced an admirably continent realization of the orchestral framework of Mozart's Piano Concerto K.467 for Emil Gilels, who played also Tchaikovsky's Concerto No. 2, a work of finer substance than the ubiquitous No. 1. I had previously heard Gilels only in a recorded performance of Chopin's Sonata Op. 35 that had left me with no interest in hearing more; and recently Van Cliburn in Tchaikovsky and Glenn Gould and Leon Fleisher in Mozart have exhibited a considerate mastery in the treatment of their instrument, a clean and finished execution, a continuous piano legato in the service of an unfailing sense for the continuing musical phrase, that make Gilels—with his unprecise slam-banging of passage-work, his percussive loud or pallid soft tone in insensitive or affected phrasing of melody, his lack of a sense for continuity—sound coarse-grained and immature.

[*Hudson Review*]

Summer 1960 The New York City Opera Company, in its third season of American opera, again ignored distinguished achievement in American opera and added Marc Blitzstein's *The Cradle Will Rock* and Menotti's *The Consul* to its undistinguished repertory. The intellectual level of *The Cradle Will Rock* is indicated in the episode in which Mrs. Mister, the wife of the owner of the steel company, bustles in to tell the minister, the Reverend Salvation, that her husband has told the President the company must have war for its profits and the President has obeyed his orders, after which she gives the Reverend Salvation a roll of bills, and he steps into the pulpit and preaches a war sermon. To call this dated today is to imply that it was valid in 1937; whereas actually it was in 1937, as it is now, the crudest agit-prop falsification suited to an audience of readers of the *Daily Worker;* and one must be depressed when a work that one would expect to be revolting to a supposedly more normally intelligent audience is laughed with and applauded instead. I have been speaking of the libretto because *The Cradle Will Rock* is not a work like *Rigoletto* or *Il Trovatore,* whose absurd libretto is something to ignore or endure for the superb music. To Blitzstein and his public the libretto of *The Cradle* is primary; and to me the music is rubbish. And I would like to believe that what Franchot Tone applauded, the night I was there, was only the excellent performance that wasted the talents of Tammy Grimes, Ruth Kobart, David Atkinson and the rest.

The larger and more important part of Leonard Bernstein's book *The Joy of Music* is a group of the *Omnibus* television talks that gave him the prominence and the audience eager to follow him into Carnegie Hall that in turn brought him the musical directorship of the New York Philharmonic, some of whose concerts he has felt impelled to transform into approximations of the television talks. And the first thing to note is that the printed words haven't the impact of the words spoken by the engaging television personality. Also, and more important, it is one thing for Bernstein, in illustration of his spoken words, to offer the actual and accurate sounds of passages of jazz or of Schönberg's String Quartet Op. 30 No. 3 and *Pierrot Lunaire* and Berg's *Lyric Suite* played by living musicians, and another thing for Bernstein, in illustration of his printed words, to depend on the reader's own realization on piano and in *Sprechstimme* of the printed musical notation of the passages: in the one case the listener heard the passages; in the other the reader will hear something very different from the passages.

But even when the millions of listeners heard the actual sounds of the passage from Schönberg's quartet—to leave the book and go back to the television talk—and were asked "Can you see that this had to be the next step after *Verklärte Nacht?*" I doubt that very many of them *could*, and really did, hear what Schönberg heard and Bernstein hears but most people do not hear—that these atonal sounds had to be the next step after the tonal ones of *Verklärte Nacht*; though I can believe that many of the television listeners were magnetized into accepting Bernstein's contention as true without being able to hear its truth themselves. And so with Bernstein's general contention in this talk—that once he had explained how the modern music they disliked had come about, his television listeners would hear that "modern music is your music" and find it a "miracle that we, now in the sixth decade of the twentieth century, have so much beauty in our music." What I am illustrating with this instance is my contention that in Bernstein's television talks his engaging personality got many people to believe they understood or learned something they didn't really understand or learn at all, and to accept as true certain positions and ideas that were questionable.

There are other instances—among them the talk on Bach, with its contention that when Bernstein had explained the technical procedures, the preoccupation with mystic numbers, the musical pictorialism in exciting passages of the *St. Matthew Passion*, he had explained what produced equally exciting music in all the "suites, partitas, sonatas, toccatas, preludes, fugues, cantatas, oratorios, masses, passions, fantasias, concertos, chorales, variations, motets, passacaglias—the white-hot creation" of a man for whom "all music was religion; writing it was an act of faith; and performing it was an act of worship"—whereas in fact

Bernstein had explained what on occasion produced deadly dull music in all those categories by a man for whom the writing of music seems at times to have been only the routine exercise of his craftsmanship. Or the talk on the American musical, with its contention that the musical is on the verge of giving us our truly American opera—in disregard of the basic and irreconcilable expressive differences in the musical idioms of the musical and opera. Or the talk on jazz, in which Bernstein's explanation of syncopation was concerned with the crude shifting of accents from strong to weak beats and not with the subtle thing one hears in jazz—what Wilder Hobson, in his *American Jazz Music*, described so well as the tension- and momentum-producing suspended rhythms created around the regular beats by players who have a feeling for these suspended rhythms and in whose playing they are a fluent principle; and in which Bernstein's demonstration of a jazz scale with flatted "blue" notes caused a jazz player I know to object that the flatting was a momentary and subtle modification of the notes of the *normal* scale, dictated by the course of the player's melodic invention, and done again by players who had a feeling for such flatting and in whose playing it was a fluent principle.

But if I must point out these things I must also say that much of the detail of the talks on Bach and the American musical was excellent, and that the talk *What Makes Opera Grand*, a demonstration of the articulation of drama by music, was mostly admirable. I only wish Bernstein had used a better work than *La Bohème* as his illustration; and regret the inexplicable omission from the book of the important point Bernstein made in the talk with the finale of *Tristan und Isolde*—that "we really don't have to understand every word that Isolde sings in order to feel the sublime exaltation of her love. You don't have to know that she is saying: 'Soll ich schlürfen, untertauchen,/ Süss in Düften

Winter 1961; 5 March 1962

mich verhauchen.'" We don't, in other words, have to have opera sung in English. [*Hudson Review*]

Winter 1961; 5 March 1962 Though the Beethoven program which the celebrated Russian pianist Sviatoslav Richter played at his first recital in New York began with the early and uninteresting Sonata Op. 2 No. 3, it didn't include even one of the last sonatas that are the greatest of the series: what it offered after the first work was another uninteresting early sonata, Op. 14 No. 1, and three sonatas of increasing consequence—Op. 26, the seldom heard Op. 54, and the familiar Op. 57 (*Appassionata*). Thus Richter provided no demonstration of his dealing with the greatest Beethoven; but he did demonstrate right at the start, in the first movement of Op. 2 No. 3, the spectacular technique that at the end produced the sensationally fast and accurate finale of Op. 57. In the slow movement of Op. 2 No. 3 he revealed further a sense for continuity and shape in the musical phrase that was evident also in the graceful performance of the opening movement of Op. 26—a performance whose blandness, however, was not what is indicated by the Beethoven markings of sforzato accents and crescendos to sudden *piano* that Richter ignored. On the other hand the contrast between the charming minuet passages and the *forte* octave passages in the first movement of Op. 54 was made excessively violent by the stepping up of the forte to fortissimo; and this excessive contrast of dynamic extremes was heard again in the first movement of Op. 57. But the middle movement of Op. 57 was played very beautifully. At all times one heard completely thought-out conceptions of the music and complete mastery in their realization; but the performances didn't achieve the largeness of expressive communication of Schnabel's less perfectly executed performances. And though they revealed impressive musical and technical powers, they didn't justify the extravagant response of the audience and press.

Similarly, the performance of Beethoven's Concerto No. 1 that Richter recorded with the Boston Symphony under Munch for RCA Victor is a good one, but is made to sound very pale by the greater animation and energy, the more enlivening phrasing and rhythm, of Glenn Gould's performance on the Columbia record. [*Hudson Review; New Republic*]

Winter 1962 The Ford Foundation, assured by the critics that its money had produced a rich sprouting of American opera whose further growth required only more of the Foundation's support, came through with a further grant; and the results of this patronage, exhibited again by the New York City Opera, elicited reviews which no doubt will persuade the Foundation to make still another grant. In Professor Paul Henry Lang's *Herald Tribune* review Douglas Moore used a "fine gift for direct musical narrative" and other talents for operatic writing to achieve in *The Wings of the Dove* a work "destined to become a . . . fixture in the American operatic repertory"; in Winthrop Sargeant's *New Yorker* review Moore achieved a work which, by virtue of "the communicative power of its music," was "the most artistically successful American opera thus far written, and . . . certainly one of the very few operas written anywhere in the past half century that seem to deserve a permanent place in the history of the art." But what Moore achieved in the City Center auditorium was a musical operation as inept and feeble as those of his earlier *The Devil and Daniel Webster* and *The Ballad of Baby Doe*. In the columns of the *New Yorker* Moore accomplished the "fascinating feat" of "[restoring] by the evocative power of the music" what was lost by the librettist's "[pruning] James's convoluted writing down to the simple dialogue of which an opera libretto must consist"; but in the auditorium one heard Moore playing at being a composer by using now this instrument or voice, now that one, to produce now these sounds, now those, and heard him accomplish the fascinating feat of achieving in these sounds unceasing inadequacy or irrelevancy even to the simple changed words and situations that were a falsification of James's novel. And one therefore regretted the waste of the talents and work of those involved in the production.

Robert Ward's *The Crucible*, about which Professor Lang had reservations (for one thing, "the Wagner-Strauss orchestral commentary and the 'singing opera' do not consort well together"), was a better work than Moore's—better in the greater expertness with which Ward did essentially the same thing. The composers of the American operas exhibited by the New York City Opera all have relied on what happened on the stage to capture and hold attention, and have carried this with music which in no instance has had the impress of an original creative mind, but has instead shown varying degrees of skill in the employment of a variety of existing resources for the needs of the libretto. This was what Ward did with *He Who Gets Slapped* a few years ago; and it is what he has done now with Bernard Stambler's adaptation of the Arthur Miller play and with the unoriginal but suitable music that he has put together with a skill and assurance that Moore doesn't have.

Virgil Thomson once observed of a certain American that he had written lots of music, which made him a real composer, but that it had been standardized in expression and eclectic in style, which made him not a real creator. What the Ford Foundation has wanted to achieve, with its grants, and may have been led to think it has achieved, is the work of creators; what actually has been produced is the work of composers, some of them not even good composers. [*Hudson Review*]

Spring 1962

5 *February 1962* Though reviewers persist in hearing Van Cliburn as a pianist whose playing of Tchaikovsky's and Rachmaninov's concertos has kept him from learning how to play other music, his performances of that other music reveal him as one of the most distinguished musicians we have heard play the piano. Instead of tearing through Chopin's Polonaise in A-flat, on the Victor record, with the usual speed and brilliance, he sets a moderate tempo—a true polonaise tempo—in which he fits every note into the continuous and beautiful musical shape that he produces in sound, down to the last note of the smallest detail, with marvelous accuracy of finely differentiated tonal values. He maintains this tempo and this concern with the shaping of melody in the episode with the octave ostinato in the bass that pianists usually make into a display of bravura octave-playing in fast tempo. And even when he plays the flowing melody of the later lyrical interlude with the traditional rubato retardations that I consider excessive, he does so with his unfailing sense for continuity of flow and shape. To Irving Kolodin's ear the playing is only what any number of students at the Juilliard and Eastman Schools can do; but I can't remember hearing from anyone a performance of the polonaise so beautifully made and effective as Cliburn's; and the playing remains on that level in the other pieces on the record. [*New Republic*]

Spring 1962 In a letter to this magazine not too long ago Joseph Kerman made a distinction between the newspaper reviewing of music that was concerned chiefly with performance—"performance being news and box-office while music usually isn't"—and true music criticism, about which he contended that "a music critic should concentrate on music, not on musical performance, just as a dramatic critic should center his attention on plays and playwrights, not actors." But the superiority of

Spring 1962

Stark Young's dramatic criticism to even the best of today lay in the way he applied his extraordinary perception to the total theatrical event that presented itself to him—not only to the initial work of the playwright, but to what was made of it by the operation of the director, the actors' use of vocal inflection, timing, gesture, make-up, the contribution of scenery, costumes, lighting. And in a recent article Mr. Young pointed out the inadequacy of the criticism of today that left the art of the actor undiscussed. Music too is not something we read on the printed page; it is something we experience as it is realized in sound in particular performances; and the art of the performer in the particular realization is something for the music critic to concern himself with.

Mr. Kerman himself shifted ground in his next sentence: performance, it appeared, *was* something the music critic wrote about; but he must relate the writing about it to writing about the music. "Excellence in performance is the realization of the work of art from the page to actual sound; but how can one judge this excellence without insight into the work of art itself? And so how can one write relevantly about performance without writing about music?" One cannot, of course; but writing about music, for Mr. Kerman, meant writing the detailed close analysis of a piece of music that he wrote; and relevant writing about a performance related the performance to such analysis of the piece of music. I was, he said, not to be taken seriously as a critic because I didn't write about music —by which he meant that I didn't write detailed close analyses of pieces of music; and my writing about performance was of no value because it wasn't related to such analyses. Mr. Kerman was inaccurate about me: I had, on numerous occasions, written in detail about the happenings in pieces of music. But in addition he was wrong in his idea of music criticism: it is not limited to detailed close analysis, but includes summary value judgments, like Bernard Shaw's description of one of the Brahms piano concertos—"a desperate hash of bits and scraps, with plenty of thickening in the pianoforte part"—which is a judgment based on Shaw's experience of the happenings in the work, is capable of being verified by the reader's experience of those happenings, and is therefore valid and illuminating music criticism even though it isn't a detailed account of the succession of the "bits and scraps" that add up to the "desperate hash" in the first movement of Brahms's B-flat Concerto. And criticism of performance is not always related to detailed close analysis of the piece, but may also be summary. It may, that is, say that the melodic passages in a Mozart concerto were played by Artur Rubinstein in the unsuitable mannered style in which he plays Chopin; or on the other hand describe "the subtle articulation and clear outlining of phrase, the delicacy and at the same time the cohesive tension, the limpidity and at the same time the strength" in Schnabel's playing of Mozart.

Francis Toye, then, was writing as a music critic about Bellini's music when he observed that in the arias "there is little dramatic characterization; the Bellinian phrase is lyricism *in excelsis*." And so am I when I add that Bellini's lyrical writing much of the time stays on the level of a routine exercise of his style that isn't very impressive to the ear of today, and only now and then rises to something as compelling of attention and admiration as *Casta diva* in *Norma* or *Qui la voce* in *I Puritani*; that in *La Sonnambula* in particular, which the American Opera Society presented in December, it isn't until after the long first act that one hears *Tutto è sciolto*, and not until almost the end that one gets *Ah, non credea mirarti*; that in addition to these two affecting pieces (which Rieti used in his score for Balanchine's ballet *La Sonnambula*) there are occasional passages which are charming, and even unusual, like the animated orchestral introduction (which Rieti also used); but that on the other hand with the routine and

Spring 1962

uninteresting there is a considerable amount that strikes the ear of today as ridiculous—some of the fast concluding cabalettas, and the occasional writing in mellifluous thirds and sixths. And I am writing as a music critic about performance in what I report concerning Joan Sutherland's singing in *La Sonnambula*. A few years ago Maria Callas created new interest in the operas of Bellini and Donizetti with her singing of their difficult vocal parts—the delivery of melody that was made affecting by the strangely beautiful color of her lower notes, musically distinguished by her sense for continuity and shape of phrase, and eloquent by her powers of dramatic expressiveness; the execution of florid passages that was made spectacular by her vocal agility, accuracy and range and her bravura style. And now it is Sutherland who is exciting audiences with singing which in melody also exhibits an unfailing sense for continuity and shape of phrase, with in addition a steadiness and beauty in the higher notes that in Callas's singing are now wobbly and unpleasant; and which in florid passages exhibits an agility even more spectacular than Callas's. It is the bright, crystalline upper range of Sutherland's voice that is beautiful, not the lusterless lower range, in which her singing of melody makes its effect mostly with its phrasing and style. And in this lower range she does a lot of singing in which the drab color, a low volume level, and pathetic inflection produce a succession of mournful moans—this sometimes when the words are about joy and happiness. In *La Sonnambula* one heard this moaning even in the recitative and melody of *Come per me sereno*; and in the Metropolitan performance of *Lucia di Lammermoor* one heard it even in the passage of the *Mad Scene* concerned with the demented Lucia's imagined recollection of the joyful occasion of her marriage to Edgar. [*Hudson Review*]

Summer 1962 In 1938 Paul Henry Lang, professor of musicology at Columbia University, published in the *American Scholar* an article, *Ecce Criticus,* in which he contended that newspaper criticism of music offered "a thick tangle of prejudices, inherited formulas and catchwords, a prodigious lack of information, and an unbelievable ignorance of musical literature," and that the public would get the guidance it needed only when newspapers would have musical scholars writing for them instead of ignorant journalists. He repeated these contentions at the symposium on music criticism at Harvard University in 1947; and he was answered in the *Nation* by Henry David Aiken of Harvard's department of philosophy, who wrote in a review of the published addresses that Lang's

diatribe against the "musical journalist" is a nearly perfect instance of the failure to distinguish between understanding of music and knowledge about music, which is the besetting vice of so many academic music historians. That the level of a great deal of contemporary musical journalism is pitiably low is no secret. But the cure for this is not more historical erudition, but a more intense and sensitive devotion to the felt quality of music. . . . Lang's position . . . is typical of the historicist for whom real understanding of works of art is achieved, not by attending to what one directly hears and feels in them, but rather by learning about the "soil and surroundings they grew from. . . ." The interests of music are not well served by learned minds for whom the "central aesthetic quest" is merely an incident in the history of human culture. These interests are far better served by such "journalists" as Virgil Thomson, for whom the experience of music is the cardinal musical fact.

The phrase "central aesthetic quest" was E. M. Forster's: he had used it in his own address at the Harvard symposium to make the same point as Aiken in his own fashion. Concerning the aims of criticism in dealing with the work of art Forster had said: "The first and the more important is aesthetic. It considers the object in itself, as an entity, and tells us what it can about its life. The second aim is subsidiary: the relation of the object to the rest of the world." This meant consideration of "the conditions under which the work of art was composed, the influences which formed it (criticism adores influences), the influence it has exercised on subsequent works, prenatal possibilities. . . ." And Forster had contended that when criticism strayed "from [its] central aesthetic quest to influences and psychological and historical considerations" it was no longer in contact with the work of art.

According to Aiken and Forster, then, the critic's *perception of* the work of art and the scholar's *knowledge about* it are different things. It is true that both may occur in the writing of one person, but not because they are related. When E. J. Dent, in his book on Mozart's operas, in addition to offering a large amount of valuable historical material about the operas, makes one of the most perceptive observations about Mozart's other works that has ever been made: "The theatre is the sphere in which Mozart is most completely himself; his concert works—concertos, symphonies, quartets, and sonatas—are all fundamentally evocations of the theatre," he does this by virtue not of a scholar's knowledge of history but of a critic's close contact with those works of Mozart and perception of their "felt quality." And Dent is one of the exceptions: ordinarily it is one thing or the other. Great critics like Berlioz, Bernard Shaw and W. J. Turner have had the critic's perception without the scholar's knowledge; and as for the reverse, let us consider the actual performances of two of the scholars, Lang himself and the late Alfred Einstein, as writers on music for the general public.

Some years ago a student at the University of North Carolina, who had both the critic's perception and the scholar's knowledge, wrote me about an experience involving Lang's statement in *Music in Western Civilization* that "many, if not the majority, of Gesualdo's madrigals must . . . be considered closet madrigals, because their frightful, ragged, unvocal writing makes their performance by a vocal ensemble well-nigh impossible," and Einstein's statement in his *Short History of Music* about Gesualdo's "chromaticism which . . . was to lead to extremes of daring—but not based upon clear harmonic perception and hence not fully absorbed by the main stream of development." This was still before the advent of long-playing records, and at a time when—except in the rare instance where a copy of the Gesualdo record in *L'Anthologie Sonore* or the one in *2,000 Years of Music* was available for the history and appreciation course—all that the students in this course knew about Gesualdo was the sentence or two jotted down next to his name in the notes taken at a lecture or made of outside reading. As a result, they hadn't heard a note of the actual music but they knew from Lang about Gesualdo's unvocal writing and from Einstein about his extreme chromaticism; and that was what they wrote on their examination papers in answer to the question, "Discuss the following: (a) Gesualdo." My young correspondent, however, had gone to the printed scores of the madrigals, and reported his findings: "Gesualdo's chromaticism was not based on the major-minor, tonic-dominant relationships which ultimately prevailed: why should it have been? But to claim that it is not based on clear harmonic perception is to deny the evidence of one's ears: in every example I have been able to run down it always comes off—provided one is not so hog-tied by tonic-dominant prejudice that one can't hear it for what it is." Moreover, "all this colorful patter about 'frightful, ragged, unvocal writing' is a fabrication which an examination of the madrigals disproves in a moment: I have found in them a rare augmented fourth, and occasionally a diminished fifth—which even sight-singing students are taught to sing, and which constitute the 'frightful, ragged, unvocal writing.'" In addition, my correspondent had looked up Gesualdo in the Grove *Dictionary* of that period and discovered that "the ten volumes of Gesualdo's works went through not less than twenty-five different editions between 1594 and 1626," which led him to observe: "That they are hard to sing cannot be doubted; that they are possible to sing is quite as obvious; that Gesualdo's contemporaries sang them is fully demonstrated by the bibliographical record." Not only, then, had Lang and Einstein been unable to hear the music for what it was, and thus shown themselves to be in this instance poor critics, but Lang had made his statement in ignorance or disregard of the bibliographical record, and thus shown himself to be in this instance a poor scholar.

That, as I said, was before LP records; since then a half-dozen such records have appeared with performances of a large number of Gesualdo's madrigals. These have enabled us to hear that the harmonic progressions that sound strange and daring to ears accustomed to our major-minor, tonic-dominant relations invariably make a harmonic sense of their own to ears that can free themselves from major-minor, tonic-dominant prejudice; they have enabled us to hear that Gesualdo wrote some of the most remarkable, powerful and affecting pieces in the musical literature; and they have provided additional evidence that his madrigals can be sung. But even these recorded performances have not kept Lang from writing in a recent *Herald Tribune* article that the music attempts to render "every whim and fleeting emotion . . . in harmonies never before heard, in an exaggerated chromaticism"; that as a result it is "often bizarre and almost senseless, and when in that mood goes far beyond the confines of the madrigal: it can no longer be sung." Again we find not only that Lang is unable to attend to the music he is concerned with and hear it for what it is, but that he speaks with ignorance or disregard of the evidence of the twenty-five editions of Gesualdo's music in his own day, and disregard of the evidence of the recorded performances of today—the result being statements that have misled his readers about the music.

Summer 1962

Einstein in Germany reviewed musical events for a Berlin newspaper; but in this country the general public knows him through his books: the *Short History of Music, Greatness in Music, Mozart: His Character, His Work, Music in the Romantic Era*. And these show the scholar to be without the critic's perception. Thus, a few years before my North Carolina correspondent wrote me about the Gesualdo statement, I noted the statements about Berlioz in the *Short History* that showed Einstein to be no more able to hear Berlioz's music for what it was than Gesualdo's. According to Einstein, "the full orchestra was [Berlioz's] principal medium; only very occasionally did he handle smaller musical forces, preoccupied as he was with extreme and gigantic aims"—the implication, entirely incorrect, being that the full orchestra could be, and was for Berlioz, the medium only for extreme and gigantic aims. And Berlioz "forged anew the poetry of *Faust* and *Romeo and Juliet* to his own ends, and monstrous works came forth, half oratorio, half symphony, half lyrical and half dramatic, all blazing with color." From all of which it was evident that Einstein was not reporting what was actually to be heard in the exquisite writing of much of Berlioz's *Faust* and *Romeo*, but merely restating the old colorful legends —the "inherited formulas and catchwords"—about Berlioz in new colorful language.

As for the best-known *Mozart*, in his review of the book Virgil Thomson remarked on "the author's assumption that his undoubted familiarity with the facts of Mozart's life, including his working habits, gives him automatically a true insight into the meaning of Mozart's works." Thomson then cited, as typical, this statement: "And the Little Sonata in B flat major (K.570), dating from February, 1789—perhaps the most completely rounded of them all, the ideal of his piano sonata—also contains counterpoint used humorously in the finale as if in open reference to the secrets of which the work is full." And Thomson

Summer 1962

commented that he found Einstein, in this pontifical obscurity, more secretive than the piece he was talking about. The book is full of similar statements that tell us as little about other works: we get the same flowery chit-chat about the Piano Concerto K.595, for example, but nothing about the exciting happenings that constitute the life a critic would perceive in the development of the first movement. The critic concerned with such life would speak of the musically climactic moment in *The Marriage of Figaro*, the *Contessa, perdono* passage, with its sublimity from which we are eased down to earth again by the solemn octaves of the strings below distant wind chords. But the scholar has nothing to say about it; he is concerned instead with the fact that "in Susanna there is a bit of Columbine left, in Figaro of Arlecchino; that Don Bartolo and Marcellina are pure *buffo* figures. But the Countess? The Count? Cherubino? The tiny roles of Barberina and her father, the gardener Antonio? It took courage to see the *opera buffa* possibilities in this work and to realize them—courage that Mozart and da Ponte can have gathered only from pieces like those of Bertati and Casti." The critic would speak of what makes the minuet movement of the String Quintet K.515 extraordinary—the somber strangeness of the Minuet and the first part of the Trio, the violent intensities of the amazingly dissonant middle part of the Trio; but all that the scholar finds to speak of is that the movement "is more of a *tempo di minuetto*, with a Trio in the subdominant, which itself grows into complete song-form."

Moreover, in view of the contention that the scholar's information is essential to the proper guidance of the public, it should be noted that what this scholar gave the public included misinformation. It was again my North Carolina correspondent * who wrote me that the statements in *Mozart* about Boccherini's

---
* See pages 107-8.

quintets—that they were becoming famous in the late 1760's and must therefore have been known to Mozart in 1770, and that they were really works not for two cellos but, like Mozart's quintets, for two violas—were incorrect; and that the available documentary evidence established the date of composition of Boccherini's first set of quintets as 1771 and the date of publication as 1774, and also established the fact that his quintets were works for two cellos. Einstein's *Mozart* appeared in 1945; already in 1948 the erroneous statement about the Boccherini quintets being really works for two violas was referred to in Homer Ulrich's book on chamber music; later the statement was quoted on the envelopes of the Budapest Quartet recordings of Mozart's quintets; this enabled record-reviewers to refer knowingly to Boccherini's quintets as being really for two violas; and the proliferation will continue, causing increasing numbers of people in years to come to believe something about Boccherini's quintets that isn't true.

Numerous other statements seem to represent a belief on Einstein's part that his having operated with rigorous correlation of statement and evidence in some area of musical scholarship gave him the privilege to operate thereafter without the constraint of this rigorous procedure, but nevertheless with an authority that carried over from the rigorous to the unrigorous operation. Actually, writing informally for the general public rather than formally for scholars, he writes not only, as he says, "with no learned annotations," but with his scholar's discipline relaxed below the requirements even of informal intellectual activity—the requirement of sufficient evidence for a statement even without the learned annotation regarding its source, and the requirement of mere order in succession of statements. In *Greatness in Music* the scholar, writing informally out of the riches of his scholarship, his reading, his philosophical meditations, takes the informality of the occasion as an excuse for shirking the burdensome obligation to integrate the material of each chapter into a clear and coherent progression, the chapters into a unified treatment of the book's subject, and for producing instead a number of causeries such as are given on the lecture circuit—each with an impressive rather than descriptive title, and each a confused clutter to impress minds as pretentious and confused as Einstein's own.

The book on Mozart has more of this clutter of pontifical generalizations and tangential allusions displaying the extensiveness of Einstein's background of knowledge and culture, and also statements that are mere assertion not based on any evidence. An example is the passage about Mozart's

> independence in regard to the new currents that heralded the approach of the nineteenth century, the period of Romanticism whose full flowering he might well have lived to witness. Anything that belonged simply to change or transition did not concern him. He was completely a child of the eighteenth century, perhaps, but also of the twentieth; which is another way of saying that he belonged to the eternity of art, and was in no sense a "forerunner." Beethoven found a great deal in Haydn that he could take as a point of departure, but very little in Mozart. How should one try to continue Mozart's work? It was possible to strive for perfection on another level, and perhaps even to achieve it; but Mozart's perfection could not be surpassed on its own level. With Haydn, on the other hand, one could in many respects compete on his own terms. Now, Mozart lived in the middle of the period of *Sturm und Drang*, the age of "sensibility," the age of Jean-Jacques Rousseau. Mozart never mentions Rousseau, although he composed a *Singspiel* on Rousseau's *Devin du Village*, and he must have heard Rousseau's name often enough in Paris. Presumably he would have had no use for the philosopher and musical amateur of Geneva, whose call "Back to Nature" would have meant very little to him. Mozart was on the side of Voltaire, in spite of the ill-tempered words he pronounced upon the sage of Ferney as an obituary. Voltaire, too, belongs to the eighteenth century and to eternity; and he has the same power of dry and pitiless observation, the same irony, the

Summer 1962

same fierce satire, and the same profound fatalism. Between *Candide* and the G minor Symphony there is a real kinship.

I find in all this no continuity of thought; I hear in the G-minor no kinship with *Candide*; I know no evidence that Mozart was on the side of Voltaire and didn't mean what he wrote about his death.

Nor do I know any evidence for Einstein's statement that Mozart's "deep intuition pierced the cultural tendencies of his time." Indeed, Einstein's mind being as confused as it is, he adds immediately, with no awareness of largely contradicting what he has just said, that "although he had no eye for . . . architecture, sculpture, or painting, he had as a dramatist the finest sense of poetry, both lyric and dramatic." And as evidence that "he must have read a great deal," Einstein describes his library; but it turns out that "whether he actually read all this, nobody knows." However, "we do know that he read Metastasio and Gellert. He also knew Fénélon's *Télémaque* and Tasso's *Aminta*; he found amusement in the tales of *The Thousand and One Nights*; and above all he knew a large part of the boundless Italian libretto literature." In the end Einstein appears to have evidence for a limited statement about what Mozart read, but none for his statement about Mozart's deep intuition into the cultural tendencies of his time.

After all this it is not surprising to find that Einstein was not always rigorous in his scholarly work. A friend told me of being taken to see the manuscript of *Don Giovanni* at the Paris Conservatory by a composer who showed him important changes made by Mozart that Einstein failed to include in his list of such changes in his edition of the work.

As for Lang, his first Sunday article for the *Herald Tribune* in 1954 was a new rewriting of his old attack on the big orchestra, concerned with our continuing "bondage to the times when artists shed their tears before a mirror, gloried in their sorrows

in stentorian tones that shook the decor, were possessed of pathos to overflowing, and in their simulated anger slashed the air with tin swords, whereupon the scared bourgeois had to be humored and reassured with bonbons. . . . As we push toward the new century, the twentieth, the gestures become even more expansive, the passions more violent, the colors more intense. . . ."
This appallingly conceived and phrased stuff was, as I have said, a new restatement of an old position: in *Ecce Criticus* Lang had accused the critics of encouraging "the worship of the big, the long, the ponderous, and the loud" that was a product of the Romantic period. "The musicians of the last century, from Berlioz to Strauss . . . expressed their thoughts by large gestures and used a complicated, at times even enormous, technical apparatus. . . . Today we wonder why musicians of judgment were captivated by orchestral scores which when dispossessed of their tremendous orchestral ornaments show an astonishingly meager invention and vague construction." In this period Brahms was for Lang "the lonely retrospective musician who was trying to save the glory of classical art in a world engulfed in the dramatic frenzy of the Neo-German school"; and his First Symphony was "a work of great merit and beauty, especially great on account of its noble tone, in its hysterical environment."

A perceptive English critic, Martin Cooper, observed that "if you really listen to Berlioz's music, really follow it . . . it is perfectly coherent and alive with the most astonishing vitality"; "for all the richness of his palette . . . Berlioz is not a sensualist"; the four brass bands and eighteen kettledrums of the *Tuba mirum* of the *Requiem* "are used by a mind so completely in the grip of a poetic idea, so absolutely alien to all exploitation of sound for its own sake (the sensualist's music), that the listener's soul and not his nerves are affected." And I would say that someone who really listened to what was to be heard on the one hand in Berlioz's *Romeo and Juliet* and *Harold in Italy*, which don't use the extra brass bands and drums of the *Requiem* but only the normal symphonic orchestra, and on the other hand in Brahms's concertos and First Symphony—such a person would have to write that Berlioz used a large orchestra with economy and finesse, whereas Brahms used it to achieve "the big, the ponderous and the loud," and that the orchestral coloring in Berlioz's writing added to the effectiveness of an invention that was distinguished even without the coloring. But Lang was not such a person: he was no more able to hear Berlioz's and Brahms's music for what they were than he was able to hear Gesualdo's; and he merely repeated the "inherited formulas and catchwords" about them.

The worship of "the big, the ponderous and the loud," said Lang in *Ecce Criticus,* made the public "oblivious of the fundamental approach to an understanding of music—the road of intimate choral music, chamber music, piano music, and songs," performed in the home, as they were originally in past centuries, and not transferred to "a huge auditorium" where the songs were "bellowed . . . by an operatic prima donna intent on bringing down the house," and where music that was originally something people "literally lived with" and "a most personal experience" became instead something "we face . . . as exhibition." Here the scholar was using history not for the public's guidance but for its deprivation. The historical fact that the madrigal for a few voices preceded in time the symphony for large orchestra doesn't make the madrigal rather than the symphony the "fundamental" approach to music (any more than the line drawing rather than the oil painting is the fundamental approach to pictorial art). Nor does the historical fact that a Mozart quartet or a Purcell song was heard originally in a small room mean that it must not be heard today by those who have to hear it in a concert hall (any more than a painting which the original owner lived with in a room of his palace must not be looked at today

Summer 1962

by those who have to see it in a room of a museum). Nor does the fact that it provided "a most personal experience" for someone who heard it in the room mean that it does not provide such an experience for the person who hears it in the concert hall. And the distorted performances in "a huge auditorium" that Lang spoke of were products of his imagination with no resemblance to the actual performances of Elisabeth Rethberg, Elisabeth Schumann and Irmgard Seefried in Town Hall.

Lang, indeed, seems to have shared Einstein's belief that the authority of his rigorous operation on one occasion in some area of musical scholarship carried over thereafter to anything he found to say—even if it did not represent the scrupulous correlation of statement with evidence, and even if it represented only the activity of his imagination. My North Carolina correspondent wrote me about having read on page 829 of *Music in Western Civilization* Lang's statement that Auber's *La Muette de Portici* was a success, and a few pages later the statement that "the modest beginnings of *La Muette* had been forgotten," which had struck him as absurd on the face of it: a successful opera wasn't forgotten in three years. He had therefore looked up the factual record in de Lajarte's *Bibliothèque Musicale du Théâtre de l'Opéra* (1878), which showed *La Muette* to have been continuously in the repertory of the Paris Opera from 1828 to 1854 and to have received 471 performances by 1876.

What Lang could achieve in this way was demonstrated by the article on chamber music that he contributed to a New Friends of Music program booklet. According to Lang, chamber music was reduced in the ninteenth century to "the private affair of a musical minority, a musical élite," which was "able to derive enjoyment from 'absolute' music," while the public musical scene was dominated by the "Bengal light" orchestral sonorities of program music, the music with extramusical meaning that was "dictated" by the new concert hall public "composed of the large mass of the middle classes" who "possessed the necessary general culture but whose musical capabilities could not rise to pure music." Bernard Shaw once described how a philosopher, "having pieced an illusory humanity and art out of the effects produced by his library on his imagination, [could] build some silly systematization of his worthless ideas over the abyss of his own nescience." One could make a similar observation concerning Lang's systematization of inventions about the change in the nineteenth century from an aristocratic public with elevated musical taste that listened to the pure—that is, superior—music for chamber groups, to a middle-class public with low musical taste that "dictated" the composition of impure—that is, inferior—program music for large orchestra.

One must point out in this the long-accepted myth that has converted the eighteenth-century aristocracy of birth and rank into an aristocracy of mind and taste, and the change from the eighteenth-century aristocratic to the nineteenth-century middle-class public into a change from a musically cultivated and enlightened to a musically uncultivated and unenlightened public. Actually, eighteenth-century aristocratic patronage of the arts was part of the ritual of aristocratic existence—a part that was performed by many aristocrats of birth and rank who, if we may believe Mozart, lacked aristocracy of mind and taste; and on the other hand, while the nineteenth-century middle-class audience included people who attended concerts because it was the thing to do, it also included people who attended them because of the enlightened interest in music that was part of their culture.

Another thing to say is that Mozart, as far as I know, didn't consider the pure music of his quartets, symphonies and concertos to be superior to the impure music with extramusical meaning in his operas; and the operas were listened to in the theater by the same people who listened to symphonies and concertos in the concert room and to quartets in their homes.

And in the nineteenth century Schubert and Schumann and Brahms and the other composers who wrote impure music with extramusical meaning in the form of songs and poetic piano pieces didn't consider this music inferior to the pure chamber music they also wrote—the chamber music that was listened to in the concert hall by the same people who performed it or listened to it being performed in their homes, and who listened also to the new orchestral program music. As for the latter, Edwin Denby's observation that "to recognize poetic suggestion through dancing one has to be susceptible to poetic values and susceptible to dance values as well" has its analogy in music: to recognize poetic suggestion through music one has to be susceptible not only to poetic values but to musical values. And the communication of the poetic content of the *Love Scene* and *Queen Mab* Scherzo of Berlioz's *Romeo and Juliet*—pieces "dictated" solely by the poetic stimulation of Berlioz's imagination—was effected through exquisite musical writing that represented in him, and required in his listeners, not only a susceptibility to poetic values, but the same susceptibility to musical values, the same "musical capabilities," as did the exquisite writing in a Mozart or Schubert quartet.

I have discussed only the substance of Lang's writing, allowing the quality of its phraseology to proclaim itself. But what the phraseology can attain to, on an occasion when the professor-turned-journalist unbends in what he thinks of as gaiety, humor and charm, is demonstrated by his review of a performance of Respighi's *The Fountains of Rome*. This is a wholly inconsequential piece of agreeable-sounding tonal scene painting; but for Lang it "conjured up an unforgettable scene of Roman ladies gathering about the fountains with the wash to be done while they chat about the world. One of the signoras brought the socks a faun left one afternoon in the woods, another rinsed a big bundle of dead and transfigured underwear, while a third

Summer 1962 (1964)

struggled with a whole bag of rumpled nightshirts a sorcerer's apprentice soiled while fixing the plumbing. Neither of the ladies had water softener with her, therefore they dumped the clean clothes in a bucket of ninth chords and they came out nice and limp, flat, odorless and tasteless." And the musical perceptions expressed in the metaphors—of the alleged relations of the sections of the piece to Debussy's *The Afternoon of a Faun*, Strauss's *Death and Transfiguration* and Dukas's *The Sorcerer's Apprentice*—are incorrect.

If one judges by Einstein's and Lang's performances, writing about music for the enlightenment of the general public doesn't seem the right activity for musical scholars. As for what that right activity is, it was stated very well on one occasion by Virgil Thomson. To Lang's contention that the musicologists should have the task of teaching music in the colleges, Thomson answered that the thing for the musicologists to do was to teach musicology. [*American Scholar*]

Postscript 1964 I am not sure that even this is something for Lang to do, after the less than a scholar's rigor that he exhibited in his handling—in the *Musical Quarterly* of July 1946—of the *Bombastes Furioso* appendix in the fourth volume of Ernest Newman's *The Life of Richard Wagner*.* In this appendix Newman quoted a paragraph from Carl Engel's review of the third volume, and argued that it showed Engel to be unacquainted with the documentary material on the physicians' certification of King Ludwig's mental derangement in 1886. Lang omitted the Engel paragraph and Newman's comment on it; instead he quoted Newman's description of his own exhaustive study of the documentary material, and then said that as a result of this study Newman "rehabilitates the King, pronounces

* See the article in the *Nation* of 29 March 1947 or the footnotes on pages 352-4 of *Music in the Nation*.

Winter 1963; 27 August 1962

him hale and hearty"—which Newman did *not* do; after which Lang argued at length against the statement he had incorrectly imputed to Newman. Nor was this the only instance of its kind in the Lang piece, which hardly made him seem the predestined person to teach students of musicology at a great university rigor and accuracy in their scholarly activity. And I don't need to say what would happen to a physicist or geneticist who, discussing in a learned journal a piece of work by another physicist or geneticist, indulged in such suppression and misrepresentation of what he wrote about.

Winter 1963; 27 August 1962   In April 1959, in a New York Philharmonic performance of Mozart's Piano Concerto K.491, Glenn Gould kept his playing of the solo part within a dynamic range that didn't go above mezzo forte and that seemed to represent an intention to create an image of the music as it was produced on the piano of Mozart's day. Listening to his more recent performance of the work with the Canadian Broadcasting Company Symphony under Susskind, on Columbia records, and expecting what I heard in 1959, I was surprised to hear instead the exact opposite: the piano part delivered with a bold and powerful sculpturing of phrase, a purposeful energy in every note of fast runs and figurations, a sustained tension and momentum, that I had never before heard in the playing of this music, and that made it one of the greatest performances I have ever heard. It is, I must add, a performance flawed by two familiar practices of Gould's for which his reasons, as I apprehend them from his accompanying notes, seem to me wrong. The "chromatic fugal manner" employing both hands, in which Mozart writes the variation for piano alone in the finale, Gould considers the proper way of employing the pianist and his instrument; whereas the left-hand accompaniments of right-hand melody in Mozart's more usual homophonic writing sound to Gould like "unrealized continuos." This leads him to play the homophonic writing sometimes as though it were contrapuntal, and to produce the left hand's thumping out of unimportant Alberti basses, its expressive treatment of unmelodic accompaniment material as though it were melody, even to the point of making it predominate over the actual melody of the right hand. And the desire to activate the left hand may also be responsible for the arpeggiating of what Mozart writes and intends as solid chords, the inserting of such arpeggiated chords where he writes single notes. This all seems to me wrong: Mozart's homophonic writing is not unrealized contrapuntal writing; and the practices with which Gould attempts to make it contrapuntal flaw his performance.

Gould's notes make it clear that the oddities and perversities that have appeared in his performances as far back as the recorded Beethoven Sonata Op. 109, and that presumably will continue to appear in them in what one hopes will be many years to come, represent carefully thought-out purpose. One is free to decide that the thought is mistaken, and that its result in the performance is a defect; but one must consider these things in their context: one must not fail to see that the mistaken ideas are those of someone with possibly the most remarkable and exciting musical intelligence operating in musical performance today, and that the defects occur in the course of playing which attains overwhelming greatness. One may, that is, dissent with respect; but one may not jeer and sneer as Harold C. Schonberg did in his *Times* review of Gould's eccentrically paced performance of the Brahms D-minor Concerto—a review unprecedented in the ostentatious vulgarity of its writing and offensiveness of its content: "Between you, me and the corner lamppost, Ossip, maybe the reason he plays it so slow is maybe his technique is not so good." [*Yale Review; New Republic*]

Winter 1963 After a few experiences in Philharmonic Hall it was a relief and a pleasure to hear again the normal sound of music in a normal concert hall. Actually what I heard was the exceptional sound of the Philadelphia Orchestra in Carnegie Hall, at the first of a special series of concerts of this orchestra presented by the Carnegie Hall Corporation. And actually I was there because of my interest in Klemperer's performances of Beethoven's *Pastoral* and *Eroica* Symphonies. There has been in England recently the same excitement about Klemperer, and specifically about his performances of Beethoven, as there used to be about Toscanini, with talk of the similarity of Klemperer's operation to Toscanini's in its strict obedience to the letter of the score, and the consequent similarity of Klemperer's performances to Toscanini's in authenticity and effectiveness. This talk was contradicted by the performances I heard in Carnegie Hall. It is true that Klemperer, like Toscanini, had the orchestra play with strict obedience to Beethoven's every direction for loud and soft, for crescendo and decrescendo, for legato and staccato. But he did not exact from the orchestra the obedience Toscanini exacted to Beethoven's directions for tempo. The English writer Spike Hughes reports in his book, *The Toscanini Legacy*, that at the rehearsal of the *Eroica* in London in 1937 Toscanini stopped the orchestra after the first few moments and shouted: "Is not Napoleon! Is not Hitler! Is not Mussolini! Is *Allegro con brio!*" And an NBC musician told me of his stopping the orchestra in the second movement to say: "You play *funebre*; I want *marcia*." His concern for the meaning of the words was of course a concern for the expressive character of the music that dictated the words; and it produced a performance of the *Pas-*

toral in which each movement had the lilting flow called for not only by the directions *Allegro ma non troppo, Andante molto moto* and so on, but by the character of the movement, a performance of the *Eroica* with the energy, the tension and intensity this work calls for. Whereas Klemperer's disregard of Beethoven's directions and the character of the music produced strange slow-motion performances which made the *Pastoral* graceless, the *Eroica* nerveless. But these somnolent performances excited the audience in Carnegie Hall to cheers.

The opening of the first building of Lincoln Center was the occasion for a *Times* supplement that included an article by Virgil Thomson on opera in America, in which he wrote that our composers have been unable to satisfy the public's interest with viable works because they haven't been taught to deal with the specifically operatic problems of choosing a text with suitable verbal and dramatic values and of writing for the English language and for the human voice. But I would say the composers have exhibited these deficiencies in addition to the primary one that Thomson didn't mention. A composer of good opera must be first of all a composer of good music, and the writing he adapts to words and voices must be worth listening to for its intrinsic quality. It was such music that made Thomson's *The Mother of Us All* and Copland's *The Tender Land* works which deserved the places in its repertory that the New York City Opera persists in not giving them. And it is their lack of such music that has been the important deficiency of the works of Carlisle Floyd, Douglas Moore, Vittorio Giannini and the rest that the company has wasted productions on. Later in his article Thomson wrote that "with every composer in the country writing operas and every house ... producing them, the mere volume of this effort will give birth to a 'school' "; and "if this happens, quality will develop automatically; it always does." But again I must point out that it does, and will, only if the members of the school have the powers as composers that Floyd, Moore and Giannini lack.

For the *New Yorker's* Winthrop Sargeant the quality has already been achieved in notable degree in those works of Floyd, Moore and Giannini; and not only quality but interesting growth, which was shown last year in Moore's *The Wings of the Dove*, one of "the strongest and most effective new operas produced anywhere in many decades," and this year in Floyd's *The Passion of Jonathan Wade*, a "musically quite inspired work" by one of "the most gifted of America's younger operatic composers." One can understand that all this would be heard by a critic who hears in Stravinsky's *Le Sacre du Printemps* a mere famous musical conversation piece that is beginning to sound dated, but hears a great opera in Montemezzi's *L'Amore dei Tre Re* and "the closest thing to a great work of art that has appeared in music during the past generation" in Shostakovitch's *Leningrad* Symphony. But what actually was to be heard in Moore's attempt at something more sophisticated than the simple inanities of *The Ballad of Baby Doe* was the painfully feeble results achieved with more inept use of more elaborate means; and this is true also of Floyd's attempts at something more advanced than *Susannah:* his *Wuthering Heights* two or three years ago, and *The Passion of Jonathan Wade*, produced by the New York City Opera last fall. This work exhibited the deficiencies of text (Floyd's own) and of writing for the voice that Virgil Thomson spoke of; but the cruelly prolonged screaming in her highest range that Phyllis Curtin was required to do several times was not just bad writing for the voice: it was bad music, the result of an attempt at expressive intensity that failed abysmally. And the work was a series of such attempts and failures—concerning which I must report however that every attempt which failed for me succeeded for the enthusiastically applauding audience in City Center. [*Hudson Review*]

Winter 1963

Winter 1963 Much of what Stravinsky, talking ostensibly in answer to questions of Robert Craft, has to say in his three volumes of conversations *—about music, about the now historic artistic events he observed or was involved in, about the famous persons who were involved in them with him—is fascinating, revealing him as one of the artists who are perceptive and articulate about their art, and as the possessor of a powerful mind that tends to go in unexpected directions, a sharp eye for human character and behavior, a grim sense of humor, a gift of pungent statement. Thus, jazz "has nothing to do with composed music and when it seeks to be influenced by contemporary music it isn't jazz and it isn't good." Or, "Translation changes the character of a [musical] work and destroys its cultural unity." Or, "Rimsky's Meyerbeerization of Musorgsky's 'technically imperfect' music could no longer be tolerated." Or, "I would like to admit all Strauss operas to whichever purgatory punishes triumphant banality." Or a composer's "good intentions have got to be paved with Hell." Or Nijinsky's face "could become the most powerful actor's mask I have ever seen, and as Petrushka he was the most exciting human being I have ever seen on the stage."

But reading Stravinsky's statement that Nijinsky's choreography for *Le Sacre du Printemps* was unsuited to the music and represented Nijinsky's ignorance of music and of its proper relation to movement, one remembers that it is contradicted by what Emile Vuillermoz, Jacques Rivière and André Levinson wrote at the time about Nijinsky's achievement. And it may be that the composer could see only "rhythmic chaos" where the critic—in this instance Levinson—saw that "in their simplified gymnastics the dancers express the respective duration and force of the sounds; they bend their knees and straighten them again, they raise their heels and fall back on them, they stamp in place, in-

---

* *Conversations with Igor Stravinsky, Memories and Commentaries,* and *Expositions and Developments,* by Igor Stravinsky and Robert Craft.

sistently marking the accented notes. . . . An all-powerful constraint dominates them, disjoints their limbs, lies heavy on the necks of their bent heads." There is no way of knowing today whether Stravinsky or Levinson is right about Nijinsky's *Sacre*; and I cite the disagreement merely to illustrate the important fact that Stravinsky, looking through the lenses of his practice, his attitudes, his interests of a doer in his art, often sees something the non-doer does not see.

Thus, for Stravinsky as a doer his recent *Movements* is made interesting and valuable by the doing in it—by the fact that "every aspect of the composition was guided by serial forms, the sixes, the quadrilaterals, triangles, etc. The fifth movement . . . uses a construction of twelve verticals. The gamma and delta hexachords in this movement are more important than the A and B, too. Five orders are rotated instead of four, with six alternates for each of the five, while, at the same time, the six work in all directions, as though through a crystal." All this, for him, makes *Movements* as interesting and valuable as the doing in *Le Baiser de la Fée* makes that piece; and there are other people, certainly, who feel the same. "When I compose something I use the language of music, and my statement in my grammar will be clear to the musician who has followed music up to where my contemporaries and I have brought it"; and certainly, for those who have been able to follow music to that point, the doing in *Movements* makes it as interesting and valuable as the doing in *Le Baiser* makes that piece, and Stravinsky's description of it is as intelligible as the piece itself. But certainly these people are few; and for the majority of non-doing listeners who have not been able to follow music to where Stravinsky and his contemporaries have brought it, *Movements* makes no musical sense and Stravinsky's description of its construction is equally unintelligible. And this is true of the other recent and contemporary works that Stravinsky talks about in these volumes.

Nor is it only new music that Stravinsky looks at through those lenses that cause him to see what the non-doer does not see. His doer's interest in the manner of doing, and his own practice in doing, cause him to hear that "Berlioz's basses are sometimes uncertain and the inner harmonic voices unclear. The problem of orchestral distribution is therefore insurmountable, and balance is regulated superficially, by dynamics"—a defect for Stravinsky, whose practice is to write intrinsic and automatic balance into the scoring.* But the basses, the inner harmonic voices, the orchestral balance regulated by dynamics don't trouble the non-doer listening to Berlioz's music. Nor is he troubled by what makes the first movement of Beethoven's Ninth, for Stravinsky, "a late and terrible example" of Beethoven's frequent lapses into banality: "such quadrilateral phrase-building and pedantic development (of Bars 387-400), such poor rhythmic invention . . . , and such patently false pathos."

So with performance. For a composer of new music the only good performers are the few who "have attained new instrumental and musical powers through their performances of new music"; and Boulez and Maderna, because as composers they have performed new music, are "the conductors today who have most advanced the techniques of conducting (communication between musicians)." Indeed, their involvement with new music makes composers the most interesting conductors of any music, "for the reason that they are the only ones who can have a really new insight into music itself"; and for Stravinsky with his interest in the composer's doing there is another reason for finding composers—for example Mahler—to be the best conductors even of older music: their performances exhibit the understanding of

* But I heard Stravinsky, at a rehearsal of *Le Baiser de la Fée*, say to the Boston Symphony basses: "Stronger. You are covered by the trombones, but I don't want to touch the trombones," and repeat the passage, in which now the basses were not covered by the untouched trombones.

the way music is put together, which conductors who are only conductors don't have.

One thinks of Toscanini's beautifully articulated performances of Beethoven that were achieved without the new powers and insights derived from new music; but Stravinsky reports hearing in the recorded performance of Beethoven's First that Toscanini's *allegro* for the first movement was "an absurdly fast Rossini-like tempo that obliterated phrase accents and articulations"; and "Toscanini's ambition throughout the movement seems to have been to create climaxes, whether or not they coincided with Beethoven's own climaxes and, especially, Beethoven's own scale of climax. The second movement was also badly played. At one place in the development section the strings performed strict thirty-second notes after dotted notes. Then, a few bars later, the winds doubly shortened these thirty-seconds (as indeed they were right so to do). The strings, hearing themselves corrected, followed suit in the next statement of this rhythm. But can Toscanini have failed to hear such a thing? In any case, he did not hear that the *ritardando* he applied to the beginning of the recapitulation was insufferably gross." This caused me to listen again to the performance on RCA Victor LM-6009 or 6901, in which I heard that the tempo of the first movement was suited to the character of the music and not too fast for the phrase accents and articulations to be all clearly audible, and that the climaxes were the ones in Beethoven's score and in right scale. As for the second movement, I found a passage such as Stravinsky describes not in the development section but in measures 42-49 of the exposition; and what became clear was not only the fact that Toscanini had instructed the winds and strings to shorten the thirty-seconds and thus to sharpen the rhythm in the second four measures, but his reason for so instructing them (which it is astonishing that Stravinsky didn't perceive): the energetic character of those four measures, marked *f*, as against the quiet first four, marked *p*. And I heard no *ritardando* at the beginning of the recapitulation.

And so with criticism, which Stravinsky not only comments on briefly in the earlier volumes but devotes an appendix to in the latest volume. Critics are incompetent because "they do not see how a musical phrase is constructed, do not know how music is written; they are incompetent in the technique of the contemporary musical language." That is, competence in writing about music, for Stravinsky, consists in knowing what the contemporary composer knows; and he suggests in the appendix that the composers oppose to the ignorance of "the journalist-reviewer pest" a new magazine that will be "a composers'—i.e. a professional—review." But what criticism calls for is not the knowledge of the composer, the doer, the insider, but rather the perception, the judgment, the taste of the non-doer, the outsider —i.e. the listener. And what the composer writes as a doer, an insider, is likely to be intelligible, interesting and valid for other composers and a few performers and listeners who share his special interest and viewpoint, but not for the majority of non-professional listeners for whom the critic writes as a professional listener. We have seen that some of Stravinsky's writing in these volumes provides an illustration of this; and I have found another in a few articles a reader sent me that were written by the new critic of the *Nation*, a composer named Benjamin Boretz. Whether he discusses contemporary works, or old works and their performances—the weaknesses of Schubert's C-major Symphony, with respect to which Furtwängler's recorded performance is good; the strengths of Beethoven's Eighth, with respect to which Wallenstein's concert performance was bad; the characteristics of Mendelssohn's writing, with respect to which several Klemperer performances are exemplary—my experience of what he is talking about (including a new look at the Schubert and Beethoven scores) doesn't enable me to recognize what he describes in the music or to accept his evaluations of the performances. And I would suppose that his *Nation* readers got no more from the writing than I.

And actually what makes the two critics whom Stravinsky denounces in his appendix contemptible is not their lack of the composer's knowledge he thinks necessary, but initially their deficiencies of critical perception, judgment and taste. In Winthrop Sargeant's writing these deficiencies appear not in his rejection of Stravinsky's recent works but in his boredom with the earlier Stravinsky works that are twentieth-century classics, and on the other hand in his enthusiasm over Menotti, Giannini, Carlisle Floyd and Douglas Moore. And I call these deficiencies initial because Sargeant exhibits others in addition—among them a lack of intellectual rigor. His mind has developed enormous proficiency in coming up with whatever will achieve momentary advantage or escape momentary difficulty in a discussion; so that when Stravinsky attacks him with the statement that "[Sargeant's] giants are Giannini, Jello Doio, Gian Carlo, etc.; his dwarfs are Schönberg and myself," Sargeant's way of parrying this is to assure Stravinsky that he "does not find the present world of musical composition to be generally populated by giants, and he regards Mr. Stravinsky, by comparison with his contemporaries, as a giant of a pretty fair stature"—under cover of which he says nothing about his overestimation of Menotti, Giannini and the rest. This is for readers of the *New Yorker* of March 3, who he must hope will not see the April issue of *Show*, with an article written some months earlier in which Sargeant describes Stravinsky as one who covers his "lack of creative capacity" with his "master[y] of the artificialities of music," such as orchestration, and predicts that the only works that are likely to survive are things like *Pulcinella* and *Le Baiser de la Fée*, "largely because the[ir] basic inspiration ... is not Stravinsky's own. They are ... Stravinsky orchestrations of music written in the style of others."

For Sargeant "even that most famous of all musical conversation pieces, 'Le Sacre du Printemps,' is beginning to sound dated." (*Petrushka* apparently isn't even worth mentioning; and the deficiency even in mere perception appears in the fact that listening to *Le Baiser de la Fée*—in which one hears the Stravinsky mind in characteristic operation on the Tchaikovsky fragments that it transforms and fits together with materials of his own—Sargeant hears only a "Stravinsky orchestration of music written in the style of [Tchaikovsky].")

As for Paul Henry Lang, this man who is confident of the critical powers that he believes, erroneously, only a scholar's knowledge can provide is actually unperceptive enough to hear that "Stravinsky . . . is not the best conductor of his own works," and ignorant enough to add that in the performance of *Movements* "the top-notch musicians . . . needed only the first beat to make their own way"—which Stravinsky rightly calls vicious nonsense, pointing out that "no orchestra in the world can make 'its own way' through even five measures of my *Movements* . . . and only a very skillful conductor can manage the piece at all." And Lang's deficiencies in judgment and taste are evident in, among other things, the statements about Gesualdo that create, in Stravinsky's words, "the mystery of how anyone with even rudimentary musical background could write so stupidly about such obvious questions." Moreover, with Lang too there are additional deficiencies. For one thing there is the confusion of mind that expressed itself with characteristic aggressiveness in the outpouring of incoherent pontifical pronouncement that was Lang's review of the first volume of the Stravinsky-Craft conversations. Stravinsky replies to some of the statements in the review with understandable fury, but he is strangely silent about one which—in the light of what we know about Stravinsky—was not only grotesquely improbable but highly offensive: the contention, which Lang kept repeating without once citing an example, that in these conversations Stravinsky was little more than a ventriloquist's dummy speaking what a sinister Robert Craft contrived, with his loaded questions, to get him to speak.* And in Lang's review there were also the atrocious writing and the personal nastiness that Stravinsky speaks of as things that make Lang worse than Sargeant.

It has been interesting, finally, to observe the reactions to the appendix on criticism. For it wasn't only Lang who, professedly "more in sorrow than in anger," deplored it as "unworthy of a great artist." Even Arthur Berger, a devoted admirer of Stravinsky, feared "that attention may be deflected from the really illuminating passages" of the book by "a sensational attack" which he referred to also as a "descent into polemic." Both men were speaking out of an experience in which no composer had

---

* Just as the appendix was not Stravinsky's reaction merely to "the most temperate dissent by a critic," as Lang contended in his reply in the *Herald Tribune* of March 11, so Stravinsky's enraged telegram to the paper after Lang's review of *The Flood* in June was his reaction to Lang's continuing offensive statements about Stravinsky's association with Craft. Thus, in his March 11 article Lang wrote: "In a special appendix, Mr. Stravinsky and/or Mr. Craft (by now the collaboration has reached a stage where Mr. Stravinsky should use the business designation 'A Division of Craft Products Inc.') launches a hysterical attack etc." In this article Lang deplored Stravinsky's insulting garbling of his name in the appendix, but himself referred to Stravinsky's "amanuensis, Robert Anton Schindler Craft," who put to "the great composer . . . questions, some straight, some leading, some loaded," and whom Lang described as "the 'ventriloquist of God' "—one who "makes Mr. Stravinsky concern himself with matters a great composer should leave to his musical accountants." That "makes" continued the view of Craft as dominating Stravinsky and being the real author of their books—the view that appeared again in Lang's concluding sentence: "I am afraid that when these controversial volumes are finished we may discover that what protrudes from Mr. Craft's head is not Mephistophelian horns, as once suspected, but donkey's ears." And in his review of *The Flood* Lang's offensiveness reached a climax in his references to "the direction of the venerable maestro himself and his amanuensis, librettist, and *valet de chambre*, Robert Craft." It was the personal nastiness in all this that elicited the rage in Stravinsky's telegram to the editor of the *Herald Tribune*, and the phrase which described the review as "suppurating with gratuitous malice."

ever done anything of this kind, and it had therefore come to be considered not a proper thing for a composer—or for anyone else—to do. Many years ago Bernard Shaw contended that "musical criticisms, like sermons, are of low average quality simply because they are never discussed or contradicted," and advocated setting up a "vigilance committee of musicians for the exposure of incompetent critics"; but musicians continued to be silent. And, as the Strauss-Hofmannsthal correspondence* shows, this was not because the occasion and desire to speak were lacking.

To those who value the operas Strauss composed to the librettos of Hofmannsthal, the correspondence is interesting mostly for what it reveals of the joint operation that produced those works. But to those who care nothing about the operas, the correspondence is fascinating for what it reveals about the two men, for what they say about the greats of their time—e.g. Bruno Walter, Max Reinhardt, Diaghilev, Nijinsky—with whom their activities involved them, and for what they report of the private operations in their world of artistic creation—the maneuvering with and about royal ministers, directors of the royal opera companies, conductors, singers, designers—that led up to what in the end was presented to the public in the opera house. And one of the objects of the maneuvering is the press—the "stupid, uncomprehending Berlin press" that Strauss refers to, the "newspaper louts" and "*canaille*" that Hofmannsthal speaks of. Quite possibly they would feel angry contempt even for a competent and disinterested critic who scrupulously considered nothing beyond the work that was presented to him but who reported that he didn't like it. But some of the critics they hate are *not* competent, disinterested and scrupulous: the powerful Julius Korngold of the Vienna *Neue Freie Presse* not only was a pompously

* A *Working Friendship: the Correspondence between Richard Strauss and Hugo von Hofmannsthal*, translated by Hanns Hammelmann and Ewald Osers.

stupid critic but shamelessly misused his position in the interest of his composer son—one such misuse being his campaign against Strauss as co-director and principal conductor of the Vienna Opera. Such stupidity and unscrupulousness are no less a proper subject of discussion when they appear in criticism than when they appear anywhere else; and certainly their victims are entitled to speak out about them; but although Strauss exclaims indignantly once: "Must one really take all this nonsense lying down?" he and Hofmannsthal speak about it only in private and are silent in public. With the Vienna première of their version of *Le Bourgeois Gentilhomme* at hand, Hofmannsthal writes of Korngold's "systematic campaign to undermine every single thing you do and so eventually poison your existence in Vienna and drive you away," and fears that he "might easily turn the scale against a work so delicate and unusual as this Molière with your music." But he attempts only a private maneuver: he tries to persuade the *Neue Freie Presse* that the work calls for review by the drama critic as well as the music critic, calculating that if the drama critic writes about the dramatic aspect Korngold will be unable "to discredit, in his perfidious way, the whole piece through an attack on the libretto (not, at first sight, directed against you [Strauss] at all), and so to destroy its success in the theatre." And the reason for the public silence comes out in the letter in which Hofmannsthal advises Strauss, who is considering an open break with the Munich Court Opera, not to get into a "theatre quarrel—where regrettably the artist has always, always the worst of it against the officials," or into a "newspaper squabble in which by virtue merely of their office the officials must inevitably prevail." That is, in a dispute with a critic it would again be the critic who by virtue of his office—i.e. his control of the printed page—would prevail in this instance and be able to take his revenge on the next work.

Fear, then, has imposed public silence on the composers and

Summer 1963; 30 November 1963

performers who have raged in private over what they have endured at the hands of horrors like Henry Krehbiel, Olin Downes, Noel Straus, Jerome Bohm, Irving Kolodin, and now Harold Schonberg and Lang. And Stravinsky has acted with unprecedented courage. Probably he too would denounce even a competent and scrupulous critic who liked *Le Baiser de la Fée* and disliked *Movements*. But he isn't angered only by the criticisms of his own works; and the critics he denounces—Sargeant for his writing about Menotti and the rest; Lang for his writing about Gesualdo and for his personal nastiness—he is right in denouncing. His action deserves the gratitude of his fellow musicians and the admiration of all of us. [*Hudson Review*]

Postscript 1964 The diary in *Dialogues and a Diary*, the fourth volume of Stravinsky-Craft conversations, is Craft's, concerned with his travels with Stravinsky, including the return to Russia in 1962. Its ironically, irreverently and amusingly perceptive writing, light and deft in style, is in striking contrast to the grim and sardonic statements attributed to Stravinsky in the conversations, and provides conclusive proof that those statements are Stravinsky's own and not, as Lang contended, Craft's spoken through a ventriloquist's dummy named Stravinsky.

Summer 1963; 30 November 1963 It was understandable that when Cliburn returned from Russia in 1958 he should have repeated here the Tchaikovsky and Rachmaninov concertos with which he had triumphed in Moscow. But he made a great mistake in not repeating in addition the recital which—with its performances of a Mozart sonata and the Chopin Fantaisie—also had contributed to his triumph. For if he had done this he would have established at once the musical competence which

Summer 1963; 30 November 1963

enabled him to play Mozart effectively as well as Tchaikovsky and Rachmaninov; and there would have been nothing to give the reviewers the idea that he had mastered the flamboyantly romantic style of the two Russians but needed to learn how to play other music—the idea in which they have persisted ever since, in the face of the actual beautiful performances of this music that he has presented to their ears.

One of these was the performance of Mozart's Concerto K.503 with the New York Philharmonic in 1959, which, though I didn't hear it, I felt certain had exhibited the operation of the musical taste and competence I had heard operating in the Tchaikovsky and Rachmaninov concertos. My belief was confirmed at the time by a member of the Philadelphia Orchestra, who told me about Cliburn's beautiful playing in the Mozart work when he had rehearsed it with that orchestra for his own pleasure. And it was confirmed recently by what I was at last able to hear for myself when he played it with the Symphony of the Air under Wallenstein. The piano's very first reply to the orchestra exhibited a perfection of enunciation of musical phrase that continued to be heard in the piano's every statement thereafter; and one was moved not only by the extraordinary musical powers that one heard operating in this realization of the work, but by the way they were being exercised—the simple directness of their application to the task by this quietly, raptly concentrated youngster as though he were only—to borrow Stravinsky's phrase—the vessel through which Mozart's concerto was passing. And the risks he took in playing so unspectacular a work in so unspectacular a manner were demonstrated by the statement of a minor *Times* know-nothing that "his Mozart was so tame and relatively uninteresting that one wondered what had become of the great talent." [*Hudson Review; New Republic*]

17 August 1963

17 August 1963 When Britten's *War Requiem* was performed for the first time at the consecration of the new Coventry Cathedral in May 1962, the occasion received the kind and amount of attention in the press, here as well as in England, that in the past has been given to the première of a major work of Stravinsky; and the English reviews gave the impression that Britten's new piece was an achievement of that magnitude. One knew that English reviewers overestimated English composers; but Britten's impressive talent was something Americans had had opportunities to confirm for themselves. One knew also that the talent was an extraordinarily resourceful craftsmanship which could operate in the place of, and in the guise of, creativity, producing for *The Rape of Lucretia* years ago a hubbub that was a mere going through the motions of musical activity, and for the more recent *The Turn of the Screw* "modern"-style vocal and instrumental sounds with no expressive relation to the words and action and no attractiveness or interest in themselves. But one knew on the other hand that for *Peter Grimes* and *Albert Herring* he had applied himself to the task of real invention for the situation, sometimes with brilliantly successful results; and that for *A Midsummer Night's Dream*, given by the New York City Opera last spring, he had again provided music which established the atmosphere of the scenes and heightened the expressiveness of the words.

This was the reason for the interest with which I began to listen to the performance of the *War Requiem* conducted by Britten himself on London records, and for my excitement when I heard the superbly effective invention for the opening—the powerful two-note phrases of the orchestra to which the chorus sang "*Requiem aeternam dona eis.*" It seemed that the occasion had impelled Britten to unusual effort, with results which the English reviewers had been right in pronouncing the best he had

17 August 1963

ever achieved. But then the boys' chorus entered with writing for *"Te decet hymnus"* that said nothing at all; and the solo tenor, with writing that did no more for Wilfred Owen's poem *What passing-bells for these who die as cattle*. And thereafter there was the same alternation of now and then a passage of impressively effective writing, and more often a passage that was a mere resourceful craftsman's spinning of notes.

A press build-up of George Szell—including articles in the news magazines and elsewhere that are essentially publicity stories with built-in critical praise—is going on, similar to the one of Leonard Bernstein that preceded his appointment to the New York Philharmonic; and it gives credibility to the rumor that Szell will be taking over the Philharmonic in a couple of years. The Bernstein build-up included an article in *Harper's* by Harold Schonberg, who more recently has been pointing out the Bernstein limitations and deficiencies that were just as evident then; and if Szell does become conductor of the Philharmonic we may begin to read about the limitations and deficiencies of his that are evident today. Szell's strength, like Reiner's, is technical, revealing itself in the precision and beautiful tone with which he can get an orchestra to play; his weakness, like Reiner's, is musical, revealing itself in defects in the pacing and shaping of the work the orchestra is playing. The strength has made the Cleveland Orchestra a superb instrument; the weakness has produced stiff, insensitive, hard-driven performances of the German classical repertory from Haydn through Schubert; but Szell has operated effectively with modern works—for example in the Strauss *Don Quixote* on Epic records. [*New Republic*]

28 September 1963; Winter 1964

28 September 1963; Winter 1964 Perhaps the most outrageous of the silly inventions in the Marsh book on Toscanini * was the statement that works he played many times "had all the life played out of them," so that the performances were mechanically perfect but without meaning. Those who speak out of knowledge—musicians of the New York Philharmonic and NBC Symphony—invariably recall how moving and inspiring it was that to the very end Toscanini's return to a work he had played innumerable times was never a mere repetition of the performance the year or years before, as it might have been, but always an occasion for new study of the score that brought him to the rehearsal with new insights and new details in place of what he now deplored as earlier mistakes. Confirmation of this can be heard in Victor recordings of works he recorded more than once: one would think that by the time he recorded Mozart's *Haffner* Symphony in 1929, Rossini's *Semiramide* Overture

---

* Marsh's original announced purpose was merely to comment on the entire series of Toscanini's recorded performances—on the character of the performances themselves, and on the fidelity with which they were reproduced. And his actual comments on these in the completed book were those of someone who could hear that the Prelude to Act 1 of *Die Meistersinger* on Victor 11-9385 was slower and more relaxed than the one on the later LM-6020, which in fact was merely the LP transfer of the earlier one; and who on the other hand—encountering at No. 48 in the second movement of the recorded Debussy *Ibéria* a spliced-in passage whose sound was strikingly less bright, clear, solid and spacious than the sound before and after it—reported that the splicing "was expertly done and cannot be heard." But the title of the completed book—*Toscanini and the Art of Orchestral Performance*—indicates the grandiose thing it developed into; and in view of the rubbish Marsh wrote about the recorded performances he knew at first-hand, it is hardly likely that he would have produced anything better about Toscanini's personality and character if he had ever talked to him, or about Toscanini's powers, method of operation, and achievements as conductor and musician if he had observed him at working rehearsals. Actually, writing without such first-hand knowledge, and putting together what an unrigorous mind picked up indiscriminately from reading or talking with others—most of whom had learned what they wrote or said in the same way as he—Marsh produced even more inaccurate rubbish on these matters than on the recorded performances.

28 September 1963; Winter 1964

in 1936, Beethoven's *Eroica* in 1939, he would have attained final conceptions of them; but the 1946 *Haffner*, 1951 *Semiramide* and 1949 and 1953 *Eroica*'s are remarkably changed in ways that illustrate the change in his performing style—from the earlier expansive style that articulated structure with much elasticity of tempo, and that inflected phrase with much sharply outlined detail, to the later simplified style that involved only slight modification of tempo and subtle inflection of phrase.

What these Victor recordings demonstrate in addition is that although Toscanini continued to produce great perfomances in his later years, he produced greater ones earlier—in his last years with the New York Philharmonic and first years with the NBC Symphony. Not only is the powerfully expansive introduction of the 1936 *Semiramide*, with its sharply outlined inflection of phrase, more effective than the simplified, swifter, tauter 1951 introduction, but the Allegro exhibits in 1936—even in the violins' first quiet statements of the principal theme, and later in their recitative-like phrases leading to the recapitulation of that theme—an extraordinary energy it doesn't have in 1951. And the rebroadcasting of the 1937–38 and 1938–39 NBC Symphony broadcasts by FM stations in New York, Washington and Boston last year provided an opportunity to hear many more of the earlier performances and to discover how different they were from the later ones, and how much more effective and exciting, in their expansive style and their energy. I should add that in the matter of style one discovered also one couldn't take Toscanini for granted: knowing only the *Eroica*'s on Victor records, one had thought the line of development to have been from the powerfully expansive 1939 performance to the simplified ones of 1949 and 1953; but listening to the 2 December 1938 broadcast last year one was amazed to discover that Toscanini had given the finest of his simplified *Eroica*'s a year before the 1939 performance. As for the energy, I should point out its relation to

28 September 1963; Winter 1964

the new situation in which Toscanini found himself. After a lifetime of conducting orchestras made up predominantly of middle-aged men with years of orchestral experience, Toscanini, in December 1937, found himself conducting an orchestra made up largely of young men—notably the large number of brilliant young string-players who had been induced to leave the concert stage and positions in string quartets for membership in the group within the NBC staff orchestra that was to play under him as the NBC Symphony. Their outstanding talent, their youthful vitality and capacity for warm response to the stimulus of greatness, not killed by years of playing in orchestras under ordinary conductors—these were something new for him, which delighted and stimulated him; and the players in turn were delighted and stimulated by his unique powers, magnetism and dedication—to the point of exceeding what they knew to be their highest capacities ("I don't play that good," was the comment of one wind-player after listening to a recorded performance). The mutual stimulation produced playing which didn't exhibit the beautifully blended tone the orchestra had after years of playing with him, but did exhibit the breathtaking energy and fire that the performances of the fifties, however marvelous in other ways, no longer had.

And now we have a major addition to the documentation of this early period: the performance of Schubert's Symphony No. 9 that Toscanini recorded with the Philadelphia Orchestra in November 1941, which Victor has issued at last on LD-2663. The work was very dear to him: he played it at his very first orchestral concert in 1896, the last subscription concert of his final season with the New York Philharmonic in 1936, his second broadcast with the NBC Symphony in 1938, the first of his 1941-42 concerts with the Philadelphia Orchestra, and an NBC broadcast a year before his retirement. And his performance—which realized the work's sustained tension, momentum and

28 September 1963; Winter 1964

grandeur as no other did—was one of his greatest achievements. But like all his performances it changed in the course of time; and whereas we have had until now, on LM-1835, the great 1953 performance, with its first movement that is a superbly effective example of his later practice of setting a tempo which he can maintain with only slight modification, now we have the greater 1941 performance, with its first movement that is one of the finest examples of his earlier practice of articulating and organizing a movement with changes of tempo, including an acceleration in the coda to a pace which binds the overlapping statements of winds, then violins, then low strings into a single magnificent large-spanned utterance. In the second movement also the alternating section in major is made more effective by richer detail of more sharply outlining inflection, and the catastrophe, later, by the slightly slower pace of the build-up, the slight broadening of the climax that breaks off into momentary silence, and the slower pace and richer inflection of the cello melody after the silence. But the earlier style produces its most extraordinary result in the coda of the finale: in 1953 the coda continues without change in its accelerated tempo; but in 1941, after its exciting accelerated build-up to a climactic statement, it slows down repeatedly for a distention of the four unison C's which makes them tremendous and creates a tension that is released each time in the answering tutti in fast tempo again. As a result the 1941 performance has a climactic force at this point of final summation which the 1953 does not have, and which—added to everything else—makes it the greatest of the Toscanini statements of the work known to us.*

[*New Republic; Yale Review*]

* In addition to the performances on Victor records, the 1936 performance with the Philharmonic and the 1938 performance with the NBC Symphony are known through air checks; and they reveal that Toscanini didn't distend the four unison C's at all in 1936, and that he distended them a little in 1938, increased the distention in 1941, and eliminated it in 1953.

Autumn 1963 A lot of talent, work and money was wasted on the televised production of Menotti's newest opera, *Labyrinth*, by NBC Opera Theater, which had commissioned it (and was similarly responsible for the earlier *Maria Golovin* and *Amahl and the Night Visitors*). The libretto of *Labyrinth* was the usual Menotti weirdie, concerned this time with what happened to a bride and groom wandering about in the corridors of a "grand hotel" in an unsuccessful search for their room, but with the difference this time that it came with new intellectual pretensions: before the performance we had Menotti himself, formerly content to deal on a realistic level with the predicaments of his twisted characters, but now the meditator on the human condition of life and death explaining the symbolic meaning of the surrealistic characters and happenings in *Labyrinth* with which he deluded himself that he was making like Kafka. And it turned out that the mind that had produced this intellectual rubbish had contrived for it the usual Menotti musical rubbish.

Bellini's last opera, *I Puritani*, rarely performed because of its formidable writing for the leading soprano and tenor, and last given in New York by the American Opera Society in 1954 with Laurel Hurley and Eugene Conley, was given again by the Society last spring with Joan Sutherland and Nicolai Gedda. The performance provided an opportunity to hear what beautiful writing Bellini had put into the work in addition to the best-known soprano aria *Qui la voce*—a notable example being the elaborate concluding ensemble of Act 1. And it also provided an opportunity to hear not only unusual singing by Sutherland but distinguished and occasionally sensational singing by Gedda. The lady behind me, catching sight of the special style of Sutherland's dress, exclaimed: "She must be pregnant!"; and this offered a possible explanation of the change in Sutherland's voice—an amplitude and glow in the vocal tone that it had never exhibited before. In addition the voice produced this time not the mannered moaning of little fragments that we had been getting from Sutherland recently but a real and sustained singing of long phrases. With the vocal beauty and style of these phrases, and the spectacular execution of florid passages, her singing was the most impressive I have heard her do. And hardly less impressive in its own way was Gedda's deployment in beautifully shaped phrases of the fine voice which took in stride—with almost no anticipatory sign of the effort involved—the sensational high D's that rang out clear and full. There was excellent singing also by the mezzo-soprano Betty Allen and the bass Justino Diaz; and Richard Bonynge, Sutherland's husband, conducted with authority and musical taste.

After curtain calls for Lynn Seymour and the other soloists of the Royal Ballet who had danced engagingly in a divertissement from Bournonville's *Napoli*, the curtain rose again for a *pas de deux* from his *Flower Festival at Genzano*. For a few moments the stage was empty; then a couple appeared at the back: Rudolf Nureyev escorting Merle Park to the center of the stage, where he released her and bowed deeply with a curving overhead sweep of the arm. It was something I had seen done many times—something that every dancer does well enough, a mere preliminary that may receive only half one's attention even when done by a good dancer; and it was almost over when I was suddenly aware that the mere flow of changing bodily configuration was extraordinary, and that with the aura of presence and style it was one of the most extraordinary things I had ever seen. And it sufficed to reveal what sets Nureyev apart from the other great male dancers known to most of us. Whether Karsavina did or did not say he was even greater than Nijinsky, anyone can see that Nureyev, on the stage, exercises—through his movements, through his mere presence when he is motionless—the kind of extraordinary compulsion we have been told Nijinsky exercised. It operates in even the quietest, the least of his movements; and it operated in those with which, in the opening adagio of the *pas de deux*, he created a heightening context for what Park did (very much as Franz Rupp's excitingly alive piano-playing creates a heightening context for the singing he is accompanying). In these movements he held one's fascinated attention legitimately, with the extraordinary way he did what the piece required him to do—not illegitimately, with anything done specifically to get attention. And the same was true of the breathtaking execution of the feats of virtuosity in his solo and in the coda.

So, a night later, with *Giselle*. For the *New Yorker's* Winthrop Sargeant, Nureyev came to life in this ballet only in his seemingly effortless execution of Albrecht's spectacular solo near the end: until then he had given the impression of being "merely a slim, decorative, graceful, and somewhat sulky young man." The solo was indeed an impressive achievement; and so, in its different way, was Sargeant's not seeing what there had been to see up to that point: Nureyev's dramatic performance, which from Albrecht's first impetuous rush onto the stage held the eye with the power of presence and expressivity that was sustained through every detail; the extraordinary things he made of Albrecht's movements in the dances with Giselle and the villagers in the first act; and above all what he made of the adagio with Giselle in the second act, with movements extraordinary not only in themselves but in the way they worked with Margot Fonteyn's to heighten their beauty and effect.

It isn't only musicians, then, who have to endure the stupidity of critics—and even worse than stupidity. The man who as critic of the *Times* wielded enormous power in the dance world for years, John Martin, had an unerring eye for greatness and an unrelenting hatred for it. A prime target of this hatred for many of those years was the work of Balanchine—until suddenly, a few years ago, one was astonished by Sunday articles in which Martin talked about Balanchine's greatness quite as though it was something he had been talking about all along. Even then what he wrote as a professed friend could be as unrelated to reality as what he had written as an enemy. Thus *Apollo*—the marvelously beautiful work of art in which Balanchine, still only in his twenties, first defined his personal classical style—Martin continued to describe as "a very young and dated effort," important only as a "historical milestone"; and when he finally accepted it, it was with the explanation that Jacques d'Amboise's performance was the first to "publish its true style and importance" and thus to "validate a masterpiece"; whereas actually he had rejected the work when its true style and beauty had been "published" by the performances of Lew Christensen in 1937 and Eglevsky in 1945, and now accepted it when the style and beauty were obscured by the stiff, angular and pompous performance of d'Amboise.

Equally unrelated to reality has been Martin's writing about Nureyev. After the dancer's single appearance here two years ago Martin denounced the folly of a gifted but insufficiently trained and undisciplined boy whose head had been turned by excessive acclaim in Paris, and who as a result had defected from the Kirov company and in so doing thrown away his chances of developing into a mature artist. And Nureyev's work with the Royal Ballet last spring elicited an even angrier denunciation, this time in the *Saturday Review,* in which Martin accused him of wrecking the performances with his single aim of attracting attention to himself at every moment—the manifestations of this aim having ranged from needlessly interpolated stage business to partnering of Fonteyn in which his every movement had competed with hers. As against these fantasies there were the realities of the situation: Nureyev's explanation that he had defected because of the stratification of the Kirov company, which

2 November 1963

he had foreseen would for years limit his opportunities and in this way hinder the development of his capacities; and his employment of these capacities in the Royal Ballet's performances last spring, which demonstrated that he, the company and the public all had gained by the desperate action that had freed him.

[*Hudson Review*]

2 November 1963 From the start, von Karajan's performances on records and in concerts here with the Philharmonia and Berlin Philharmonic Orchestras made it clear that in the manipulating of an orchestra he operated with powers of virtuoso caliber and magnitude, like Heifetz's powers for the violin or Horowitz's for the piano. Heifetz and Horowitz taught us that extraordinary powers in playing an instrument are not inevitably associated with distinguished taste in playing music; Stokowski and Koussevitzky demonstrated that this is true also of conductors; and some of von Karajan's early work provided another, though less extreme, demonstration of this. In 1956 I heard him use his technical powers to get the Berlin Philharmonic to play with remarkable delicacy in performances that he kept low-keyed not only when the music was a Mozart violin concerto but, perversely, when it was Strauss's *Don Juan* and even the first movement of Beethoven's *Eroica*. And though the recorded performance of the *Eroica* with the Philharmonia didn't exhibit this playing around with orchestra and music, it did exhibit an occasional error in musical judgment—e.g. the slowing down of the first movement after the dissonant climax in the development, breaking the continuity of flow and tension.

In the newly issued performances of Beethoven's nine symphonies on Deutsche Grammophon records there is no playing around with orchestra and music: the virtuoso who obtains bal-

Winter 1964

anced and clear textures of ear-ravishing sounds from a Berlin Philharmonic now marvelously sensitized to his direction, operates as a serious musician applying impressive skill to a pacing and shaping of the works that much of the time is highly effective and satisfying—though not, for me, as effective and satisfying as Toscanini's, and still not without occasional errors in musical judgment. Its steadiness of tempo makes the *Eroica* this time one such effective and satisfying performance; but that rigorous steadiness in the second movement keeps the fugato episode from achieving the tremendous power Toscanini builds up with his distentions of the tempo in preparation for the later entrances of the subject and for the climax. Nor does the similarly steady first movement of the Ninth have the tremendous power at the beginning of the recapitulation that Toscanini gives it with his volcanic distentions of tempo and sonority for the climaxes of the phrases. In the Ninth, moreover, the tenor solo of the finale is too fast for a march (and the bass drum is almost inaudible); and I will add that the minuet movement of the Eighth loses by its uncustomarily slow tempo, the first movement of the *Pastoral* by its unusually fast one, the second movement of the Seventh by the slowing down of the alternating sections in major and therefore of the movement's basic rhythm that should continue unchanged in the basses, the finale of the Fifth by the slowed-down bassoon statement in the coda that breaks the momentum of the movement. The Toscanini performances are, then, still the ones for the person who wants the most effective statements of the works. [*New Republic*]

Winter 1964 The three recent collections of Ernest Newman's writings in magazines and newspapers—*From the World of Music, More Essays From the World of Music,* and now

Testament of Music—have offered only a small amount of the journalism that won him his international reputation as a critic while he was winning his reputation as a scholar with the books that culminated in the four-volume *The Life of Richard Wagner*. The reputations represented the public's acceptance of the claims that Newman made for his work; and though the first important and damaging challenge to these claims was made almost thirty years ago, it was only when I read the three collections that I realized how large the discrepancy was between Newman's pretensions and his performances, and how much his writings were overestimated.

Faced with the awesomely documented text of the first volume of *The Life of Richard Wagner*, readers like myself accepted what they were in no position to question—Newman's claim to be replacing earlier *fable convenue*, as he called it, with fact established by examination of the documentary evidence; and a little later they accepted his further claim to have done the same thing in *The Man Liszt*. But Carl Engel, reviewing *The Man Liszt* in *The Musical Quarterly*, demonstrated that instead of allowing the documentary material to dictate his ideas, Newman had allowed his ideas to pervert some of the documentary material—letters of Liszt and the Countess d'Agoult in 1833, when their relation began. When I looked up the volume in which they are published I found that all of Liszt's, many undated, others with dates from August through December, are given first; then the four of the Countess—the first two undated, the others dated May 20 and 26—"*y sont joints*," says the editor, meaning that they are added in a group after Liszt's, not interpolated among his. But Newman, as Engel pointed out, coming to the last of Liszt's letters, writes: "At this stage we have apparently the first of Marie's letters to him that have been preserved. She addresses him as 'Monsieur,' and discusses points connected with literature and music." This, said Engel, is in order to make the letter support Newman's contention that the Countess was not the pursuer but the pursued: that is, as late as December, after ardent letters from Liszt, she is still formal and reserved. And Engel pointed out that Newman omits the date, May 20, of her third letter, in which she addresses Liszt as Franz (which Newman also omits) in one of several impassioned passages, including a postscript in which she explains her absurd demands by the fact that she loves him *"bêtement"* sometimes, and at these times no longer understands that she could not and ought not to be an absorbing thought for him as he is for her (Newman, at one point, translates *"je suis absurde"* as "I am not absurd"). After this demonstration—which Newman, as far as I know, didn't answer, and whose correctness I discovered when I read the letters Engel referred to—one couldn't be confident about the rigor and scrupulousness of Newman's dealing with documentary material elsewhere, and specifically in *The Life of Richard Wagner*. And as it happened, the publication in 1951 of a volume of Hanslick's music criticism enabled me to discover how Newman had misrepresented the review of Wagner's concert in Vienna in 1872 and other writings of Hanslick.* Moreover, though Newman didn't answer Engel's demonstration of his scholarly malpractice in *The Man Liszt* in 1935, he did deal in an extraordinary manner with certain highly vulnerable statements in Engel's review of the third volume of the Wagner biography in 1941—among them Engel's monstrous contention that because of the connection between Wagnerism and Nazism "we should ban and burn every scrap of Wagner's music and writings, and every book written about the amazing wizard, beginning with the books of the Anglo-Wagnerian Ernest Newman." What was extraordinary in Newman's dealing with this was that he answered it not in 1941 in a letter or article,

---

* See pages 108-11.

but in 1946, long after Engel's death, in an appendix of the final volume of the Wagner biography;* and he asked the world to believe that "if I have not made a practice of replying to Dr. Engel's ill-tempered comments . . . it is because I would as soon have thought of going round with an antiseptic cloth wiping up the slaver of a rabid dog. But I feel that I ought not to bring the present biography to a close without some exposure of the manners and the methods of this gentleman"; whereas it seemed clear that actually he had adopted the strategy of remaining silent when Engel had made a criticism that was valid and effective, and replying when Engel had said something monstrously stupid, and of claiming then that such monstrous stupidity was what he had ignored before. These methods and manners didn't restore confidence in the rigor and scrupulousness of Newman's operation as a scholar; and what he had revealed here one began to recognize in the critical writing: much of it was the writing of a bullying tooth-and-nail debater who used incorrect facts in fallacious reasoning against misstatements of what he was arguing against.

This—about which I will say more in a moment—is only one of the things one discovers in reading the three collections. Another is how poor the writing is—how verbose, and as a result, on occasion, how inexact in statement and conducive to fallacy in reasoning; and how badly it performs the critic's primary and essential task of describing and evaluating the work of art that is presented to him. This too I will say more about presently; but an interesting preliminary at this point is Newman's comment on the music criticism of Bernard Shaw collected in *Music in London 1890–94*. As a young provincial who confined his reading of criticism to men like Sainte-Beuve, Taine, Brunetière and Lessing, Newman hadn't known of the mere musical jour-

---

* See the review in the *Nation* of 21 September 1946, reprinted in *Music in the Nation*.

nalism Shaw was doing in London; and reading it for the first time in 1932 he noted that Shaw "concerned himself with music only as it came his way week by week in . . . performances, and . . . went no further into any subject than his couple of columns . . . demanded of him," and that—using in this his knowledge of what he was writing about, his "lively intellect" and a literary style with "directness . . . point . . . wit and humor"— he produced articles "not only as readable but as valuable in 1932 as they were in 1890." What is interesting about this is that the operation which produced Shaw's writing—the concert-reviewing in a newspaper which he was content to do—Newman from the beginning of his own career disdained and denounced as a worthless activity and a waste of the critic's powers that should be devoted to "lengthy and connected essays in book form" and the other loftier activities Newman carried on in addition to the concert-reviewing he was compelled to do. And worthless too, in Newman's opinion, was what Shaw accepted as his critical task in his reviewing—the task, as E. M. Forster has described it, of considering the work of art "as an object in itself . . . and [telling] us what [he can] about its life," or, as Henry D. Aiken once put it, of attending to, and reporting, "what one directly hears and feels" in the work. This Newman described contemptuously as "performing a fantasia on [one's] own 'reactions' to a work," which, he contended, told a reader nothing about the work, but only things about the critic that were of no interest or value to anyone else. Not, again, that Newman, in his own concert-reviewing, didn't do what he was contemptuous of; but in addition he professed to do what he contended was the critic's *real* task, which is to inform the reader about the operation of the composer's mind. And it is ironic that whereas Shaw, content with his modest objective, produced wonderfully perceptive writing that is fascinating today, Newman, contemptuous of that objective and pursuing his more pretentious ones, failed not only in these but in the modest one he disdained, producing not only pretentious think-pieces that were erroneous in fact and reasoning, but also descriptions and evaluations of pieces of music that reveal his lack of mere critical perception—of the ability, which Shaw had, to hear accurately what was to be heard in Mozart's G-minor and Verdi's earlier operas, among other things.

Reporting the operation of the composer's mind was one of a number of impressive-sounding things Newman thought of himself as doing that he didn't really do. What he was concerned with was that "the constitutional bias of [the composer's] mind makes him do practically the same thing again and again when he is confronted by much the same general idea to be expressed," so that "each composer's general procedure can be reduced, by analysis, to a few simple formulae." But it was Newman himself who once pointed out correctly that "the same formula lay ready to Bach's hand on a hundred occasions, but the inspiration that could vivify . . . the formula was not always at his command," and that this produced the difference between Bach's workmanlike verse and his poetry. Clearly, criticism is concerned with that difference—with what the composer achieves beyond his formulae. It is in the particularities of this in each work that we get the real, active, purposeful operation of the composer's mind, as against its mechanical operation in his general formulae; it is they that constitute the life which Forster says it is the critic's task to perceive and report; and this life produced by the real operation of the composer's mind, as we shall see, Newman often was unable to perceive.

Another impressive-sounding activity Newman thought of himself as carrying on was listening to music of the past with a mind purged, as he wrote in 1929, "of the music . . . written since the epoch when the work was written," and "with ears contemporary with itself." Only with this discipline could one, faced with an opera like *Norma,* begin to hear what "gave it its superior value in the eyes of its contemporaries," and did one's ears, "brutalized by the more highly colored music of later times," recover "the sensitiveness of contemporary ears to the finer shades of such music as Bellini's" and hear "the really vital things in it," which he said were not the "saccharine and flaccid" melodies but the "hundred passing little subtleties in the score." But in dismissing the melodies as saccharine and flaccid Newman was not hearing with the ears of Bellini's contemporaries what gave his music its superior value for *them;* he was listening with ears of today— or rather with his particular ears, which were unable to hear the beauty of melodies like *Tutto è sciolto* and *Ah, non credea* in *La Sonnambula* and *Qui la voce* in *I Puritani* that many listeners of today are able to hear. And as for Bellini's contemporaries, they may have been aware of the little subtleties in the score; but what gave it its value for them were those melodies.

I might add that this is a subject Newman wrote about many times, and with much confusion and inaccuracy. We find him writing in 1944 that he has never heard the orchestral phrase preceding Donna Anna's words *"Calma il tuo tormento"* in the aria *Non mi dir* "given its proper expressiveness, for the reason that neither conductors nor players have realized what it meant to Mozart and his contemporaries" (I can't believe the little orchestral phrase meant anything to them beyond its meaning in the performances I have heard). But two paragraphs earlier he has said: "We have to recognize frankly that it is impossible for us to play or sing in public much of the older music as its contemporaries played or sang it, because the world can never hear it with the ears and the minds of those contemporaries. The 'Messiah' sung as it was in Handel's day would sound comic to us." And he has spelled this out in 1935, printing a measure from *Messiah* as it appears in the score and is sung today and then this measure as it was sung in Handel's time, when "the soloists [indulged] in all kinds of shakes and appogiature and other coloratura embellishments," and commenting that "the feeling of the eighteenth century for the expressive power of coloratura has vanished from the earth, never to return. Are we to restore the externals of this old manner for pure antiquarianism's sake, and so drive people away from the Handel oratorios, or ignore them and let people have a Handel they can understand and admire?" Thus the man who on the one hand has argued that one must listen to old music with the ears of its contemporaries argues on the other hand that one should not listen to the actual sounds of the music that contemporary ears heard. And as against Newman's contentions the facts are that *I know that my Redeemer liveth* as it appears in the printed score and is usually sung today is not the piece of music Handel had in mind, but is an incomplete notation of that piece which he expected the singer to complete by filling in the wide intervals with scale passages and appogiaturas before long notes in the style of the period (as Joan Sutherland has done, without comic effect, in in a recent recorded performance of *Messiah*); that the excesses indulged in by exhibitionistic singers—which are what Newman is talking about—were a perversion of this normal operation that other singers performed with taste (as Sutherland did recently); and that the coloratura in Handel's, Mozart's, Bellini's and Verdi's music does have dramatic expressiveness for listeners today.

I might add further that it is Newman's habitual practice in argument to deal with the perversion of what he is arguing about instead of the thing itself, and to deal with it not as a perversion of the thing but as its normal form. Thus he argues against the perversion of the critic's operation that he refers to contemptuously at various times as the critic's performing a fantasia on his own reactions to a work, his writing about himself a propos of a work, his reporting the reactions of his soul to masterpieces—

against this not as a perversion of the operation but as though this perversion were the normal operation of the critic reporting the life he perceives in a work. And Newman's contention that this writing tells the reader nothing about the work, but only things about the critic that are of no interest to anyone else, is true only of the perversion he is attacking, not of the real critical operation, which does tell the reader things about the work. That operation may also tell him things about the critic; but these too are of interest when the critic is a Shaw, and of no interest only when he is a Newman.

Another big subject on which Newman writes repeatedly, and with pretension greater than achievement, is form. He is concerned with the distinction between the mere external appearance of it and the genuine thing—between form as a mere mold or pattern that is filled according to specifications, and form as a shape assumed by the accumulation of details which succeed each other in accordance with their mutual coherence. Discussing the instrumental composer's problem of achieving continuity and logic in a large structure, he contends that the easy way is the filling in of a mold or pattern like sonata form, the difficult way that of "the creative imagination at its best, its most logical," which is when it works "as Coleridge described Shakespeare's imagination working: 'he goes on creating,' says Coleridge, 'and evolving B out of A, and C out of B, and so on.'" The two ways, and the two kinds of form they produce, are exemplified by, on the one hand, the first movement of a Mozart symphony, and, on the other hand, the single movement of Sibelius's Symphony No. 7. The Mozart, "however marvelous . . . as a specimen of its own historical genre, is none the less the representative of a relatively primitive genre"—"the musical equivalent of that simple type of pictorial design" in which there is "a central figure with a balancing figure on either side of it"; and "it illustrates merely a stage through which the symphony has to pass in order to attain to [the] higher stage of organization . . . seen in a work such as the Sibelius No. 7"—higher, in that unity and balance are achieved by other devices than the "simple and obvious mathematical symmetries" of the Mozart. And the beginnings of the second way are seen in the last piano sonatas and string quartets of Beethoven, in which " 'sonata form' and all the rest of it have . . . gone by the board," and "Beethoven now constructs in a new way because he is thinking in a new way . . . everything that happens in the music of a movement is a proliferation of a single cell." The instrumental composers after Beethoven—because "their brains were not of the calibre of Beethoven's"—were unable to continue what he began, and took off instead from the structure of his earlier works—the result in Brahms's Symphony No. 2 being what Newman refers to as "the merest class room mechanics in the 'symphonic' manipulation" of the first movement. "But with the final liquidation of sonata form . . . the concentric way of thinking and building has become more and more attractive to the greater composers," of whom Sibelius, for Newman, is one.

All this has an appearance of truth in Newman's words, but is untrue of the realities the words are concerned with. As against Newman's opposed schematic and organic forms, the reality is in music what it is in poetry: sonata form is for the composer what the sonnet or rondeau is for the poet—a framework within which he deploys the organically coherent substance of the work. As against Newman's three sections of the primitive Mozart first movement, the reality is the Mozart first movement as it is actually experienced in a symphony—experienced not instantaneously in its schematic entirety, but as a progression presenting itself, detail after detail, in time, and producing on the mind the continuous, elaborated and cumulative effect of its successive details, with in addition the effect of departure, in the development, from what has been presented in the exposition, the effect of seeming return, at the beginning of the recapitulation, to what was presented in the exposition, and the effect of the unexpected changes, in the recapitulation, in what is repeated from the exposition. And when the first movement is that of a Mozart piano concerto the reality is that of a more elaborately organized progression, with the additional effect of the differences in what first the orchestra and then the solo piano state in the exposition, and the changes in this distribution of material between them, and in order and context of ideas, in the recapitulation. As against Newman's idea of Beethoven's discarding of sonata form in his last sonatas and quartets, there is the reality that this first-movement framework was the one Beethoven used from the beginning of his creative activity to its end, and for all the varieties of his musical thinking including the last: the explosively vehement thought of the first movement of the last piano sonata, Op. 111 (after the slow introduction), and the quiet thought of the first movement of the last quartet, Op. 135, both follow the clearly marked sonata-form course of exposition, development, recapitulation and coda—the clear markings being the prescribed "second group" in the prescribed related key in the exposition and in the prescribed tonic key in the recapitulation, and, in the sonata, the prescribed first and second endings of the exposition—the first leading back to the beginning of the exposition for its customary repetition, the second leading on to the development. As against Newman's idea of what happened after Beethoven, there is the reality that the first-movement framework he used to the last was one that Schubert used for the further varieties of *his* thinking: whereas Brahms, striving to write greater than he felt, could indeed only, in the first movement of the Symphony No. 1, fill out the framework with aridly synthetic substance contrived mechanically by formula (e.g. the sawing away in cross-rhythms), Schubert deployed in the first movement of his Symphony No. 9 the substance that issued from genuine poetic impulse—substance that occasioned unprecedented episodes in which Tovey sees Schubert, "like other great classics . . . pressing his way toward new forms." There is also the reality of Tchaikovsky's similarly expansive and episodic deployment of *his* material within the same framework, later; and Mahler's deployment within it of *his* musical thinking, in our own century. And a final reality to point out is that the kind of continuity and form Newman argues for he is unable to recognize when it is presented to him in the three movements of Debussy's *La Mer*, in each of which the evocative fragments are fitted together in a progression with coherence and superb cumulative effect: all Newman can hear in this and the other major instrumental works (he excepts *Jeux*) is evidence that "the constructive sense of Debussy . . . so far as the larger forms are concerned, was no more than that of a child."

This is one of the examples of Newman's failure in the critic's primary task of perceiving and reporting what is to be heard in a piece of music. Another is the characterization of Bellini as a "saccharine and flaccid melodist" that I mentioned earlier. And we find him, in 1911, exclaiming: "Heaven knows how empty some of these instrumental works of Mozart can be!"—this about one of the piano concertos and the G-minor Symphony, which he says made him feel sometimes that he was hearing "the nursery prattle of a bright child," as against the Strauss *Burleske, Also sprach Zarathustra* and *Dance of the Seven Veils* on the same program, which filled him "with a kind of awe before the enormous possibilities of psychological expression that music has developed." True, in 1923 he speaks of the inability of youth to appreciate the self-sufficient beauty of Mozart, and writes that "my delight in Mozart has gone on increasing since I first came completely under his spell some fifteen or twenty years ago." But those statements in 1911 were made not by a youth but by a man of forty-three. And in 1924 he asks, "Is Mozart never dull and feebly repetitious, especially in his symphonic slow movements?," citing his "dilly-dallying in the slow movement of the G-minor Symphony."

Again, we find Newman, in 1913, describing *Il Trovatore* and the other operas of Verdi's middle period as "just the awkward but fascinating sprawlings of a cub," with nothing of the real Verdi that he says is to be heard only in the *Requiem*, *Otello* and *Falstaff*. This reveals his inability to perceive the superb results of the operation of the impressive powers of the real Verdi of those earlier works—e.g. the melodic power that produces *Tacea la notte* and the other superb melodic structures. And as late as 1933 we find him exhibiting this lack of perception even about a work as late as *Don Carlo*, which is for him a major example of "how little [Verdi] really changed from first to last; time after time, in his latest works, we discover that a really fine piece of expression is actually nothing more than an old formula with a better face on it"; and "unfortunately the reverse is also true; as likely as not, a later work will show us not an improved but a degraded version of the formula." Particular illustration of this—which for him includes the ensembles in the *auto-da-fé* scene and Philip's study that actually are excellent and effective specimens of the genre—is apparently all he hears in *Don Carlo*, which he says "is often interesting because it reads like a sketch for something Verdi was to do better in 'Aida' or 'Otello.'" And by his silence about them he reveals his failure to perceive the marvelous achievements of Verdi's matured powers in the great pages of the work: not only the entire scene with Philip's famous soliloquy, his interview with the Grand Inquisitor, the quartet, Eboli's confession to Elisabetta, and her *O don fatale*, not only Elisabetta's *Tu che le vanità* in the last act, with its melodic grandeur that is unique in Verdi's writing, but the tremendous orchestral prelude to this act, and the second-act colloquies of Carlo and Elisabetta and of Philip and

5 March 1964

Rodrigo, which have the flexible and free-ranging vocal phraseology, the imaginatively resourceful supporting orchestral invention that one hears in *Otello*, and are some of Verdi's most accomplished, incandescent and affecting writing. What Newman is further unaware of is the truth and the applicability to *Don Carlo* of Tovey's observation that "the highest qualities attained in important parts of a great work are as indestructible by weaknesses elsewhere as if the weaknesses were the accidents of physical ruin," and that "neither Shakespeare nor Schubert will ever be understood by any critic or artist who regards their weaknesses and inequalities as proof that they are artists of less than the highest rank."

There are additional failures—with Musorgsky, with Stravinsky—but no magazine could provide the space to deal with all the errors of perception, fact and reasoning in these collections of Newman's critical writings.* [*Partisan Review*]

5 March 1964 Toscanini was aware that for most people—not only in business but in personal relations with him—he was someone to exploit for their own advantage; and my guess is that, regarding this as inevitable, he exploited his exploiters and accepted the exchange of benefits without complaint. But sometimes he didn't get what was owed him—from people he trusted who betrayed him; from the record or broadcasting company which failed him by issuing on records or transmitting on the air defective reproductions of his performances, or by persuading him to give up Sunday at 5 and accept for his broadcasts a time when many couldn't listen. And another exploitation from which he usually got no benefit in return was that of the journalist. I

---

* See the last paragraph of the *Nation* article of 8 and 15 September 1951.

5 March 1964

don't mean a piece of writing like Spike Hughes's book, *The Toscanini Legacy*, in which a musician with perception wrote of what he had heard in concert and on records, and from which Toscanini gained the illumination of his work for those who read the book. I mean what was written not to illuminate his work but to impress the reader with the writers' knowledge and understanding—which actually they didn't have. At one time the way to impress one's readers was to admire Toscanini extravagantly; later it was to criticize and attack him; and the attacks revealed as little understanding of the Toscanini operation and its results as the admiration. But one could be even more impressive by judiciously discriminating between strengths and weaknesses, achievements and failures—all plausible in the writer's words, but existing only in those words. One egregious example of this pseudo-discrimination was the Marsh book; another was the lead article in a *Saturday Review* birthday greeting to Toscanini, in which Irving Kolodin went "phlumph-phlumph-phlumph" on *The Meaning of Toscanini* and demonstrated his discriminating perception by citing "a stiff 'Magic Flute' Overture" as against "a superbly flexible 'Freischütz,'" "an overwrought 'Lenore No. 3'" as against "a wonderfully proclamative 'Meistersinger.'" However, the greeting also included truth in the form of an article, *Playing with the Maestro*, by a member of the NBC Symphony, Samuel Antek; and this accurately informative article he later elaborated into the text published now in *This Was Toscanini*.

When an NBC Symphony musican once remarked to me that Toscanini had been written about only by outsiders, and there was need of a book by the insiders—the men who had worked with him—he meant that even an outsider like Hughes who reported what he had heard in performances and observed at working rehearsals couldn't describe what it meant to sit in an orchestra and rehearse or perform under Toscanini. And the

5 March 1964

Antek text is the first written by an insider, telling us the things only an insider can tell, which in addition are made vividly real by the marvelous photographs Robert Hupka took of Toscanini in action at rehearsals. We learn of the extraordinary powers with which Toscanini operated; of the complete, selfless and intense dedication to the artistic task he made into a moral quest for truth, which for the men in his orchestra set him apart from all other conductors; and of the wonderful personal qualities that made him someone his musicians loved. (The only one whom some of them speak of in similar fashion is Cantelli.)

Working with Toscanini, we learn, gave each player the same feeling of personal artistic fulfillment as he would have had from performing alone: "we were inspired to . . . satisfy our own highest standards and instincts, in pursuit of our common goal." And concerning the resulting performances Antek reveals that although the ones heard by the audience—the outsiders—were extraordinary, the greatest were the performances heard only by the insiders—the musicians of the orchestra—at the working rehearsals (as distinguished from semi-public dress rehearsals). For there Toscanini was relaxed, was uninhibited in his gestures, and could even "shout, bellow, and sing"; whereas "at concerts he seemed to freeze," and "sensing his tension, the men themselves became tense and nervous and often could not give their utmost." Also, whereas the performance was what mattered for the audience, his greatness for the players was what they felt in their relation with him—"the unimpeachable honesty and integrity, the warm humanity . . . in his working process," and the "tremendous power and incandescence he inspired" in them. It was this that "set apart the experience of playing with Toscanini from that of playing with any other conductor."

For Toscanini, one might add, it was a relation with one group he could feel sure would not betray him. Text and photographs support his statement once: "Conducting is great suffering for

5 March 1964

me"; but his orchestra was one group of human beings about whom he could feel confident that they wanted nothing from him beyond what it meant most to him in life to give and he was happiest in giving, and who—as some of the photographs testify —gave him moments of the greatest happiness he experienced in his life. [*New York Review of Books*]

Index

Abraham, Gerald, 100-101, 134
Aiken, Henry D., 98, 233, 280
Aitken, Webster, 22, 23, 25-6, 194
Allen, Betty, 271
American Broadcasting Company, 64, 68
Anderson, Marian, 72-3
Antek, Samuel, 290-92
Armstrong, Louis, 58-60, 105-6

B

Bach, J. S., 17, 18-20, 74n, 140, 199-200, 281
Backhaus, Wilhelm, 160-62, 187
Balanchine, George, 21-2, 74, 76-9, 174, 203-6, 222, 231, 273-4
Barber, Samuel, 92-3, 135, 219
Barbieri, Fedora, 185
Barbirolli, Sir John, 30, 32, 197-8
Barzun, Jacques, 97-101, 111-13, 125-6, 164, 189-91
Beecham, Sir Thomas, 6, 7, 23, 101-2, 141, 145n, 167
Beethoven, Ludwig van, 5, 6, 13, 23, 24-5, 35-8, 43, 84, 104-5, 129-30, 143, 149, 161-2, 176-7, 184, 193, 226-7, 249, 250-51, 255, 256-7, 267-8, 275-6, 285-6
Bellini, Vincenzo, 201, 231-2, 271, 281-2, 283, 287
Berger, Arthur, 260
Berlin Philharmonic, 12, 275, 276
Berlioz, Hector, 3, 23, 146, 188-91, 219-20, 234, 237, 242-3, 246, 255

Berman, Eugene, 135, 145
Bernstein, Leonard, 93-4, 102-3, 114-15, 169-71, 178-9, 206-7, 209-10, 213, 214, 218-21, 223-6, 266
Bing, Rudolf, 126-7, 134-5, 142, 175-6, 186
Bjoerling, Jussi, 127, 185, 216
Blesh, Rudi, 60
Blitzstein, Marc, 211-12, 212n, 222-3
Bloch, Ernest, 13
Boccherini, Luigi, 107-8
Bodanzky, Artur, 20
Bonynge, Richard, 271
Boretz, Benjamin, 257-8
Boston Symphony, 7, 35, 36, 43-4, 64, 68, 155n, 197, 255n
Brahms, Johannes, 3, 4, 8, 14, 16, 25, 26, 231, 242, 243, 246, 249-50, 285, 286
British Broadcasting Corporation, 65, 66-7, 68, 69-70, 154-5
Britten, Benjamin, 172, 265-6
Broadcasting, 60-73, 152-5
Bruckner, Anton, 11, 13
Bucci, Marc, 209
Budapest Quartet, 41, 168

C

Callas, Maria, 184-5, 186, 232
Cantelli, Guido, 90-91, 143, 145, 146, 166-7, 186-8
Cardus, Neville, 193
Casals, Pablo, 6, 129, 167

293

Index

Chaliapin, Feodor, 173
Chasins, Abram, 181-4
Chopin, Frédéric, 161, 181, 183, 222, 229, 231
Chotzinoff, Samuel, 28, 30, 31, 33-4, 172-4
Cleveland Orchestra, 266
Cliburn, Van, 214-16, 222, 229, 263-4
Columbia Broadcasting System, 68
Cooper, Martin, 242
Copland, Aaron, 54, 55, 83, 147-8, 212, 251
Criticism, 4, 7-9, 30-31, 54-7, 115-16, 135-7, 145-6, 164-5, 198, 229-31, 257, 280-84
Crosby, John, 67-9, 121

D

Damrosch, Walter, 31, 33n
Danilova, Alexandra, 79
Debussy, Claude, 11, 13, 75-6, 173-4, 201, 246-7, 287
Del Monaco, Mario, 127, 185-6
de los Angeles, Victoria, 145, 185
Denby, Edwin, 246
Dent, Edward J., 234
De Sabata, Victor, 90, 113-14, 166
Diaz, Justino, 271
Di Stefano, Giuseppe, 166
Donizetti, Gaetano, 232
Downes, Olin, 3, 16, 28, 31, 33, 34, 88-9, 98, 160-61, 162, 194-8, 237-41, 263
Dukas, Paul, 246-7

E

Einstein, Alfred, 107-8, 111-13, 124-5, 234-6, 237-41
Ellington, Duke, 59, 83-4
Engel, Carl, 247, 277-8

F

Farrar, Geraldine, 5, 20
Farrell, Charles B., 107-8, 112, 234-6, 238-9, 244
Flagstad, Kirsten, 20-21, 22-3, 103-5, 155-9, 163-4, 216
Fleisher, Leon, 222
Floyd, Carlisle, 208-9, 217, 251, 252
Fonteyn, Margot, 273, 274
Ford Foundation, 208, 217, 227, 228
Form, 284-7
Forster, E. M., 198, 233-4, 280, 281
Furtwängler, Wilhelm, 11, 12, 13, 14, 159, 176-8

G

Gatti-Casazza, Giulio, 20, 33
Gedda, Nicolai, 271-2
Gelatt, Roland, 149-50
Gerhardt, Elena, 17
Gershwin, George, 84, 214
Gesualdo, Carlo, 234-6
Giannini, Vittorio, 209, 217, 251, 252, 258
Gilels, Emil, 180, 222
Gilman, Lawrence, 28, 30, 31, 32-4
Gould, Glenn, 26, 216, 218, 222, 227, 248-50
Graf, Herbert, 40, 48
Gray, Cecil, 14, 15
Gutman, John, 51-2

H

Hammerstein, Oscar, 33
Handel, George Frideric, 134, 282-3
Hanslick, Eduard, 108-11, 116-17, 278
Harris, Roy, 41-2, 83
Harrison, Jay S., 121

Index

Harshaw, Margaret, 142, 185-6
Haydn, Franz Josef, 143, 167, 266
Heifetz, Jascha, 6-7, 24, 72, 176, 275
Henderson, William J., 31-2, 138
Hobson, Wilder, 59, 105, 225
Hofmann, Josef, 6, 181-4, 215
Hofmannsthal, Hugo von, 261-2
Horowitz, Vladimir, 88-9, 149-52, 162, 176, 275
Hughes, Spike, 250, 290
Hupka, Robert, 291
Hurley, Laurel, 174

I

Israel Philharmonic, 102
Iturbi, José, 18
Ives, Charles, 103, 219

J

Jarrell, Randall, 82
Jazz, 57-60, 225
Judson, Arthur, 197
Juilliard Quartet, 168

K

Karajan Herbert von, 275-6
Kemp, Barbara, 20
Kempff, Wilhelm, 168
Kerman, Joseph, 198-202, 229-31
Klemperer, Otto, 250-51
Kolodin, Irving, 137-40, 145, 166-7, 188, 229, 263, 290
Kondrashin, Kiril, 221-2
Korngold, Julius, 261-2
Koussevitzky, Serge, 5, 6, 7, 35, 36, 37, 102, 119, 143, 275
Kreisler, Fritz, 73, 129

L

Lambert, Constant, 14
Lang, Paul Henry, 38-41, 60, 98, 99, 159, 179-80, 214-15, 227, 228, 233, 234-6, 241-8, 259-60, 263
Lehmann, Lotte, 26-8, 79, 104-5, 160
Leider, Frida, 20
Leinsdorf, Erich, 135
Lhevinne, Josef, 215
Lipatti, Dinu, 202-3

M

Mahler, Gustav, 3, 11, 167, 169-70, 192-3, 196-7, 255, 287
Markova, Alicia, 45, 79
Marsh, Robert C., 267, 290
Martin, John, 206, 273-5
Mengelberg, Willem, 5, 143
Menotti, Gian-Carlo, 95-7, 120-21, 207-8, 217, 222, 258, 271
Menuhin, Yehudi, 128, 195-6
Merrill, Robert, 144
Metropolitan Opera, 5, 20-21, 33, 44-5, 47-8, 48-52, 67, 104-5, 126-7, 128, 131-5, 139-40, 141, 142, 143-5, 155-7, 184-5, 186
Milanov, Zinka, 127, 128, 141
Miller, Philip L., 165-6
Mitropoulos, Dimitri, 42-3, 186
Modern music, 52-4, 82-3
Montemezzi, Italo, 252
Monteux, Pierre, 127-8, 141, 186
Moore, Douglas, 208-9, 217, 227-8, 251, 252
Moscow State Symphony, 221
Mozart, W. A., 18, 23, 24-5, 45-8, 51, 74n, 77, 79, 84, 124, 134, 146-7, 167, 168, 170-71, 174, 184, 193, 198, 200, 214, 220, 222, 231, 234, 237-9, 240-41, 245-6, 248, 263-4, 267-8, 275, 282, 283, 284-6, 287-8
Muck, Karl, 33n, 44

Index

Musical show, American, 106, 148-9, 210-12, 213-14
Musicologists, 38-41, 57, 60, 82-3, 247
Musorgsky, Modeste, 87-9, 131-4, 150, 175-6, 253, 289

N

Nat, Yves, 168
National Broadcasting Company, 66, 152-5
NBC Symphony, 68, 79-80, 152-5, 187-8, 268-70, 292
NBC-TV Opera Theater, 174, 192
Nelli, Herva, 76
Newman, Ernest, 14-16, 18-19, 42, 99, 109-11, 133-4, 247-8, 276-89
News stories with built-in critical praise, 127-8, 141, 142, 266
New York City Opera, 147, 148-9, 208-13, 216-18
New York Philharmonic, 23, 24, 30, 32, 35-8, 43-4, 45, 64, 68, 186-8, 197-8, 218-21, 268, 269, 270n
Nijinsky, Vaslav, 253-4, 272-3
Nureyev, Rudolf, 272-3, 274-5

O

Oistrakh, David, 179-81
Opera, 48-51, 173, 201-2, 206-12, 213-14, 251-2

P

Performance, 6-7
Peters, Roberta, 144-5
Philadelphia Orchestra, 7, 23, 35, 36, 68, 250-51, 269-70
Philharmonia Orchestra, 187, 275
Pons, Lily, 72
Program music, 246
Prokofiev, Sergei, 192
Public, musical, 245

R

Rachmaninov, Sergei, 129, 214, 215
Ravel, Maurice, 150
Respighi, Ottorino, 246-7
Rethberg, Elisabeth, 17, 216, 244
Richter, Sviatoslav, 226-7
Rimsky-Korsakov, Nikolai, 87-8, 132-4, 253
Robbins, Jerome, 94-5
Rodzinski, Artur, 197
Rosenfeld, Paul, 53-4, 99
Rossi-Lemeni, Nicola, 142
Rossini, Gioacchino, 143-5, 201, 267-8
Rubinstein, Artur, 231
Rudolf, Max, 134
Rupp, Franz, 73, 273

S

Sachs, Curt, 39-40, 57, 83
Sackville-West, Edward, 134
Sargeant, Winthrop, 96-7, 112, 176, 186-7, 215, 217, 227-8, 252, 258-9, 263, 273
Sayao, Bidu, 47-8
Scherchen, Hermann, 167
Schnabel, Artur, 6, 23-4, 129-30, 150, 151, 184, 216, 231
Schneider-Miller-Horszowski, 142-3
Schneider Quartet, 168
Scholars, musical, 107-12, 234-48
Schönberg, Arnold, 52, 91-2, 223-4
Schonberg, Harold C., 26, 168, 249-50, 263, 266
Schubart, Mark, 98, 124, 125
Schubert, Franz, 25, 26-7, 28, 84-7, 142, 143, 149, 150-52, 168, 175, 193, 246, 266, 269-70, 286-7
Schuman, William, 83
Schumann, Elisabeth, 41, 79, 129, 244
Schumann, Robert, 17, 27, 168, 246

Index

Schwarzkopf, Elisabeth, 159-60, 166
Seefried, Irmgard, 244
Serkin, Rudolf, 24-5
Sessions, Roger, 113, 121-5
Shaw, Bernard, 28-30, 31, 56-7, 92, 146, 219, 231, 234, 245, 260, 279-80
Shawe-Taylor, Desmond, 134
Shostakovitch, Dmitri, 41, 135, 219, 252
Sibelius, Jean, 14-16, 198, 285
Siepi, Cesare, 143-4, 185
Solomon, 129-30
Spaeth, Sigmund, 42, 71
Steber, Eleanor, 47-8, 63, 127, 128, 166, 185
Stiedry, Fritz, 135
Stokowski, Leopold, 7, 30, 35, 36, 88, 143, 150, 176, 187, 275
Straus, Noel, 26, 263
Strauss, Richard, 11, 13, 72, 193, 242, 246-7, 253, 261-2, 266, 275, 287
Stravinsky, Igor, 52, 73-4, 131, 141, 178-9, 198, 203, 220, 252, 253-60, 263, 289
Sutherland, Joan, 232, 271-2, 283
Symphony of the Air, 169, 170
Szell, George, 186, 266
Szigeti, Joseph, 6, 7, 8, 19, 22, 216

T

Taubman, Howard, 112, 117-20
Taylor, Deems, 31, 33, 42, 67
Tchaikovsky, 5, 143, 147, 214-16, 221-2, 287
Tebaldi, Renata, 127, 164
Telephone Hour, 60-62, 64-5, 67
Teyte, Maggie, 60-61
Thomson, Virgil, 18, 42-5, 52-3, 54, 83, 93, 96, 113-17, 125, 136-7, 143-4, 159, 198, 212-13, 228, 237-8, 247, 251-2

Times, New York, 26
Toscanini, Arturo, 5-6, 7, 17-18, 24-5, 35-8, 43, 44, 45, 68, 75-6, 79-82, 89-90, 114-15, 117-20, 129, 140, 146-7, 152-5, 163-4, 166, 170, 187-8, 192, 193, 215, 216, 250-51, 256-7, 267-70, 276, 289-92
Tourel, Jennie, 172
Tovey, Donald F., 11, 42, 175, 198, 289
Toye, Francis, 231
Traubel, Helen, 141
Turner, W. J., 4, 75-6, 99, 146, 219-20, 234

V

Valdengo, Giuseppe, 76
Valletti, Cesare, 144, 185
Verdi, Giuseppe, 50, 75-6, 138, 147, 166, 202, 283, 288-9
Vienna, music in, 11-14
Vinay, Ramon, 76
Vishnevskaya, Galina, 221-2

W

Wagner, Richard, 20-21, 103-4, 109-11, 147, 165-6, 177, 200, 207
Walter, Bruno, 48, 169-70, 186, 192-4
Ward, Robert, 217, 228
Weill, Kurt, 83-4, 210-11, 217-18
Weinstock, Herbert, 98
Weisgall, Hugo, 217
Wilson, Edmund, 178
WNYC, 65-6
Wolf, Hugo, 17, 160, 204
Wotton, Tom S., 99, 108
WQXR, 65
Wührer, Friedrich, 168

Y

Young, Stark, 229-30

NOTE
(1974)

1. The following indented paragraph—omitted from *Music Observed* in deference to someone's insistence that it was "nasty," which I did not agree with and should not have deferred to—is for insertion between the two paragraphs on p. 200.

> All this is recalled to mind by Mr. Kerman's first book, *Opera as Drama*. On the jacket one reads that he was born in 1924; he was, then, twenty-four when he wrote those articles in *The Hudson Review*; and this makes their quality even more impressive. It also suggests an explanation of the ostentation: Mr. Kerman was engaging in the activity of the young that I heard a young man describe once as defining one's personality in public. Nor was it only that as a young man beginning to write for professional publication Mr. Kerman was putting on a performance to establish his claim to the public's attention: he was putting on a particular performance of being very learned, very intellectual, very severe, for the particular public of *The Hudson Review*. And it seems to have become a habit which persists: there is in the book a certain amount of the ostentatious intellectualism and severity of the articles, in addition to much of their critical perception and excellent writing.

2. The estimate of Van Cliburn in this book has been confirmed, in the years since the book's first appearance, by his recorded performances of Beethoven's Sonata Op. 57 (*Appassionata*) and Concerto No. 3 and Chopin's Sonatas Opp. 35 and 58 and Concerto No. 1—the performances of one of the greatest musicians who have played the piano in this century. It seemed reasonable to expect this musician to employ his outstanding musical powers in performance of the great works that required them—the concertos of Mozart, the last sonatas of Beethoven, the later sonatas and smaller pieces of Schubert, the Fantasy,

Symphonic Etudes and other major works of Schumann. And it has been a saddening experience to have the years pass without even a beginning of the fulfillment of this expectation.

With Glenn Gould there has been not only a similar failure to perform the concertos of Mozart and great works of Schubert, Schumann and Chopin, but an increasing eccentricity in tempo, touch and phrasing in the music he has performed—Bach's *Well-Tempered Clavier,* Mozart's sonatas, the Concerto No. 5 and earlier sonatas of Beethoven—to the point where many of the performances have been not worthy of a serious listener's attention. Mozart's Sonata K.330, for example, which he played so marvelously on Columbia ML-5274 fifteen years ago, he now rips through on M-31078 at a speed which makes the performance absurd and the music meaningless.

Acknowledgments

I am indebted to

William H. Youngren, for all the time and interest he gave to reading and evaluating my tentative assemblage of material and helping to make the final selection.

Sheldon Meyer of the Oxford University Press, for his interest in publishing the collection and the help of his editor's judgment in putting it together.

Leonard Conversi, for additional suggestions of material.

Roger Dakin, for advice in a few editorial matters.

Charles B. Farrell, for his information about the unscholarly errors of Alfred Einstein and Paul Henry Lang.

The publications in which the material appeared originally, for making it available.